Fodor's InFocus

PANAMA

1 Panama Beaches

With some 1,500 miles total of Pacific and Caribbean coastlines and with no spot in the country more than 50 miles from a coast, Panama is a country fringed by beautiful beaches. *(Ch. 3–7)*

2 Handicraft Markets

Exploring Panama City's handicraft markets is a must even for non-shoppers. Browse the colorful stalls and learn about local cultures from shop owners who are often indigenous people. *(Ch. 1)*

3 The Panama Canal

One of the world's remarkable engineering achievements, the Panama Canal is all the more amazing when you consider its construction took place a century ago. *(Ch. 3)*

4 Barro Colorado

Hop a boat on Gatún Lake to explore the island of Barro Colorado, one of the world's first wildlife reserves and home to more than 400 bird species and 120 kinds of mammals. *(Ch. 3)*

5 Jungle Adventures

The Darién is a lush region cloaked with dense jungle. For an unforgettable journey, explore this remote land with an experienced guide. *(Ch. 6, 7)*

6 Bicoastal Diving

In Panama you can dive the Pacific and Caribbean on the same day. Pacific dives have bigger schools of fish; Caribbean sites offer sponge, coral, and wreck diving. *(Ch. 3, 4, 5, 7)*

7 The Emberá

The Darién province was the original homeland of Panama's indigenous Emberá people, and if you venture there, you'll see this group at its most authentic. *(Ch. 6)*

8 Surf Tours

Hot-shot surfers flock to Panama for the challenging reef breaks, but many operators offer lessons for beginners. Take a surf tour to access Panama's best waves. *(Ch. 4, 5, 7)*

9 Seafood

A trip to a country whose name means "abundance of fish" isn't complete without a fresh seafood meal. One Panamanian specialty not to be missed is ceviche (marinated, raw fish). *(Ch. 1, 2)*

10 Bocas del Toro Town

Slow down and unwind in Bocas Town, where there are almost no cars but plenty of bicycles. Stroll or pedal its wide streets lined with brightly colored, wooden Caribbean houses. *(Ch. 5)*

11 Casco Viejo

Stroll beneath latticework balconies on brick streets and discover this historic Panama City neighborhood, a World Heritage Site with a pastel patchwork of ancient churches, convents, shops, and homes. *(Ch. 2)*

12 Land of the Guna

The indigenous Guna people hold the deed to what is arguably Panama's most stunning scenery: white-sand beaches, coconut palms, and 300-plus islands off the northeast Caribbean coast. *(Ch. 6)*

CONTENTS

MAPS

ABOUT THIS BOOK

Fodor's Ratings

Everything in this guide is worth doing—we don't cover what isn't—but exceptional sights, hotels, and restaurants are recognized with additional accolades. Fodor's Choice★ indicates our top recommendations; ★ highlights places we deem highly recommended. Care to nominate a new place? Visit Fodors.com/contact-us.

Trip Costs

We list prices wherever possible to help you budget well. Hotel and restaurant price categories from **$** to **$$$$** are noted alongside each recommendation. For hotels, we include the lowest cost of a standard double room in high season. For restaurants, we cite the average price of a main course at dinner or, if dinner isn't served, at lunch. For attractions, we always list adult admission fees; discounts are usually available for children, students, and senior citizens.

Hotels

Our local writers vet every hotel to recommend the best overnights in each price category, from budget to expensive. Unless otherwise specified, you can expect private bath, phone, and TV in your room. For expanded hotel reviews, facilities, and deals visit Fodors.com.

Restaurants

Unless we state otherwise, restaurants are open for lunch and dinner daily. We mention dress code only when there's a specific requirement and reservations only when they're essential or not accepted. To make restaurant reservations, visit Fodors.com.

Credit Cards

The hotels and restaurants in this guide typically accept credit cards. If not, we'll say so.

Ratings
- ★ Fodor's Choice
- ★ Highly recommended
- Family-friendly

Listings
- Address
- Branch address
- Mailing address
- Telephone
- Fax
- Website
- E-mail
- Admission fee
- Open/closed times
- Subway
- Directions or Map coordinates

Hotels & Restaurants
- Hotel
- Number of rooms
- Meal plans
- Restaurant
- Reservations
- Dress code
- No credit cards
- Price

Other
- See also
- Take note
- Golf facilities

Experience Panama

WORD OF MOUTH

"We just came back from a couple of weeks in Panama. It was way more than what we expected. Two weeks was not enough time."

—ninabaile

www.fodors.com/forums

WELCOME TO PANAMA

Five centuries after Spanish explorer Vasco Núñez de Balboa's debut as Panama's premier tourist—he gets credit for "discovering" the Pacific Ocean—new waves of travelers are discovering this squiggly shape isthmus of a country. A record 2 million tourists passed through the visitor turnstiles for the first time in 2011.

Literally and figuratively, all roads lead to **Panama City**. Unless you sneak in from the west via Costa Rica, Panama's sparkling capital will be your first introduction to the country. Panama City mixes old and (mostly) new. Pay homage to the ruins of Panama Viejo, the first, now-abandoned settlement, and the Casco Viejo, which survives as a charming colonial quarter with new boutique hotels. You can also marvel at the dense skyline, the glitzy shopping, the fine dining, and the rocking nightlife in Central America's most cosmopolitan city.

Much of the center slice of the country can be done as a day trip from the capital putting **Central Panama**'s rain forests, wildlife, colonial fortresses, hill towns, beaches, tropical islands, and indigenous communities within easy striking distance. (We recommend getting out of the city and overnighting at least one day here.) Of course, no trip to Panama is complete without a visit to its namesake canal. Partake of partial (once or twice a week) or full (once or twice a month) transits of the waterway. Landside, observation platforms at the Miraflores Locks just outside Panama City give you a perspective on the enormity of one of history's great engineering feats.

Booming **Chiriquí** is Panama's breadbasket and economic powerhouse. The western province provides you with a pleasing combination of lowland tropics and mountain vistas, and the greatest climate variation of any of the country's nine provinces. Here, you can enjoy some of Panama's top scuba diving, surfing, and sport fishing. To hike and bird-watch in the highland cloud forests head to Boquete, Volcán, Bambito, and Cerro Punta. Don't forget your jacket, you'll be surprised at how chilly it can be. The highland town of Boquete is also the heart of Panama's newfound real estate boom. Singled out in many circles as one of the world's best retirement destinations, it hosts an astonishingly international population.

The laid-back, tropical, archipelago of **Bocas del Toro** may remind some of Jamaica. There are around 250 islands and islets scattered over the turquoise waters of northwest Panama's Almirante Bay, but you'll likely just visit one or two of the largest. There are tons of options here—rain-forest hiking, bird-watching, surfing, scuba diving, snorkeling, canopy touring, boating, visiting indigenous Ngöbe communities—but if you're like most visitors, you'll settle into island life right away, and choose your activities selectively so as not to play the crazed tourist in Panama's most relaxing destination.

Eastern Panama's Guna Yala and Darién regions are another story. Remoteness means you'll need reserves of time and, frankly, money to take in this lesser traveled sector of Panama. Accommodation here is rustic, though pricey—all goods must be flown or boated in—but few who make the trip express regrets. You may choose the utterly fascinating indigenous Guna culture. Their colorful clothing against a backdrop of coral beaches and sparkling islands evokes classic *National Geographic* photos, but remember the cardinal rule of travel here: You accept the Guna on their terms. It is never the other way around. The east's other adventure is the dense forest of the Darién and some of the country's best wildlife viewing. Proximity of the Colombian border and the wilderness conditions mean you should never visit the Darién without a guide.

Of course, all the top-notch tourist attractions lose their value if you can't access them, and here's where Panama truly shines in recent years. The current intensely pro-growth government is fighting corruption and making all citizens pay their taxes—both problems bedevil every Latin American government—and is investing that added revenue in infrastructure, tourist and otherwise. In particular, a flurry of highway construction has made getting around Panama easier than ever. The capital's sleek, efficient Tocumen International Airport is vastly improving in response to the tourism and economic surge.

Nothing symbolizes Panama's boom like the canal. The world-famous waterway marks its **centenary in 2014** with an expansion that will permit every ship in the world to pass through its locks. "Post-Panamax" ships, so known because their size prevents them from using the canal, will be a thing of the past. Panamanians have done themselves proud since taking over operations in 1999, and, as an added benefit, they've made tourist visits to the canal easier than ever. The country's new economic development and rave notices in world tourism circles are cause for celebration as the canal turns 100 and Balboa's expedition marks its 500th anniversary.

WHAT'S WHERE

2 Panama City. The capital is an obligatory stop, and a surprisingly pleasant hub for exploring the country. It is a vibrant and diverse metropolis with excellent dining, lodging, and nightlife, and an abundance of day-trip options.

3 The Canal and Central Panama. Central Panama holds an array of landscapes and attractions in a relatively small area. The Panama Canal is the region's biggest attraction, literally, and it can be admired from half a dozen vantage points or navigated on day trips that cost a fraction of what a cruise does.

4 Chiriquí Province. The western province of Chiriquí comprises everything from cloud forest to coral reefs, and white-water rivers to white-sand beaches. World-class surfing, river rafting, sportfishing, bird-watching, skin diving, and hiking make Chiriquí a destination meant for lovers of the great outdoors.

5 Bocas del Toro Archipelago. The Bocas del Toro Archipelago holds an impressive mix of beaches, jungle, idyllic cays, and coral reefs. The archipelago's dozens of islands are surrounded by turquoise waters and lined with pristine strands that provide access to great skin diving or surfing, according to the season.

6 Eastern Panama. The eastern provinces of Guna Yala and the Darién are Panama at its wildest, where every trip is an adventure. This region also has the country's best sportfishing and fishing lodges.

Caribbean Sea
Portobelo
El Porvenir
Naraganá
Colón
Rio Sidra
KUNA YALA
Sabanitas
El Llano
Ailigandí
Chilibre
Ustupu
COLÓN
Pacora
PANAMA
Mulatupu
Arraiján
PANAMA CITY
COCLÉ
La Chorrera
Puerto Obaldia
La Pintada
Cerro Gaitál
Nueva Gorgona
Bahia de Panama
Meteti
Penonomé
San Carlos
San Miguel
Anton
Farallon
La Palma
Yaviza
Aguadulce
Isla del Rey
DARIÉN
Divisa
El Real
Chitré
Golfo de Panama
Garachiné
Sambú
HERRERA
Las Tablas
Pocrí
Puerto Piña
LOS SANTOS
Punta Piña
Pedasí
Jaqué
Tonosí
COLOMBIA
0
50 mi
0
50 km

PANAMA PLANNER

Visitor Resources

The Panamanian Tourism Authority, ATP, is Panama's official tourism organization. Its website (🌐 *www.visitpanama.com*) is an excellent pretrip planning resource with overviews of Panama's regions and points of interest.

ATP has 17 offices around Panama, open weekdays 8–3:30. The English-speaking staff at ATP offices are friendly and helpful. Their resources—mostly brochures—tend to plug local tour companies rather than aid independent exploration.

Other resources include *The Visitor,* a small, free paper that can be found at most hotels and travel agencies, and *Panama Planner* an excellent tourism magazine, available at large hotels.

Getting Here and Around

Air Travel: Copa, a United partner, is Panama's flagship carrier. It operates flights from Chicago, Las Vegas, Los Angeles, Miami, New York–JFK, Orlando, Toronto, and Washington Dulles. Copa also flies to many Central and South American cities. You can fly to Panama from Houston and Newark on United, from Atlanta on Delta, from Miami Dallas, New York, and Newark on American, and from Fort Lauderdale on Spirit.

Air Panama is Panama's domestic carrier and serves destinations all over the country, including Guna Yala, Bocas del Toro, David, and the Darién. Domestic flights usually cost $100 to $200 round-trip; you can buy tickets directly from the airline or through a travel agent. Air Panama offers charter flights as well, although these tend to be quite pricey.

Rental Cars: Driving is a great way to see Panama. The Panamerican Highway takes you to or near most towns in the country, and with a car you can also visit small villages and explore remote areas more easily. Most secondary roads are well signposted and in reasonable condition.

Compact cars like a Kia Pinto, Ford Fiesta, VW Fox, or Toyota Yaris start at around $35 a day; for $40–$50 you can rent a Mitsubishi Lancer, a VW Golf, or a Polo. Four-wheel-drive pickups start at $70 a day. International agencies sometimes have cheaper per-day rates, but locals undercut them on longer rentals. Stick shift is the norm in Panama, so check with the rental agency if you only drive an automatic.

Where to Stay

"Hotel" isn't the only tag you'll find in Panama: *hospedaje, pensión, casa de huespedes,* and *posada* also denote somewhere to stay. Hotels and *posadas* tend to be higher-end, whereas *hospedajes, pensiones,* and *casas de huespedes* are sometimes smaller and family run. A *residencial* might be a by-the-hour sort of place.

Resorts: Big international chain hotels (Westin, Radisson, Marriott, InterContinental, and more) are found throughout Panama City. They have rooms and facilities equal to those at home, but can lack a sense of place. If five-star luxury isn't your top priority, the best deals are undoubtedly with mid-range local hotels.

Rentals: Short-term furnished rentals aren't common in Panama. Villas International offers several premium villa and apartment rentals. Sublet.com and VRBO deal mostly with modest apartments, often as cheap as $700 a week.

Bed-and-Breakfasts: In Panama the term *B&B* is frequently extended to luxury hotels that happen to include breakfast in their price. Indeed, these make up most of the pickings at Bed & Breakfast.com and BnB Finder. Ah! Panamá includes a few homier mid-range establishments.

Eco-Lodges: Found throughout the Guna Yala and the Darién, eco-lodges can be luxurious, but most are rustic, and all are way off the beaten path, so plan on staying a few nights. The term *eco-lodge* sometimes describes a property in a rural or jungle location rather than somewhere that is truly sustainable. The International Ecotourism Society has online resources to help you pick somewhere truly green.

Panama Tips and Safety

Packing: Insect repellent, sunscreen, and sunglasses are essential to help protect you from the relentless sun and persistent mosquitoes. Panama's rainy season lasts from mid-April to December, and rain is common at other times, too, so a foldable umbrella or waterproof jacket is advisable.

Trouble Spots: Poorer neighborhoods in the capital (shaded on our Panama City maps), the city of Colón (other than the Colón 2000 cruise port, the free zone, the train station, and the hotels we list), and the border area with Colombia in the Darién. Using standard travel precautions, the majority of visitors have a hassle-free trip here.

Pacific or Caribbean? You can incorporate both coastlines during your visit. If you're in the center of the country, a highway zips you from Panama City to Colón in 45 minutes. The Caribbean side receives more rain, but myriad fans of Bocas del Toro, Portobelo, and Guna Yala don't seem to mind.

WHEN TO GO

Hotels often fill up between Christmas and Easter, especially on weekends. Reserve rooms weeks or months in advance if you plan to be here during Christmas week or Semana Santa (Holy Week). Holidays mean crowded times at the beach, but they hardly affect Guna Yala and the Darién. Check the Panama Tourism Authority's website (🌐 *www.visitpanama.com*) for holiday and festival dates.

Most visitors come during the December–May dry season, but there's no bad time to visit. Just choose your activity.

Bird-watching is best from October to March, when northern migrants boost the native population.

Fishing excels from January to March, though Pacific sailfish run from April to July, and there are plenty of fish biting from July to January.

Surfing is best from June to December in the Pacific, whereas the Caribbean gets more waves between November and March, and some swells in July and August.

White-water rafting and **kayaking** are best June to December, when you have half a dozen rivers to choose from.

Scuba diving varies according to the region. The Caribbean's best diving conditions are between August and November, though March and April can also be good. The Gulf of Panama has better visibility from June to December, but the trade winds make the sea progressively colder and murkier there from December through to May. Those winds have less of an impact on the Gulf of Chiriquí and Isla de Coiba, where the diving is best from December to July.

Get the idea? It's all in what you plan to do.

Dry Season/Wet Season

Panama is an unmistakably tropical country, where temperatures fluctuate between 70°F and 90°F year-round, and humidity hovers around 80%. The country experiences only two seasons: dry, from late December to May, and rainy from early May to December. January through April are the sunniest months for most of the country. Panama experiences a mini dry season in July and August, where you may have long stretches of sunny days. Count on downpours most afternoons in May, June, September, October, and November. Bocas del Toro province gets plenty of rain in December and January. The Darién receives more rain than the rest of the country, and has a slightly shorter dry season.

IF YOU LIKE

Adventure Sports

The options for enjoying Panama's great outdoors range from hiking through the cloud forest to paddling down a white-water river. The country's world-class fishing, surfing, diving, and bird-watching draw plenty of people focused on just one activity, but Panama is also a great destination for travelers who want to dabble in several adventure sports.

Hiking. Panama's hiking options range from short walks into the rain forest near Panama City to longer hikes though the mountains above El Valle de Antón, Boquete, or Cerro Punta, to a two-week trek through the jungles of the Darién.

Horseback Riding. Equestrian tours take you through the mountain forests of Cerro Azul, El Valle de Antón, Boquete, Volcán, Cerro Punta, or the rain forest of Bocas del Toro.

Kayaking. Sit-on-top kayaks are available at many lodges for exploring reefs and mangroves, but serious kayakers can join tours to paddle the lower Chagres River, the Panama Canal's Pacific entrance, or the San Blas Islands of Guna Yala.

Rafting. The Chagres and Chiriquí Viejo Rivers have exciting white-water rafting routes that pass through pristine rain forest. From June to December they are complemented by half a dozen smaller rivers near Boquete.

Surfing. With dozens of surf spots on two oceans, Panama has waves most of the year. Expert-only reef breaks are the norm, but a handful of beach breaks are good for neophytes, too. Try Playa Santa Catalina, Morro Negrito, Bocas del Toro, and Isla Grande.

Zipline Tours. These high-adrenaline tours send you gliding through the forest canopy on cables strung between platforms high in trees, providing a monkey's perspective of the jungle.

Diving

With two oceans, 1,600 islands, and countless acres of coral, Panama is a world-class dive destination. Its Caribbean reefs and wrecks are adorned with dozens of sponge and coral species and a mind-boggling array of fish and invertebrates. But the Pacific has the country's most spectacular dives, with schools of big fish, manta rays, sharks, and other marine creatures.

Bocas del Toro. With plenty of coral reefs and several dive shops, this popular Caribbean archipelago is perfect for scuba divers and snorkeling enthusiasts alike.

The Canal. Scuba Panama offers a unique dive in the Panama Canal, where steam shovels and trains used to dig it lie submerged in the murky depths.

Escribano Bank. This barrier reef east of Isla Grande is so remote that few divers visit it, but it lies near the eco-resort Coral Lodge.

Isla Coiba. Protected within a vast national park, Coiba is surrounded by the country's best diving, with immense reefs, submerged pinnacles, and legions of fish. Explore it on one-week dive cruises or shorter trips from Play Santa Catalina.

Islas Secas. This remote archipelago in the Gulf of Chiriquí has extensive reefs teeming with marine life that can be explored from the exclusive resort on the islands, or on day trips from Boca Chica.

Guna Yala. Though scuba diving is prohibited in Guna Yala, the province has impressive reefs, especially at the Cayos Holandeses, which can be visited on cruises with San Blas Sailing.

History

The site of the first Spanish colony on the American mainland, Panama has remnants of five centuries of European influence, including ancient fortresses and colonial churches, as well as indigenous cultures that have hardly changed since Columbus sailed down the country's coast.

The Canal. The Panama Canal's creation only a century ago was a historic event that is celebrated by displays in the visitor center at Miraflores Locks and murals in the Canal Administration Building.

Casco Viejo. Panama City's historic quarter holds an enchanting mix of colonial churches, abandoned monasteries, 19th-century buildings, and timeless plazas that are perfect for a drink, or meal.

Indigenous Panama. The country's indigenous communities are living history, preserving centuries-old customs. Visiting them provides glimpses of the Panama that Spanish explorers discovered five centuries ago.

Panama Viejo. The ruins of Panama's first city—founded almost five centuries ago, and sacked by the pirate Henry Morgan in 1671—evoke the nation's start as a trade center.

Portobelo. Together with nearby Fuerte San Lorenzo, these colonial fortresses hemmed by jungle and perched over aquamarine waters are stunning reminders of the days when pirates cruised the Caribbean in search of booty.

Nature Lodges

With more than 960 bird species, 9,000 kinds of flowering plants, and such rare animals as tapirs and ocelots, Panama is a great place for nature lovers. And there's no better way to experience that wildlife than a stay at a nature lodge, where you can bird-watch from your porch or bed.

Cana Field Station. Nestled in Parque Nacional Darién, this remote and rustic lodge is surrounded by jungle that is home to more than 400 bird species and an array of other wildlife, making it the best place in Panama to see animals.

Canopy Tower. This refurbished radar station in Parque Nacional Soberanía has good bird-watching from the restaurant, the rooftop deck, and every room. Expert guides and daily hikes help guests see as much as possible, whereas the property's sister Canopy Lodge, in El Valle de Antón, provides more comfort in a gorgeous setting.

Finca Lerida. Rooms on this coffee farm at the edge of Parque Nacional Volcán Barú are near a cloud forest where guests regularly see resplendent quetzals, emerald toucanets, and hundreds of other birds.

La Loma Jungle Lodge. With just three open-air bungalows inside the rain forest on Isla Bastamentos, in Bocas del Toro, this intimate lodge provides constant exposure to nature.

Los Quetzales Lodge. Cabins inside the cloud forest here feature amazing views and bird-watching, whereas guests at the main lodge can choose from hikes in two national parks.

Sierra Llorona. Surrounded by a 500-acre private nature reserve traversed by miles of trails, this small, affordable lodge has more than 200 bird species, various types of monkeys, and other wildlife on the property.

Caribbean Sea
Puerto Limón
Parque Nacional Cahuita
Bribri
Las Tablas
Guabito
Isla Colón
Changuinola
Reserva Forestal Palo Seco
Bocas del Toro
Parque Nacional Marino Isla Bastimentos
Almirante
BOCAS DEL TORO
Parque Internacional La Amistad
11
COSTA RICA
Chiriquí Grande
Golfo de los Mosquitos
COLÓN
Cerro Punta
Bájo Boquete
Volcán
Caldera
NGÖBE BUGLE
COCLÉ
Parque Nacional Omar Torrijos
El Valle de Antón
La Pintada
Santa Fe
Paso Canosas
CHIRIQUÍ
La Concepción
4
Penonomé
Puerto Armuelles
David
San Félix
1
VERAGUAS
91
Antón
Aguadulce
Parque Nacional Sariqua
Interamericana
Divisa
Santiago
3
Quebrada del Medio
Punta Burica
Parque Nacional Marino Golfo de Chiriqui
Soná
Ocú
Chitré
HERRERA
Los Santos
Las Minas
Las Tablas
Macaracas
Golfo de Montijo
Parque Nacional Coiba
Isla de Coiba
LOS SANTOS
Reserva Forestal La Tronosa
Tonosí
Parque Nacional Cerro Hoya
KEY
Bird watching
Diving/Snorkeling
Fishing
Golf
Hiking
Horseback riding
Kayaking
Rafting
Surfing

National Parks and Activities

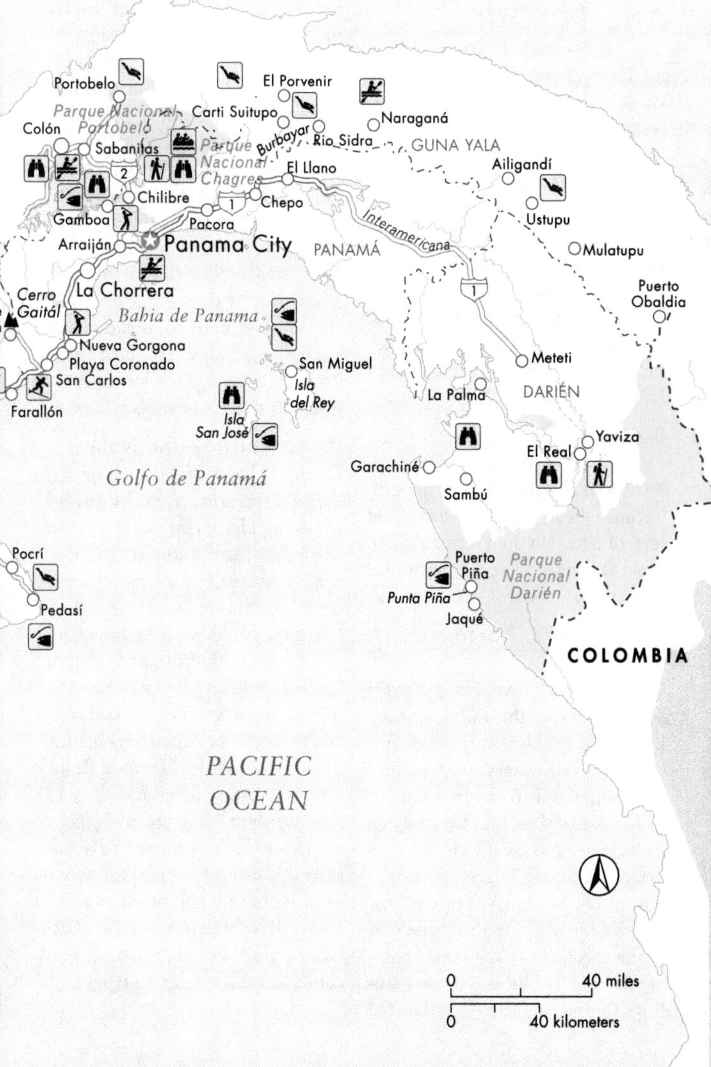

GREAT ITINERARIES

CITY, CANAL, AND BEYOND

The quintessential three-day Panama itinerary is perfect for a long weekend. It takes in the country's capital and its famous canal, as well as gives you a taste of the adventure that waits in the interior. It requires some judicious planning, but it's entirely possible to get a sampling of the best of Panama's urban and wilderness offerings in such a short time, thanks to short distances and the number of attractions easily reached from Panama City.

Base yourself in the capital for one, two, or three days of your trip. ■TIP→ **Use taxis while in the city because they are much cheaper and less of a hassle than renting a car, even for taking short trips to the outskirts of town.**

Days 1 and 2: Panama City and Canal

On your first day, get an early start to avoid the midday heat. Head to the Casco Viejo, the capital's restored colonial quarter, for a morning of old-world exploration. The pastel colors and latticework gates evoke old New Orleans, sans Bourbon Street of course. In the afternoon, head to Miraflores, just outside the city, for a ringside seat to the spectacle of huge ships passing through the locks. Narration in English and Spanish describes the fascinating process, and an adjoining museum documents the history of the canal. If you want to be on the waterway rather than alongside it, start Day 2 with a partial canal transit; billed as half-day tours, it frequently takes up three-quarters of a day. Less-frequently offered full canal transits take you end to end and do take up a full day with a return to Panama City in the evening. A visit to the Biomuseo or an afternoon of shopping in an air-conditioned mall rounds out any Panama City day. The port facility at Calzada de Amador is a great place for sunset cocktails or dinner.

Day 3: Railway and Nature

Get up early on your third day to take the Panama Canal Railway to Colón. Here, you can spend the day exploring the country's Caribbean coast, fortresses, rain forest, or the beaches of Portobelo or San Lorenzo. You'll leave Panama City at 7:15 am and return at 5:15 pm, but that allows plenty of time to see the coast. Another option keeps you closer to the capital: Spend one or two days at the Gamboa Rainforest Resort, which is less than an hour north of Panama City by taxi. This option is rather expensive but provides several choices for activities, including the popular rainforest aerial tram and trips onto Lago Gatún. No matter what you choose, you'll be sure to marvel at how close wilderness is to a major urban area.

Logistics

Schedule carefully: Partial canal transit tours operate one or two days a week; full canal transits operate one or two days a month.

In Colón, arrange a pick-up in advance through a tour company or take a shuttle to Colón 2000 cruise port (these shuttles always meet the Panama Railway trains), and hire a taxi there, not at the train station.

THE BEST OF PANAMA

With some serious picking and choosing you can put together an almost perfect dream itinerary. Panama's decent highway system makes travel quite easy, and its good domestic air network puts even the farthest-flung places an hour or less from the capital.

Days 1 to 3: Panama City and Canal

The Panama City and Canal itinerary above makes a good base from which to start. (*See itinerary above.*) The capital, canal, and Central Panama are a good introduction to the country for most visitors. Added time gives you more flexibility to include other Central Panama destinations. Active travelers may prefer to head to El Valle de Antón for bird-watching, hiking, biking, or horseback riding. Several excellent lodging choices will make sure you sleep in comfort and eat in style. You could also combine a night at Sierra Llorona or Burbayar lodge (both in the highlands northeast of Panama City) with a visit to an indigenous Emberá village.

Days 4 to 7: Bocas del Toro

An early-morning flight from Panama City puts you in Bocas del Toro in less than an hour, and you'll be pleasantly surprised at how quickly you slow down to island time. Check into your hotel in Bocas town, where most visitors stay. ■TIP→ **If you're staying at one of the outer islands, arrange to have a hotel representative meet you at the airport and transfer you by boat. The farther-flung lodgings lie 45–60 minutes away.** Nearby botanical and butterfly gardens on the main island can occupy your first day. Your second day should be spent on Isla Bastimentos, about 15 minutes away by boat. Traditionally, visitors come here to visit the indigenous Ngöbe communities, the islands' original inhabitants. These days, more Bastimentos visitors head for the popular zip-line canopy tour at Red Frog Beach. Don't worry, time allows to do both. Bocas means underwater activities, too. If you've always wanted to try scuba diving, the sev-

LOGISTICS

- If flying domestically, opt for morning flights during the rainy season. Skies are usually clearer, and you'll appreciate the smoother conditions on Air Panama's smallish planes.
- Do not schedule international-to-domestic flight connections (or vice-versa) the same day. Invariably, there will be a delay.
- The small airstrips in the Darién and Guna Yala receive one early-morning flight from Panama City. David and Bocas del Toro offer morning and afternoon flight options.
- The trip from David to Almirante, the ferry port for Bocas del Toro, is three hours overland, making it easy to combine Boquete and Bocas without backtracking to Panama City.
- Elevation makes all the difference at these latitudes. Lowland Panama swelters year-round, but you'll appreciate long sleeves at highland elevations such as Boquete and El Valle de Antón.

eral dive shops here offer a one-day intro course. You won't get certified, but you'll see if you want to pursue the activity. Of course, a full diving course will take up several days here. And for much less muss and fuss, anyone who can swim can snorkel.

Days 7 to 9: Boquete and Chiriquí

Fly to the western city of David, a business hub where travelers rarely linger. Rent a car or take a taxi for the 45-minute drive over a new four-lane highway to highland Boquete. The elevation change makes temperatures noticeably cooler. Get your bearings that first day exploring the town. Early European settlers created a community that could have been transported from the Swiss Alps. Any number of expert guides can take you bird-watching—this is one of Panama's premier destinations and is the haunt of the beautiful resplendent quetzal. An early-morning horseback tour can kick off your third day. The highlands are Panama's coffee country, and a few processors offer tours that acquaint you with the life and times of the dark beverage. If you're a rafter, you've likely come to Chiriquí for white-water sports. The Estí, Dolega, and one sector of the Chiriquí Viejo rivers are apt for beginners and take up full- or half-day excursions.

PANAMANIAN CUISINE

Signature dishes and flavors

One of Panama's best-known dishes, *carimañola*, consists of the tuber yuca, ground and boiled and made into a dumpling that's filled with minced beef or chicken and pieces of boiled egg. They're a Panamanian breakfast staple. *Sancocho* is the other dish that truly says "Panama." This chicken and yuca soup—sometimes prepared as thick as a stew—is flavored with *culantro*. (Think "cilantro," but slightly more aromatic.) It's reputed to be good for whatever ails you and also makes for a surprisingly cooling dish on a sweltering day. To make the descriptively named *ropa vieja* ("old clothes"), a Panamanian cook uses whatever is left over in the kitchen to jazz up a dish that is, at its most basic, shredded flank steak with rice and tomato sauce. Ropa vieja is one of the few Panamanian dishes that can be quite spicy.

Cooks here make a variation on Mexican *tamales*—the singular is *tamal*—with a filling of chicken, peas, onions, and cornmeal boiled inside tied plantain leaves. You eat the filling but not the leaves, and certainly not the string. Every Latin American country claims its own variation on empanadas. Panamanians make semi-circular ones with a filling of ground beef and cheese fried in dough and served as appetizers. Caribbean cooks often add plantain to the filling.

Almojábana, corn-flour bread, and *patacones,* salted green plantains fried golden brown and pounded into crispy chips, accompany many meals. *Hojaldras* make a tasty side dish to any breakfast. When made sweet and sprinkled with powdered sugar, they're like doughnuts, but they are often prepared with ham and cheese.

Seafood

With 1,500 miles of coastline, seafood is everywhere. (What else would you expect in a nation whose name means "abundance of fish"?) Corvina, a white sea bass, frequently shows up as the main ingredient in *ceviche.* Whatever the cubed pieces of fish or seafood used, Panamanian ceviche is marinated in lime juice, with onion and celery and sometimes hot pepper and served chilled as an appetizer.

Beverages

Seco, a distilled sugarcane firewater, is commonly tempered with chilled milk. For a smooth easy beverage, try *chicheme*, a blend of milk, cornmeal, cinnamon, and vanilla. And beverages don't come more basic than the ubiquitous *pipa.* Poke a hole in an unripe coconut, stick in a straw, and you have a refreshing drink of coconut juice. Roadside stands everywhere sell them.

LIVING IN PANAMA

Panama gets high marks as the Western Hemisphere's up-and-coming retirement destination. Moderate cost of living, ease of owning real estate for foreigners, quality health-care facilities in the hub cities of Panama City and David, decent in-country transportation and communication, and proximity to the United States draw thousands of Americans, who make up the majority of foreigners who retire to Panama.

The expat population congregates mostly in four enclaves around Panama. The former Canal Zone came ready-made with U.S.-style housing and amenities and a California or Florida look and feel when Panama took over the canal in 1999. In the northwest, Bocas del Toro is Panama's version of slow-paced Caribbean-island life. Central Panama's El Valle de Antón and Chiriquí province's Boquete offer higher-elevation respites from the lowland heat. The latter, in particular, is growing at an astonishing pace. Each is rich in opportunities for foreigners to meet up for events or volunteer work.

Retirement and relocation give you three status options to look into:

Pensioner. Most popular for foreigners is the pensionado route. You need a guaranteed monthly income from a pension, public or private, of at least $1,000. You are allowed a one-time duty-free import of your household goods up $10,000 as well as the tax-free purchase of a car every two years. In addition, various Panamanian businesses and institutions offer you a wide variety of discounts.

Investor. As an inversionista, you incorporate a business under Panamanian law and provide full-time employment to at least five citizens. (Household employees do not count.)

Person of Means. To qualify for solvencia económica propia, you must deposit at least $300,000 in a fixed-term account in a Panamanian bank for at least three years.

Note that none of these options permits you to work, and all require a clean police record. A good attorney here can help navigate the bureaucracy.

Don't fall prey to "Sunshine Syndrome." Pause and take a deep breath if you find yourself uttering the words "Honey, we met that nice real estate agent in the hotel bar. Let's buy a house." Some succumb and move to Panama, only to find that living here bears scant resemblance to vacationing here. Experts suggest a trial run. Rent a house or apartment for a few months and see if day-to-day life in Panama agrees with you.

Panama City

2

WORD OF MOUTH

"I would absolutely stay in Casco Viejo—really lovely colonial part of town, friendly people, good restaurants, shops and nightlife . . . can walk everywhere fun for the kids."

—carrom

www.fodors.com/forums

By David Dudenhoefer

FOUNDED NEARLY FIVE CENTURIES AGO, Panama city is steeped in history, yet much of it is remarkably modern. The baroque facades of the city's old quarter appear frozen in time, while the area around Punta Paitilla (Paitilla Point) is positively vaulting into the 21st century, with gleaming skyscrapers towering over the waterfront.

Panama City is home to races, religions, and cultures from around the world. Whereas the high-rises of Punta Paitilla and the Área Bancária (banking district) create a skyline more impressive than that of Miami (really!), the brick streets and balconies of the Casco Viejo evoke the French Quarter of New Orleans. The tree-lined boulevards of Balboa are a mixture of early-20th-century American architecture and exuberant tropical vegetation. The islands reached by the nearby Calzada de Amador (Amador Causeway) are full of bars and restaurants and a marina.

The city's proximity to tropical nature is astounding, with significant patches of forest protected within city limits on Cerro Ancón (Ancón Hill) and in Parque Metropolitano, and the national parks of Camino de Cruces and Soberanía just to the northwest of town. You could spend a morning hiking through the rain forest of the Parque Metropolitano to see parrots and toucans, then watch pelicans dive into the sea while sipping a sunset drink at one of Amador Causeway's restaurants. There are plenty of spots in and around the city to view massive ships moving in and out of the Panama Canal.

An array of restaurants, an abundance of shops and handicraft markets, and a vibrant nightlife scene round out Panama City's charm. Panama City can also serve as a base for a bunch of day trips, including Panama Canal transit tours, a boat ride to Isla Taboga or Isla Contadora, a trip on the Panama Canal Railway, a day exploring the colonial fortresses, beaches, and coral reefs of Portobelo, or hikes through various rain-forest reserves.

Included in Panama City's colorful contrasts are many of the unfortunate aspects of urban life in the developing world. It has its fair share of slums, including several around must-see Casco Viejo. Traffic is often downright terrible, and the ocean along its coast is very polluted. Crime is a problem in some neighborhoods. Be careful where you walk around alone, especially at night. The city as a whole is quite safe, especially the downtown area, where you'll find its bustling hotels, restaurants, and bars.

TOP REASONS TO GO

The Panama Canal. Fifty miles long, the interoceanic canal is literally Panama's biggest attraction. There are half a dozen spots in or near the capital from which to admire it. The Calzada de Amador, the Balboa Yacht Club, and the visitor center at Miraflores Locks all offer impressive vistas of the "big ditch."

Casco Viejo. The balconies, brick streets, and quiet plazas of the historic Casco Viejo have a European air, and the neighborhood's ancient churches and monasteries stand as testimony to the country's rich colonial history. Though much of it is dilapidated, the neighborhood has some of the city's nicest restaurants and bars.

Calzada de Amador. Stretching 3 km (2 miles) into the Pacific to connect three islands to the mainland, the Amador Causeway has panoramic views of the city's skyline, the canal's Pacific entrance, and the Bay of Panama, as well as a good selection of restaurants and bars—all of them cooled by ocean breezes.

Day Trips. Panama City is close to some of the most accessible rain forests in the world; jungle trails are a short drive from most hotels. In addition to boat trips on the Panama Canal or wildlife watching on Gatún Lake, you can visit an Emberá Indian village; go white-water rafting, fishing, kayaking, or hiking through the jungle; ferry out to the island of Isla Contadora, or Isla Taboga; or visit the Caribbean fortresses of Portobelo, where the history is complemented by beaches and coral reefs.

2

ORIENTATION AND PLANNING

GETTING ORIENTED

Panama City is a sprawling urban area, stretching for 20 km (12 miles) along the Bahía de Panamá (Bay of Panama), on the Pacific Coast and deep into the sultry hinterland. Most of its attractions and accommodations are within a few miles of one another in the city's southwest corner, near the Panama Canal's Pacific entrance. The eastern edge of the canal's entrance—because Panama snakes west to east, the canal runs north from the Pacific to the Atlantic—is defined by the former American Canal Zone, which includes the Calzada de Amador (the breakwater connecting several islands to the mainland) and the neighborhoods of Balboa,

Albrook, and Cerro Ancón, a forested hill topped by a big Panamanian flag that is a landmark visible from most of the city. To the east of Cerro Ancón is the busy Avenida de los Mártires, which was once on the border between the Canal Zone and Panama City. To the east of that former border lie the slums of Chorrillo and Santa Ana, both of which should be avoided; the Plaza Cinco de Mayo (where the country's congress is located); and the Avenida Central pedestrian mall, which runs southeastward into the historic Casco Viejo.

Avenida Balboa, one of the city's main east–west routes, runs along the Bay of Panama between the Casco Viejo and modern Paitilla Point. It runs through an attractive waterfront promenade called the Cinta Costera. The neighborhood along its western half is sketchy, so you should only stroll the Cinta Costera to the east of the Balboa monument. Avenida Balboa ends at Punta Paitilla, with its Multicentro shopping mall, skyscrapers, and private hospitals. There it branches into the Corredor Sur, an expressway to the international airport, and the inland Vía Israel, which eventually turns into Avenida Cincuentenario, and leads to the ruins of Panamá Viejo.

The main eastbound street to the north of Avenida Balboa is Avenida Justo Arosemena, which runs east from Plaza Cinco de Mayo and flows into Calle 50 (Cincuenta) (also called Calle Nicanor de Obarrio). The main westbound route is Vía España, a busy boulevard lined with banks and shopping centers that curves south to become the Avenida Central, which in turn becomes a pedestrian mall at Plaza Cinco de Mayo, after which it curves eastward to become the main avenue in the Casco Viejo.

PANAMA CITY PLANNER

WHEN TO GO

Unlike the rest of the country, Panama City hardly has a low season, because the bulk of its visitors are business travelers. Most tourists head here during the dry season, from December to May; this is when the city's hotels are packed. Carnaval, around mid-February, is a fun time to be in the capital, because that long weekend is celebrated with parades and lots of partying. The city is fairly quiet during Easter week, on the other hand, since many businesses close from Thursday to Easter Sunday and every resident who can leaves town.

May, June, and September through November are the rainiest months in Panama City, though most of that rain falls in the afternoon or evening. The rains let up a bit in July and August, which is a good time to visit, because you can share the place with fewer tourists than during the dry season.

Because Panama City has the country's only international airport and is the transportation hub for domestic flights and buses, you may return here several times during your trip. This means you can explore the capital bit by bit over the course of your stay in the country.

GETTING HERE AND AROUND

AIR TRAVEL

All international flights land at Panama City's Aeropuerto Internacional de Tocumen (PTY), 26 km (16 miles) northeast of Panama City. Panama has one domestic airline, Air Panama, which flies to about two-dozen destinations out of Aeropuerto Marcos A. Gelabert; it's in the Canal Zone.

CAR TRAVEL

Driving a car in Panama City is not an undertaking for the meek, but renting a car is an excellent way to explore the surrounding countryside. Rentals usually cost $40 to $50 per day, whereas four-wheel-drive vehicles cost $60 to $90. All the big car-rental companies offer GPS rentals, and have offices downtown and at the airports.

Car-Rental Agencies **Avis** ☎ *507/278–9444.* **Budget** ☎ *507/263–8777.* **Dollar** ☎ *507/270–0355.* **Hertz** ☎ *507/301–2611.* **National** ☎ *507/265–3333.* **Thrifty** ☎ *507/204–9555.*

TAXI TRAVEL

Taxis in Panama City are all independently owned, tend to be smaller cars, and don't have meters. The city is divided into zones, the flat fare for one person being $1.50, to which they add 50¢ each time you cross into another zone, plus 50¢ for each additional person. Fares also increase about 20% after 10 pm and on Sunday. A short trip should cost about $3 for two people, whereas a trip to the domestic airport in Albrook or the Calzada de Amador can run about $5–$7. Tips are not expected. You will be charged double, or several times the standard rate, by the taxi drivers who wait outside hotels, but they drive vans or SUVs, and are likely to speak some English. Flagging a cab in the street is widely considered to be safe. If you're alone, you may be expected to share a taxi, a common practice in Panama, as is sitting in the passenger seat next to the driver.

Panamataxi Turismo provides personal transportation and various cultural tours for individuals and small groups.

Contacts **Panamataxi Turismo** ☎ *507/263–8311, 507/6663–1092* 🌐 *www.panamataxi.com.*

SAFETY

Most of the city is safe for walking, even at night, especially El Cangrejo, the Área Bancária, and Paitilla, where the bulk of the city's hotels and restaurants are located. The Casco Viejo and Avenida Central pedestrian mall are safe by day, but after dark don't wander west of Calle 10, or Plaza Herrera. Even during the day you should leave most valuables and money in your hotel safe. At night you should travel to and from the Casco Viejo only by taxi or rental car, but by day walking there from Plaza Cinco de Mayo on Avenida Central is fine. You don't need a map or a Geiger counter to realize you've headed into a bad neighborhood, though the Casco Viejo looks more dangerous than it is. If you're on foot and feel any apprehension about where you've ended up, flag down the first taxi, even if it has another passenger in it, and go someplace you know is safe. Between 11 am and 3 pm, the heat is usually oppressive, so serious strolling should be limited to the morning and evening hours. ⚠ **Areas that should be avoided at all hours are El Chorrillo and Santa Ana, just west of the Casco Viejo; the southwestern half of Caledonia, including the Avenida Balboa west of the Balboa Monument; and Curundú, just to the west of Caledonia.**

ABOUT THE RESTAURANTS

Cuisine selection that pretty much spans the globe, from Indian and Italian to Lebanese and Panamanian (needless to say). The seafood tends to be quite fresh, which shouldn't come as a surprise, since the word "*Panama*" means "abundance of fish," and it's relatively inexpensive, with the exception of lobster and crab. Panama produces decent beef, but the best beef is imported from the United States and can be more expensive. A typical entrée at an expensive restaurant runs about $17, whereas a main dish at a less expensive eatery averages around $9. It's customary to tip at least 10%, but some restaurants automatically add a 10% *servicio* charge, so be sure to have a good look at the check.

Some restaurants close Sunday, and many close between lunch and dinner (approximately 2:30 to 6:30). Reservations aren't usually required, but are a good idea on the weekends. Jackets and ties aren't necessary, but don't wear shorts and sandals unless the restaurant is outdoors.

Prices in the reviews are the average cost of a main course at dinner or, if dinner is not served, at lunch.

ABOUT THE HOTELS

Panama City has experienced a boom in hotel construction, which means you won't need to reserve too far ahead except for the small B&Bs and boutique hotels. If you reserve through the websites of the big hotels, or travel search engines, you can usually get a room for considerably less than the rack rate. The city's best hotels are quite nice and varied enough in what they offer to suit most tastes, but some can suffer from poor service. Travelers on a budget can find a variety of comfortable accommodations for less than $120, which often includes a swimming pool. All hotels listed here have private bathrooms with hot water, air-conditioning, and Wi-Fi; most have a telephone and cable TV in the room.

Prices in the reviews are the lowest cost of a standard double room in high season. For expanded hotel reviews, facilities, and current deals, visit Fodors.com.

ESSENTIALS

EMERGENCIES

Ambulance ☎ *911.* **Fire department** ☎ *103.* **Hospital Punta Pacífica** ✉ *Boulevard Pacífica y Vía Punta Darién, Punta Pacífica* ☎ *507/204–8000.* **National police** ☎ *104.*

TOURS

Panama City has a plethora of tour companies, all of which offer tours of the city, canal, and nearby parks, but not all of them have guides of the same caliber, and few have true naturalist guides. The premier ecotourism company is **Ancon Expeditions,** but the comparable **Ecocircuitos** also has good guides and environmentally friendly policies. Smaller, newer companies that can often provide a more customized service include **Panoramic Panama, Sendero Panama,** and **Advantage Panama,** which specializes in bird-watching and nature tours. Well-established tour operators that offer day trips are **Margo Tours** and **Pesantez Tours.** An inexpensive city tour option is to board one of the red double-decker buses of **Citysightseeing Panama,** which stop at the Amador Cause-

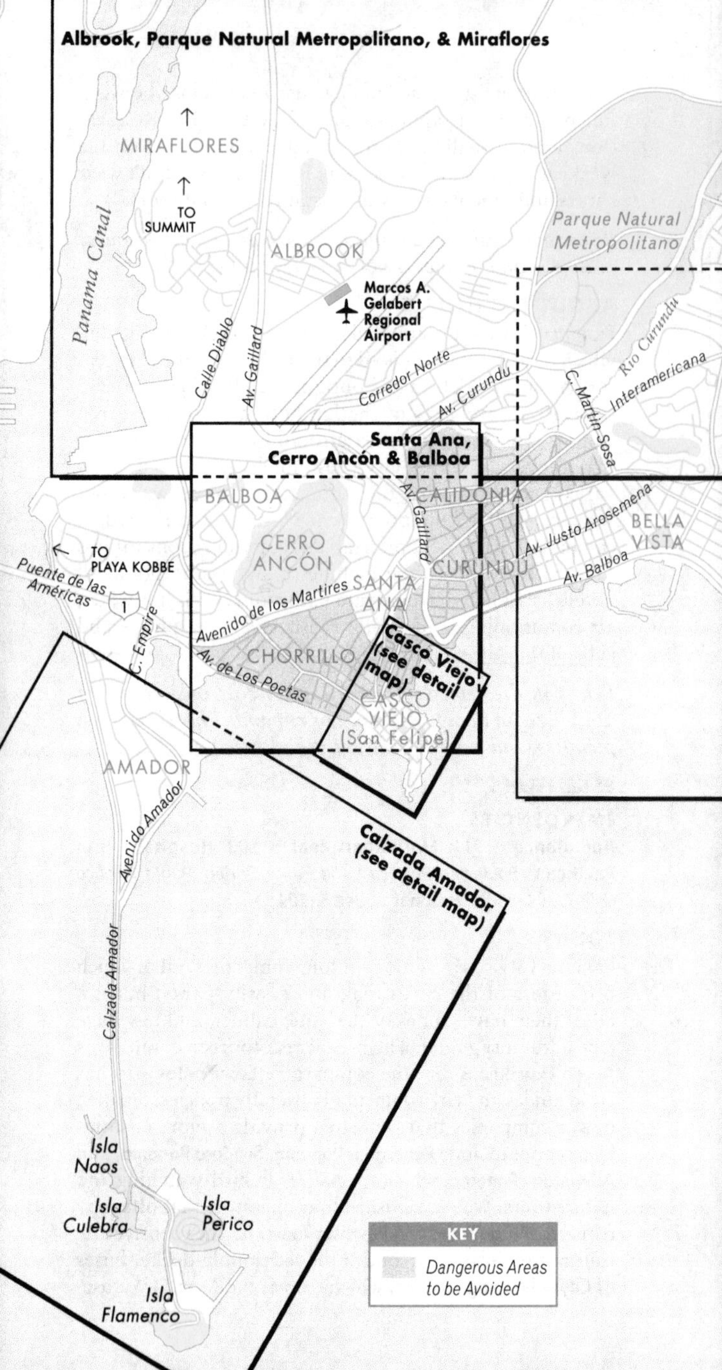

Albrook, Parque Natural Metropolitano, & Miraflores
MIRAFLORES
TO SUMMIT
Panama Canal
ALBROOK
Marcos A. Gelabert Regional Airport
Parque Natural Metropolitano
Calle Diablo
Av. Gaillard
Corredor Norte
Av. Curundu
Rio Curundu
C. Martin Sosa
Interamericana
Santa Ana, Cerro Ancón & Balboa
BALBOA
CALIDONIA
Av. Gaillard
CERRO ANCÓN
CURUNDU
Av. Justo Arosemena
BELLA VISTA
Av. Balboa
TO PLAYA KOBBE
Puente de las Américas
1
Avenido de los Martires
SANTA ANA
C. Empire
CHORRILLO
Casco Viejo (see detail map)
Av. de Los Poetas
CASCO VIEJO (San Felipe)
AMADOR
Avenido Amador
Calzada Amador (see detail map)
Calzada Amador
Isla Naos
Isla Culebra
Isla Perico
Isla Flamenco
KEY
Dangerous Areas to be Avoided

TO
BAHA'I TEMPLE

BETANIA

Ricardo J. Alfaro
(Tumba Muerto)

San Francisco & Panama Viejo

Downtown Panama City

Rio Matasnillo

Rio Gallinera

Via Simón Bolívar

Via Brasil

EL
CANGREJO

Via España

Gran Morrison Via España

Parque
Recreativo
OMAR

Av. Ernesto T. Lefevre

Av. Santa Elena

Av. Balisario Porras

OBARRIO

PANAMÁ
VIEJO

Av. Nicanor de Obarrio

SAN
FRANCISCO

Via Cincuentenario

Via Cincuentenario

MARBELLA

Av. Balboa

SAN
SABASTIÁN

Via Israel

Corredor Sur

TO
TOCUMEN INT'L. AIRPORT

PUNTA
PAITILLA

PUNTA
PACÍFICA

Bahía de Panama

0 1/2 mile

0 1/2 kilometer

PACIFIC
OCEAN

Panama City

PANAMA CITY EXPLORING TIPS

Panama City is a hassle-free place to explore on your own: many people speak English, the U.S. dollar is legal tender, and there are ATMs, restaurants, pharmacies, shops, and taxis just about everywhere. You can explore some areas on foot, though distances between neighborhoods make taxis necessary for most trips. If you ever feel uneasy about a location or situation and there aren't any police around, just flag down a taxi, which are safe and everywhere. Tourism police patrol the Casco Viejo and Panama Viejo on bicycles. If you have a medical problem, go to Hospital Punta Pacífica, the best private clinic in the city. It also has a dental clinic. If your health insurance doesn't cover expenses incurred abroad, check into the Panamanian government's free health insurance for tourists who have been in the country less than 30 days (🌐 www.visitpanama.com).

It's best to get rolling early, take a long break around lunch (when the weather is hottest), and head back into the street around 3 or 4 pm, when the heat begins to subside. If you're there during the rainy season, you can expect downpours every afternoon: the best thing to do when it starts to pour is find a restaurant and have a cup of coffee or a drink. Rest your feet until the deluge subsides, which is usually within 20 minutes. Keep in mind that most, though not all, museums are closed on Monday. The most convenient COTEL, or post office, is on the lower floor of the Plaza Concordia mall, on Vía España. Farmacia Arrocha has a dozen large pharmacies scattered around the city that are open 24 hours. Maps, brochures, and basic information are available at the Autoridad de Turismo Panama stands in the the Tocumen and Allbrook airports.

way, Miraflores Locks, Casco Viejo and several malls once an hour, allowing you to get off, explore, then board the next bus. **Panama Marine Adventures** runs a two-hour Aqua Bus City Tour in a duck bus, combining a traditional bus tour with navigation of the Pacific Ocean and the Panama Canal. To head off the beaten path, check out **Explora Eco-Adventures Panama** or **Aventuras Panama,** a white-water rafting outfitter that also offers kayaking tours in the Panama Canal and the Caribbean.

Tour Companies **Advantage Panama** ✉ *Llanos de Curundú No. 2006, Curundú* ☎ *507/6676–2466* 🌐 *www.advantagepanama.com.*

Ancon Expeditions ✉ *Calle Elvira Mendez, Edificio El Dorado No. 3, Area Bancária* ☎ *507/269–9415* 🌐 *www.anconexpeditions.com.* **Aventuras Panama** ✉ *Calle El Parcial, 1½ blocks west of Transístmica, Edif. Celma Of. 3, El Dorado* ☎ *507/260–0044, 507/6679–4404* 🌐 *www.aventuraspanama.com.* **Eco Circuitos Panama** ✉ *Albrook Plaza, No. 31, Urbanización Albrook, Albrook* ☎ *507/315–1305, 800/830–7142 Toll free in US* 🌐 *www.ecocircuitos.com.* **Margo Tours** ✉ *Centro Comercial Plaza Paitilla, local 36, Paitilla* ☎ *507/264–8888* 🌐 *www.margotours.com.* **Panoramic Panama** ✉ *Quarry Heights, casa #35, Cerro Ancón* ☎ *507/314–1417* 🌐 *www.panoramicpanama.com.* **Pesantez Tours** ✉ *Plaza Balboa oficina #2, Punta Paitilla* ☎ *507/366–9100* 🌐 *www.pesantez-tours.com.*

VISITOR INFORMATION

Autoridad de Turismo Panama (*ATP*). The Autoridad de Turismo Panama has a decent Web page and information offices in the Tocumen and Allbrook airports where they answer basic questions and hand out brochures. ✉ *Aeropuerto de Tocumen, Tocumen* ☎ *507/238–4356* 🌐 *www.visitpanama.com.*

EXPLORING PANAMA CITY

CASCO VIEJO

Panama City's historic quarter is known as the Casco Viejo (pronounced CAS-coh Bee-EH-hoh), which translates as "old shell." It's spread over a small point in the city's southeast corner, where timeless streets and plazas are complemented by views of a modern skyline and the Bahía de Panamá. The Casco Viejo's narrow brick streets, wrought-iron balconies, and intricate cornices evoke visions of Panama's glorious history as a major trade center. A stroll here offers opportunities to admire a beautiful mix of Spanish colonial, neoclassical, and art nouveau architecture. And though many of its buildings are in a lamentable state of neglect, and the neighborhood is predominantly poor, it is a lively and colorful place, where soccer balls bounce off the walls of 300-year-old churches and radios blare Latin music.

TIMING AND PRECAUTIONS

The Casco Viejo is best explored on foot, though due to the intensity of the tropical heat, try to do your walking in the morning or late in the afternoon. Four o'clock in the afternoon is a great time to stroll around, when you

can enjoy the evening light at Plaza Francia, have a drink on Plaza Bolívar, then dine at a nearby restaurant. Give yourself at least two hours to tour this neighborhood, more if you plan to shop.

Casco Viejo is predominantly poor, but it isn't as dangerous as it looks. Nevertheless, precautions should be taken: leave jewelry and passport in your hotel safe, don't bring heaps of money, and be discreet with camera or video equipment. The crime problem is not so much in Casco Viejo but in the adjacent neighborhoods, so you shouldn't stray from the areas covered in the walking tour. The area is patrolled by Tourism Police, who work out of a station behind the Teatro Nacional.

WHAT TO SEE

Iglesia de La Merced (*Mercy Church*). One of the oldest structures in the Casco Viejo, La Merced's timeworn, baroque facade was actually removed from a church of the same name in Panamá Viejo and reconstructed here, stone by stone, in 1680. Flanked by white bell towers and tiny chapels, it's a charming sight, especially in late-afternoon light. The interior was destroyed by fires and rebuilt in the early 20th century, when some bad decisions were made, such as covering massive cement pillars with bathroom tiles. ✉ *Calle 9 and Av. Central, Casco Viejo* ⏲ *Mon.–Fri. 6:30 am–noon and 2–7 pm; Sat. 4–7 pm; Sun. 6:30–11 am.*

★ **Iglesia de San José** (*Saint Joseph's Church*). This church is an exact replica of the temple of the same name in Panamá Viejo. It is the sanctuary of the country's famous golden altar, the most valuable object to survive pirate Henry Morgan's razing of the old city. According to legend, a wily priest painted the altar with mud to discourage its theft. Not only did Morgan refrain from pilfering it, but the priest even managed to extract a donation from the pirate. The ornate baroque altar is made of carved mahogany covered with gold leaf. It is the only real attraction of the small church, though it does have several other wooden altars and a couple of lovely stained-glass windows. ✉ *Av. A at Calle 8, Casco Viejo* 🎫 *Free* ⏲ *Mon.–Sat. 7 am–5 pm, Sun. 8–11:30 am.*

La Catedral (*Catedral de Nuestra Señora de la Asunción*). Built between 1688 and 1796, Panama City's stately cathedral is one of the Casco Viejos most impressive structures. The interior is vast, but rather bleak, but for the marble altar, made in 1884, beautiful stained glass, and a few religious paintings. The stone facade, flanked by painted bell towers, is quite lovely, with its many niches filled with small statues. The bell towers are decorated with mother-of-pearl from the Pearl Islands, and the bells in the left tower were salvaged from the city's first cathedral, in Panamá Viejo. ✉ *Av. Central and Calle 7, Casco Viejo* ☎ *507/262–3720* ⏲ *Mon.–Fri. 8–2, Sat. 9–2, Sun. 9–11.*

Las Bóvedas. The arched chambers in the wall on the eastern side of Plaza Francia, which originally formed part of the city's battlements, served various purposes during the colonial era, from storage chambers to dungeons. Dating from the late 1600s, when the city was relocated to what is now Casco Viejo, the Bóvedas were abandoned for centuries. In the 1980s the Panama Tourist Board initiated the renovation of the cells, two of which are used by the Instituto Nacional de Cultura for ocassional art exhibits. Three cells hold a French restaurant called Las Bóvedas, which also has tables on the plaza where you can enjoy drinks in the afternoon, or evening. ✉ *Plaza Francia, Calle 1, Casco Viejo* ☎ *507/228–8058* 🎫 *Free.*

Museo del Canal Interoceánico (*Interoceanic Canal Museum*). Once the only museum dedicated to the Panama Canal, the Museo del Canal Interoceánico has been put to shame by the visitor center at Miraflores Locks. The museum is packed with artifacts, paintings, photographs, and videos about the Panama Canal, but, unfortunately, the information is only in Spanish, so you may want to spend $5 for a recorded tour in English. Though the building was constructed in 1875 to be the Gran Hotel, it soon became the offices of the Compagnie Universelle du Canal Interoceanique, the French company that made the first attempt to dig a canal in Panama. After that effort went bust, the building became government property, and before being converted to a museum in the 1990s it was the central post office. ✉ *Plaza Catedral, Casco Viejo* ☎ *507/211–1995* 💵 *$2, audio guide $5* ⏲ *Tues.–Sun. 9–5.*

★ **Palacio de las Garzas** (*Palacio Presidential*). The neoclassical lines of the stunning, white presidential palace stand out against the Casco Viejo's skyline. Originally built in the 17th century by an official of the Spanish crown, the palace was a customs house for a while, and passed through various mutations before being renovated to its current shape in 1922, under the administration of Belisario Porras. President Porras also started the tradition of keeping pet herons, or egrets, in the fountain of the building's front courtyard, which led to its popular name: "Palace of the Herons." Because the building houses the president's offices and is surrounded by ministries, security is tight in the area, though nothing compared to the White House. During the day the guards may let you peek into the palace's Moorish foyer at its avian inhabitants, but to get inside you'll need to reserve a free tour by email (✉ *gbernal@presidencia.gob.pa*) at least two weeks ahead of time. Tours are given Tuesday through Friday. ✉ *Av. Alfaro, 2 blocks north of Plaza Catedral, Casco Viejo* ☎ *507/527–9656.*

★ **Paseo Esteban Huertas.** This promenade built atop the old city's outer wall is named for one of Panama's independence leaders. It stretches around the eastern edge of the point at the Casco Viejo's southern tip. From the Paseo you can admire views of the Bay of Panama, the Amador Causeway, the Bridge of the Americas, the tenements of El Chorrillo, and ships awaiting passage through the canal. As it passes behind the Instituto Nacional de Cultura, the Paseo is shaded by a bougainvillea canopy where Kuna women sell handicrafts and couples cuddle on the benches.

Bougainvillea arches frame the modern skyline across the bay, creating a nice photo op: the new city viewed from the old city. ✉ *Plaza Francia, between the stairway at the back of the plaza and Calle 1, Casco Viejo* 🎟 *Free.*

★ Fodor'sChoice **Plaza Bolívar.** A small plaza surrounded by 19th-century architecture, this is one of the Casco Viejo's most pleasant spots, especially at night, when people gather at its various cafés for drinks and dinner, and street musicians perform for tips. It's centered around a monument to the Venezuelan general Simón Bolívar, the "Liberator of Latin America," with decorative friezes marking events of his life and an Andean condor perched above him. In 1926 Bolívar organized a meeting of independence with leaders from all over Latin America in the Franciscan monastery in front of the plaza, which in the end, he was unable to attend. The original San Francisco Church was destroyed by fire in the 18th century and restored twice in the 20th century. The church is only open for Mass on Sunday evening, and the former monastery is now occupied by a Catholic school. Across the plaza from it, on the corner of Avenida B and Calle 4, is the smaller church, the **Iglesia de San Felipe de Neri,** which was recently restored but only opens two days a year—on Good Friday and the saint's feast day, May 26. The **Hotel Colombia,** across the street from it, was one of the country's best when it opened its doors in 1937, but it fell into neglect during the late 20th century until it was renovated in the 1990s and converted to luxury apartments. ✉ *Av. B between Calles 3 and 4, Casco Viejo.*

★ **Plaza Catedral.** The old city's main square is also known as Plaza Mayor, or Plaza de la Independencia, since the country's independence from both Spain and Colombia were celebrated here. Busts of Panama's founding fathers are scattered around the plaza, at the center of which is a large gazebo. The plaza is surrounded by historic buildings such as the Palacio Municipal, the Museo del Canal Interoceánico, and the Hotel Central, which once held the city's best accommodations and is slowly being renovated. Plaza Catedral is shaded by some large *tabebuia* trees, which are ablaze with pink blossoms in January and February. The plaza is the site of ocassional craft fairs, weekend concerts, and other events. ✉ *Av. Central between Calles 5 and 7, Casco Viejo.*

★ Fodor'sChoice **Plaza de Francia.** Designed by Leonardo de Villanueva, this attractive plaza on the southeastern corner of the Casco Viejo peninsula is dedicated to the French effort to build the canal, and the thousands who perished in the process. An obelisk towers over the monument at the end of the plaza, where a dozen marble plaques recount the arduous task. Busts of Ferdinand de Lesseps and his lieutenants gaze across the plaza at the French Embassy—the large baby-blue building to the north of it. Next to them is a bust of Dr. Carlos Finlay, a Cuban physician who later discovered that yellow fever, which killed thousands during the French effort, originated from a mosquito bite—information that prompted the American campaign to eradicate mosquitoes from the area before they began digging. The plaza itself is a pleasant spot shaded by poinciana trees, which carry bright-orange blossoms from May to July. At the front of the plaza is a statue of Pablo Arosemena, one of Panama's founding fathers and one of its first presidents. The plaza covers part of a small peninsula that served as a bastion for the walled city's defence during its early years. The former dungeons of Las Bóvedas line the plaza's eastern edge, and next door stands a large white building that was once the city's main courthouse but now houses the Instituto Nacional de Cultura (National Culture Institute) ✉ *End of Calle 1 Este, Casco Viejo.*

Plaza Herrera. This large plaza a block off the Avenida Central is surrounded by some lovely old buildings, several of which have been renovated, or are in the process of renovation. At the center of the plaza is a statue of local hero General Tomás Herrera, looking rather regal on horseback. Herrera fought in South America's wars for independence from Spain and later led Panama's first attempt to gain independence from Colombia, in 1840. Half a block west of it stands the last remaining chunk of the ancient wall that once enclosed the Casco Viejo, called the Baluarte de la Mano de Tigre (Tiger's Hand Bulwark), beyond which the neighborhood grows increasingly sketchty. ✉ *Av. A and Calle 9, Casco Viejo.*

Santo Domingo. A catastrophic fire ruined this 17th-century church and Dominican monastery centuries ago. What's left at the entrance is the Arco Chato, or flat arch, a relatively precarious structure that served as proof that the country was not subject to earthquakes, tipping the scales in favor of Panama over Nicaragua for the construction of the transoceanic canal. The arch finally collapsed in 2003, without the help of an earthquake, but the city fathers considered it such an important landmark that they had it rebuilt. ✉ *Av. A at Calle 3, Casco Viejo* ☎ *507/209–6300 for museum.*

NEED A BREAK? Gran Clement. Exploring Casco Viejo's narrow streets can be a hot and exhausting affair, which makes the gourmet ice-cream shop of Gran Clement an almost obligatory stop. Located in the ground floor of a restored mansion one block west of the Policía de Turismo station, the shop serves a wide assortment of ice creams including ginger, coconut, passion fruit, and mango. Gran Clement is also open at night, and until 9:30 pm on weekends. ✉ ***Av. Central and Calle 3*** ☎ ***507/228–0737.***

2

Teatro Nacional (*National Theater*). The interior of this theater is truly posh, with ceiling murals, gold balconies, and glittering chandeliers—a little bit of Europe in the heart of old Panama City. After serving as a convent and, later, an army barracks, the building was remodeled by Italian architect Genaro Ruggieri in 1908. Paintings inside by Panamanian artist Roberto Lewis depict Panama's history via Greek mythology. Check the local papers, or call to find out if the national symphony orchestra, or another group, is playing while you're in town, as attending a concert is the best way to experience the building. ✉ *Av. B and Calle 3, Casco Viejo* ☎ *507/262–3525* *$1* *Mon.–Fri. 9–4.*

CERRO ANCÓN, BALBOA, AND THE CALZADA DE AMADOR

For the better part of the 20th century, the area to the west of Casco Viejo held the border between the American Canal Zone and Panama City proper, and it continues to be an area of stark contrasts. The busy Avenida de Los Mártires (which separates the neighborhoods of El Chorrillo and Santa Ana from Cerro Ancón [Ancón Hill]) was once lined with a chain-link fence; it was named for Panamanian students killed during demonstrations against American control of the zone in 1964. To the west of that busy avenue, which leads to the Bridge of the Americas and the other side of the canal, rises the verdure and stately buildings of the former Canal Zone, whereas the area to the east of it is dominated by slums. Aside from Casco Viejo, and the pedestrian mall on the Avenida Central south of the Plaza Cinco de Mayo, the areas to the east of that avenue should be avoided. The eastern side of Cerro Ancón holds the Museo de Arte Contemporáneo (Museum of Modern Art) and the tourist village of Mi Pueblito. The western slope of Cerro Ancón holds the stately **Edificio de la Administración del Canal** (Panama Canal Administration Building), which overlooks the lawns, trees, and buildings of Balboa from a ridge. Just south of Balboa is the former U.S. military base of Amador, a relatively empty area that is connected to three islands by a breakwater called the Calzada de Amador (Amador Causeway). The Causeway was constructed as a breakwater from the trainloads of rock and earth removed while the digging the canal. Years later, a road was paved atop it, which is now lined with a sidewalk and palm trees. It stretches almost 3 km (2 miles) into the Pacific Ocean to connect the mainland to three islands: **Isla Naos, Isla Perico,** and **Isla Flamenco,** which hold strip malls, dozens of bars and restaurants and a couple marinas. Those islands are a popular destination for people who want to escape the heat and traffic jams, and enjoy the views of the surrounding sea, massive ships passing through the adjacent canal, and the city's modern skyline.

TIMING AND PRECAUTIONS

As with most of Panama City, you are better off exploring Balboa and Cerro Ancón in the morning or late afternoon; the Calzada de Amador is a great spot for lunch, a sunset cocktail, or night time revelry. On Sunday afternoon, the promenade fills with joggers, bikers, and roller skaters. Balboa and the Calzada de Amador are perfectly safe, but you'll want to avoid the neighborhoods on the other side of the Avenida de los Martires from Cerro Ancón.

WHAT TO SEE

Balboa. The heart of the former Canal Zone is quite a switch from the rest of Panama City, with its wide tree-shaded lawns and stately old buildings. It sometimes feels like a bit of a ghost town, especially after you spend time on the busy streets of Panama City proper, but it's a peacefull area with lots of greenery. You may spot toucans, or *agoutis* (large jungle rodents) on the slopes of Ancon Hill, or near the Panama Canal Administration Building. The Friday's restaurant next to the Country Inn & Suites Panama Canal has a front-row view of the canal and Bridge of the Americas. ✉ *Av. Arnulfo Arias and Av. Amador, Balboa.*

Cerro Ancón Summit. The rain forest that covers most of Cerro Ancón is a remarkably vibrant natural oasis in the midst of the city. The best area to see wildlife is on the road to the Cerro Ancón Summit, which is topped by radio towers and a giant Panamanian flag. The road ascends the hill's

2

DAY TRIPS FROM PANAMA CITY

The following excursions are areas covered in "The Canal and Central Panama" chapter. There are about a dozen day-trip options for exploring the canal and surrounding rain forest, which you can visit on your own or with a guide on a bird-watching or hiking tour. The canal is best experienced on a transit tour, which takes you through the series of locks, but you can also get onto the water on one of several nature tours on Gatún Lake. One of the best nature tours on Gatún Lake is the Smithsonian Tropical Research Institute's day tour to the island of **Barro Colorado** (*⇨ Barro Colorado in "The Canal and Central Panama"*), one of the world's oldest nature reserves. A 30- to 40-minute drive, taxi ride, or bus trip northwest from Panama City will bring you to trails that wind into the forests of **Parque Nacional Soberanía,** a vast rain-forest reserve that is home to more than 400 bird species and an array of mammals that ranges from timid tapirs to tiny tamarins. At **Gamboa,** which lies between the park and the canal, it's easy to spot wildlife on the grounds of the Gamboa Rainforest Resort, which has a rain-forest tram and an excellent restaurant, Los Lagartos, on the Chagres River (*⇨ Parque Nacional Soberanía, or Gamboa, in "The Canal and Central Panama"*).

For a fascinating day trip, ride the **Panama Canal Railway** through the forests and lakes that line the canal to the Caribbean port of Colón and spend the day exploring either the rain forests around the colonial fort of **San Lorenzo** or the colonial fortresses, beaches, and forest of **Portobelo,** a trip that can be done independently or on a tour (*⇨ Panama Canal Railway, "The Canal and Central Panama"*). There are several options for exploring nearby **Parque Nacional Chagres,** which include hiking in Cerro Azul, white-water rafting on the Chagres River, or a trip to one of several Emberá Indian communities within the park (*⇨ Parque Nacional Chagres in "The Canal and Central Panama"*).

The beaches of the Central Pacific Coast can be visited on day trips, but note that most of them require two to three hours of driving, which is why many Panamanians head to the nearby island of **Isla Taboga** on weekends (*⇨ Isla Taboga in "The Canal and Central Panama"*). For a real treat, consider taking the ferry out to **Isla Contadora,** one of the Pearl Islands, which has nicer beaches than Taboga (*⇨ Isla Taboga in "The Canal and Central Panama"*).

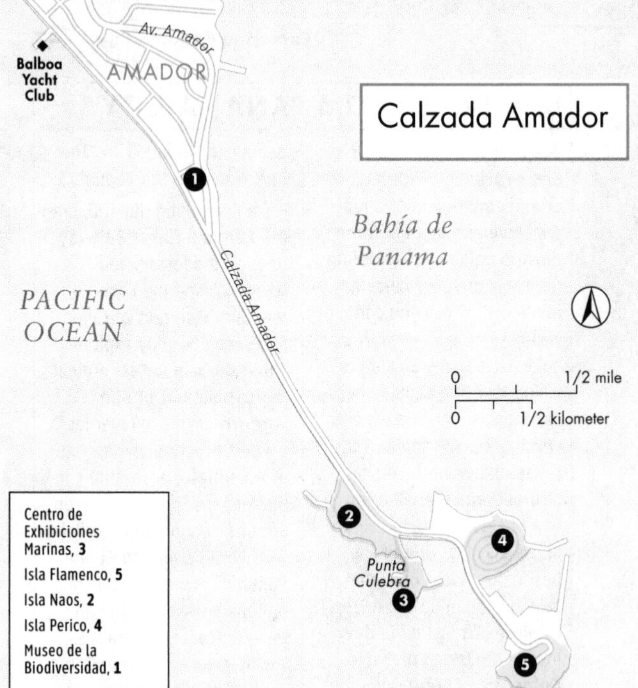

western slope from the luxuriant residential neighborhood of Quarry Heights, above Balboa. There is also a trail into the forest behind the offices of ANCON, Panama's biggest environmental group. If the gate at the end of Quarry Heights is locked, it should take 20–30 minutes to hike to the summit. It is best done early in the morning or late in the afternoon, when you are likely to see animals such as the abundant agoutis (large rodents), keel-billed toucan, and Geoffrey's tamarind—Panama's smallest simian. If you have a taxi drop you off at the trailhead (ask the driver to take you to the "Oficinas de ANCON" in Quarry Heights), you can hike down the other side of the hill to Mi Pueblito, where you should be able to flag a cab. ✉ *Quarry Heights, 400 meters south of ANCON, Cerro Ancón.*

Edificio de la Administración del Canal (*Panama Canal Administration Building*). Well worth a stop is this impressive structure set atop a ridge with a dramatic view of Balboa and the canal—a site chosen by the canal's chief engineer, George W. Goethals. The building, designed by New York architect Austin W. Lord, was inaugurated in 1914, one month before the SS *Ancon* became the first ship to navigate the canal. Since it holds the offices of the people in charge of running the canal, most of the building is off-limits to tourists, but you can enter its lovely rotunda and admire the historic murals of the canal's construction. The murals were painted by William B. Van Ingen, who also created murals for the U.S. Library of Congress and the Philadelphia Mint. They're quite dramatic, and capture the monumental nature of the canal's construction in a style that is part Norman Rockwell, part Frederic Edwin Church. The rotunda also houses busts of the three canal visionaries: Spain's King Carlos V, who first pondered the possibility in the 16th century; the Frenchman Ferdinand de Lesseps, who led the first attempt to dig it; and President Theodore Roosevelt, who launched the successful construction effort. The doors at the back of the rotunda are locked, but if you walk around the building you'll be treated to a view of the neat lawns and tree-lined boulevards of Balboa. ✉ *Calle Gorgas, Balboa* ☎ *507/272–7602* ⏲ *Daily 7–4.*

Isla Flamenco. The Amador Causeway ends at Isla Flamenco, which has two shopping centers and an assortment of restaurants. The Flamenco Marina is a popular mooring spot for yachts and fishing boats; it's the disembarkation point for cruise-ship passengers, most of whom board tour buses. Several restaurants and bars overlook the marina, which also has a great view of the city's skyline, making it a popular destination night and day. ✉ *Calzada de Amador.*

Isla Naos. The first island that you'll reach on the Amador Causeway, Isla Naos, is dominated by the marine research laboratories of the Smithsonian Tropical Research Institute (STRI). On the far side of the island are various restaurants, a large marina, which is where you catch the ferry to Isla Taboga, and the STRI Marine Exhibition Center on Punta Culebra. The dirt road that leads to the marina and Punta Culebra is on the right just in front of the restaurant Mi Ranchito, which has a high thatch roof. Just south of Mi Ranchito is a small strip mall with several bars and restaurants, one of which has a swimming pool that costs a few dollars to use. ✉ *Calzada de Amador.*

Centro de Exhibiciones Marinas Punta Culebra. Though it doesn't compare to the aquariums of other major cities, the Centro de Exhibiciones Marinas (Marine Exhibition Center) is worth a stop. It was created by the scientists and educators at the STRI and is located on a lovely, undeveloped point with examples of several ecosystems: beach, mangrove forest, rocky coast, and tropical forest. A series of signs leads visitors on a self-guided tour. There are several small tanks with fish and sea turtles, as well as pools with sea stars, sea cucumbers, and other marine creatures that kids can handle. The spyglasses are great for watching ships on the adjacent canal. ■ TIP→ **Be sure to go out to the lookout on the end of the rocky point.** ✉ *Punta Culebra, Isla Naos, Calzada de Amador* ☎ *507/212–8760* 🌐 *www.stri.si.edu/english/visit_us/index.php* 🎟 *$5, children $1* ⏲ *Tues.–Fri. 1–5, weekends 10–6.*

Isla Perico. The second island on the causeway, Isla Perico, holds a long strip mall, called Brisas de Amador, that has an array of restaurants and bars, most of which have terraces that face the canal's Pacific entrance, so you can watch the ships passing. ✉ *Calzada de Amador.*

Museo de la Biodiversidad (*Museum of Biodiversity*). The triangle of land where the Causeway begins is the site of the forthcoming Museo de la Biodiversidad. Also called the "BioMuseo," the museum was designed by the American architect Frank O. Gehry, famous for the Guggenheim Museum in Bilbao, Spain, and the pavilion at Chicago's Millennium Park. The museum was originally due to open in 2009 but at this writing had fallen considerably behind schedule; it may open in 2013. When completed, it will feature exhibits on the remarkable biodiversity of Panama's forests and oceans, as well as the isthmus's role as a biological bridge between North and South America. In the meantime, you can stop by the construction site and have a look at Gehry's model and the construction work in progress. ✉ *Beginning of Causeway, Calzada de Amador* ☎ *507/314–0097* 🌐 *www.biomuseopanama.org.*

NEED A BREAK? **Bicicletas Moses.** Behind Pencas Restaurant, on the mainland at the entrance to Calzada Amador, Bicicletas Moses rents an array of bikes, including kids' sizes. One hour for an individual mountain bike costs $3.50, or up to $18 for a six-seater. ✉ *Av. Amador, Behind Pencas Restaurant, Calzada de Amador* ☎ *507/211–3671 restaurant, call and ask for bicicletas* ⏲ *Mon.–Fri. 10–7; Sat.–Sun. 9–7.*

PARQUE NATURAL METROPOLITANO, MIRAFLORES, AND SUMMIT

The area to the north of Balboa, which was also part of the American Canal Zone, has undergone considerable development since being handed over. The former U.S. Army airfield of Albrook is now Panama City's domestic airport, Aeropuerto Marcos A. Gelabert; next to that are Albrook Mall and the city's impressive bus terminal, the Terminal de Transporte Terrestre, called "Terminal de Buses" by locals. To the northeast of Albrook is a large swath of rain forest protected within Parque Natural Metropolitano, which is home to more than 200 bird species. To the northwest, the former army base of Clayton is now called the Ciudad del Saber, or City of Knowledge; many of its buildings are occupied by international organizations. Across the road is the first set of locks on the Pacific side of the canal, the Esclusas de Miraflores (Miraflores Locks), an area that is much more visitor-friendly than it was when the canal was U.S. property. The Panamanian administration built a state-of-the-art visitor center, with a museum and observation decks, making it one of Panama City's top attractions. From there the road follows the canal northwest through the rain forest of Soberanía National Park to the small canal port and community of Gamboa, on the shore of Gatun Lake.

Follow the road north from the locks through the forest of Camino de Cruces National Park to the former American enclave of Summit, which holds Panama City's only golf course, a botanical garden and zoo, and one of the city's best hotels.

TIMING AND PRECAUTIONS

You should visit Parque Natural Metropolitano as early in the day as you can, or late in the afternoon, because those are the times when birds and other animals are most active. Bring insect repellent with you, stay on the trails, and watch your footing, because there are poisonous snakes in these areas. The visitor center at Miraflores Locks is air-conditioned, so it is one of the few places in Panama City that you can comfortably visit in the late morning or early afternoon. ■TIP→**Though the visitor center closes at 5 pm, the restaurant on its second floor is open until 10:30; it's a spectacular, albeit expensive place to dine, as the canal is busier at night than during the day.**

WHAT TO SEE

Cementerio Francés (*French Cemetery*). The pastoral Cementerio Francés sits on the left side of the road just before Summit and serves as a testament to the human toll once taken by grand construction projects. Hundreds of crosses line a hill in this pretty cemetery and mark the resting place of a fraction of the 20,000 workers who died during France's brief attempt to construct a canal across the isthmus. ✉ *Summit.*

★ Fodor's Choice **Esclusas de Miraflores** (*Miraflores Locks*). The four-story visitor center next to these double locks provides a front-row view of massive ships passing through the lock chambers. It also houses an excellent museum about the canal's history, engineering, daily operations, and environmental demands. Because most of the canal lies at 85 feet above sea level, each ship that passes through has to be raised to that level with three locks as they enter it, and brought back to sea level with three locks on the other end. Miraflores has two levels of locks, which move vessels between Pacific sea level and Miraflores Lake, a man-made stretch of water between Miraflores Locks and the Pedro Miguel Locks. Due to the proximity to Panama City, these locks have long been the preferred place to visit the canal, but the visitor center has made it even more popular.

There are observation decks on the ground and fourth floors of the massive cement building, from which you can watch vessels move through the locks, as a bilingual narrator explains the process and provides information about each ship, including the toll they paid to use the canal. The museum contains an excellent combination of historic relics, photographs, videos, models, and even a simulator of a ship passing through the locks. There is also a gift shop, a snack bar, and a restaurant on the second floor called Restaurante Miraflores, which is expensive, but has an excellent view from the tables on the balcony, and offers the only access to the locks at night. While the canal is busier at night, the largest ships pass during the day. You can call at 9 am the day before your visit to ask what time the largest ships are due through the locks. ✉ *Road to Gamboa, across from Ciudad del Saber, Clayton* ☎ *507/276–8617* 🎟 *$8, children $5; deck only $5, children $3* ⏲ *Daily 9–5.*

Parque Municipal Summit (*Jardín Botánico Summit, or Summit Botanical Garden*). About 13 miles northwest of Balboa, this large garden and zoo is surrounded by rain forest.

Started in 1923 as a U.S. government project to reproduce tropical plants with economic potential, it evolved into a botanical garden and a zoo in the 1960s. The gardens and surrounding forest hold thousands of species, but the focus is on about 150 species of ornamental, fruit, and hardwood trees from around the world that were once raised here. These range from coffee and cinnamon to the more unusual candle tree and cannonball tree. The zoo is home to 40 native animal species, most of them in cages that are depressingly small, though a few have decent quarters. Stars include jaguars, ocelots, all six of the country's monkey species, several macaw species, and the harpy eagle, Panama's national bird. A neat thing about Summit is that most of the animals exhibited in the zoo are also found in the surrounding forest, so you may spot parrots, toucans, and *agoutis* (large rodents) on the grounds. ✉ *22 km (13 miles) northwest of downtown on road to Gamboa, Summit* ☎ *232–4850* 💵 *$5* ⏲ *Daily 9–4.*

★ **Parque Natural Metropolitano** (*Metropolitan Natural Park*). A mere 20-minute drive from downtown, this 655-acre expanse of protected wilderness is a remarkably convenient place to experience the flora and fauna of Panama's tropical rain forest. Its home to 227 bird species ranging from migrant Baltimore orioles to keel-billed toucans. Five well-marked trails, covering a total of about 4.8 km (3 mi), range from a climb to the park's highest point to a fairly flat loop. On any given morning of hiking you may spot such spectacular birds as a gray-headed chachalaca, a collared aracari, or a mealy parrot. The park is also home to 45 mammal species, so keep an eye out for dark brown agoutis (large jungle rodents). Keep your ears perked for tamarins, tiny monkeys that sound like birds.

There's a visitor center near the southern end of the park, next to El Roble and Los Caobas trails, where the nonprofit organization that administers the park collects the admission fee and sells cold drinks, snacks, and nature books. **TIP→ This is the best place to begin your exploration of the park, since you can purchase a map that shows the trails. Call two days ahead to reserve an English-speaking guide ($25).**

Across the street from the visitor center is a shorter loop called Sendero Los Momótides. The Mono Titi and La Cieneguita trails head into the forest from the road about 1 km (½ mile) north of the visitor center and connect to each other to form a loop through the park's most precipitous terrain. The Smithsonian Tropical Research Institute (STRI) has a construction crane in the middle of the forest near the Mono Titi trail that is used to study life in the forest canopy, which is where the greatest diversity of flora and fauna is found. El Roble connects with La Cieneguita, so you can hike the northern loop and then continue through the forest to the visitor center; the total distance of that hike is 3½ km (2 mi).

Be sure to bring water, insect repellent, and binoculars, and be careful where you put your feet and hands, since the park does have poisonous snakes, biting insects, and spiny plants. ✉ *Av. Juan Pablo II, Altos de Curundú* ☎ *507/232–5552* 🌐 *www.parquemetropolitano.org* 🎟 *$2, children 50¢* ⏲ *Daily 7–5.*

DOWNTOWN PANAMA CITY

The area northeast of the old city, stretching from the neighborhoods of El Cangrejo to Punta Paitilla, is where you'll find most of the city's office towers, banks, hotels, restaurants, and shops. As Panama City's economy grew and diversified during the 20th century, those who had money abandoned Casco Viejo and built homes in new neighborhoods to the northeast; apartment buildings and office towers soon followed. Many of Panama City's best hotels and restaurants are clustered in **El Cangrejo** and the **Area Bancária** (Financial District), which flank the busy Via España. Calle 50, another of the city's main arteries, defines the southern edge of the Area Bancária. A few blocks southeast of Calle 50 is **Avenida Balboa,** another of the city's major thoroughfares, which curves along the coast between the Casco Viejo and Punta Paitilla and is lined by the parks and waterfront promenade of **La Cinta Costera.** Between Calle 50 and Avenida Balboa you'll find the neighborhoods of Bella Vista and Marbella, which hold an interesting mix of apartment towers, aging mansions, shops, and government offices. Just to the east of Marbella is Punta Paitilla, a small point packed with skyscrapers and a few hotels.

TIMING AND PRECAUTIONS

The downtown area is very safe to explore, although you should be careful crossing its main streets. La Cinta Costera is best strolled in the morning or evening; it skirts some rough neighborhoods to the west of the Balboa Monument, so stick to the stretch between the Monument and Punta Paitilla.

WHAT TO SEE

Area Bancária (*Financial District*). Narrow streets shaded by leafy tropical trees make the city's financial district a pleasant area to explore, though the trees are being cut to make room for more skyscrapers. Together with El Cangrejo, which lies across the Vía España from it, the Area Bancária holds a critical mass of hotels and restaurants. You'll find two of the city's highest concentration of bars and restaurants in El Cangrejo and the area around Calle Uruguay (Calle 48), between Calle 50 (Nicanor de Obarrio) and Avenida Balboa. ✉ *Between Vía España and Calle 50.*

La Cinta Costera. The busy waterfront boulevard Avenida Balboa and the linear park running alongside it is lined with palm trees and features great views of the Bay of Panama and Casco Viejo. The sidewalk that runs along the bay and the park wedged between the avenue is a popular strolling and jogging route. To the west of the Miramar towers and the Yacht Club is a small park with a monument to Vasco Nuñez de Balboa, who, after trudging through the rain forests of the Darién in 1501 became the first European to set eyes on the Pacific Ocean. That gleaming white **Monumento a Balboa** is topped by a steel sculpture of the conquistador gazing out at the Pacific. The statue was a gift to the Panamanian people from Spain's King Alfonso XIII in 1924. Do your walking to the east of the Monumento, since it passes some rough neighborhoods to the west of it. Unfortunately, a stroll along the waterfront may be punctuated by wiffs of Panama City's raw sewage, which pours into the bay from a series of pipes just off the Cinta Costera, and is especially noxious at low tide. The government is building the city's long-overdue sewage system, but it will take years to complete. ✉ *Av. Balboa, Marbella.*

SAN FRANCISCO AND PANAMÁ VIEJO

The coast to the east of Punta Paitilla has a growing supply of condominium towers, but just behind them lies the residential neighborhood of **San Francisco,** which has some up-scale streets and a growing collection of skyscrapers. The city's original convention center, **ATLAPA,** is on busy Vía Israel, which leads to the ruins of **Panamá Viejo,** or the original city. That historic site consists of little more than a museum and a collection of stone walls, but it provides an idea of what the colonial city looked like.

TIMING AND PRECAUTIONS

As with any outdoor attraction in often-sweltering Panama City, it's best to visit Panamá Viejo first thing in the morning or later in the afternoon. ■TIP→ **The museum closes at 4 pm, so make sure this is one of your first stops.** The ruins are patrolled by tourism police on mountain bikes, but the neighborhood is less tourist-friendly, so don't wander too far from the main road—Vía Cincuentenaria—and the Plaza Mayor.

WHAT TO SEE

Panamá Viejo (*Old Panama*). Crumbling ruins are all that's left of Old Panama (sometimes called Panamá la Vieja), the country's first major Spanish settlement, which was destroyed by pirate Henry Morgan in 1671.

Panamá Viejo was founded in 1519 by the conquistador Pedroarias Dávila. Built on the site of an indigenous village that had existed for centuries, the city soon became a busy colonial outpost. Expeditions to explore the Pacific coast of South America left from here. When Francisco Pizarro conquered the Incan empire, the copious gold and silver he stole arrived in Panamá Viejo, where it was loaded onto mules and taken across the isthmus to Spain-bound ships. For the next 150 years Panamá Viejo was a vital link between Spain and the gold and silver mines of South America. Year after year, ships came and went; mule trains carried precious metals to Panama's Caribbean coast and returned with Spanish goods bound for the southern colonies. The city's merchants, royal envoys, and priests accumulated enough gold to make a pirate drool. At the time of Morgan's attack, Panamá Viejo had a handful of convents and churches, one hospital, markets, and luxurious mansions. The fires started during the pirate attack reduced much of the city to ashes within days.

The paucity of the remaining ruins is not due entirely to the pirates' looting and burning: the Spanish colonists spent years dismantling buildings after they decided to rebuild their city, now known as Casco Viejo, on the peninsula to the southwest, which was deemed easier to defend against attack. The Spanish carried everything that could be moved to the new city, including the stone blocks that are today the walls of the city's current cathedral and the facade of the Iglesia de la Merced. Panamá Viejo is part of all city tours, which can be a good way to visit the site if you get a knowledgeable guide. There are also sometimes guides at the Plaza Mayor who provide free information in Spanish.

The collections of walls that you'll pass between the Visitor Center and the Plaza Mayor are all that remain of several convents, the bishop's palace, and the San Juan de Dios Hospital. The Plaza Mayor is approximately 1 km (½ mile) from the visitor center, so you may want to drive, or take a cab. Try to visit this site before 11 am, or after 3 pm. ✉ *Vía Cincuentenaria.*

Centro de Visitantes (*Visitor Center*). Start your visit to Panamá Viejo at the Centro de Visitantes—a large building on the right as you enter Panamá Viejo on Vía Cincuentenaria. From ATLAPA, that street heads inland for 2 km (1 mile) through a residential neighborhood before arriving at the ruins, which are on the coast. Once you see the ocean again, look for the two-story visitor center on your right. It holds a large museum that chronicles the site's evolution from an indigenous village to one of the wealthiest cities in the Western Hemisphere. Works on display include indigenous pottery made centuries before the arrival of the Spanish, relics of the colonial era, and a model of what the city looked like shortly before Morgan's attack. Keep that model in mind as you explore the site, since you need a good dose of imagination to evoke the city that was once home to between 7,000 and 10,000 people from the rubble that remains of it. ✉ *Vía Cincuentenaria, 2 km (1 mile) east of ATLAPA, Panamá Viejo* ☎ *507/226–1757 for Visitor Center* 🎫 *$3 museum, $4 for ruins, $6 for both* ⏲ *Tues.–Sun. 9–5.*

Plaza Mayor (*Main Plaza*). Vía Cincuentenaria curves to the left in front of what was once the city's **Plaza Mayor** (Main Plaza), a simple cobbled square backed by a stone tower that is the only part of Panamá Viejo that has undergone any significant renovation. If you have previously paid admission at the Visitor Center, then you will need to show that ticket, or you can buy a separate ticket to enter the plaza alone. Climb the metal staircase inside the **Torre de la Catedral** (Cathedral Tower)—the former bell tower of Panama's original cathedral—for a view of the surrounding ruins. The structure just south of the tower was once the city hall; walls to the north and east are all that remains of homes, a church, and a convent. The extensive ruins are shaded by tropical trees, which attract plenty of birds, so the nature and scenery are as much of an attraction as the ancient walls. ✉ *Av. Cincuentenario, about 3 km (2 mi)* *east of ATLAPA, Panamá Viejo ☎ 507/226–8915 🌐 www.panamaviejo.org 🎟 Tower and ruins $4; Plaza Mayor and visitor center $6 ⏲ Daily 9–5.*

Mercado de Artesanía (*Craft Market*). Next to the Centro de Visitantes is the Mercado de Artesanía, where dozens of independent vendors sell their wares in shops and stands. You can buy many traditional crafts here, including Emberá baskets and Kuna-made molas. Prices vary, but there are some good buys. ✉ *Av. Cincuentenaria, next to Centro de Visitantes, Panamá Viejo ☎ 507/560–0535 ⏲ Daily 9–4.*

PLAYA KOBBE (PLAYA BONITA)

7 km (4 miles) southwest of Panama City.

With a long beach on a cove of calm water backed by tropical forest, Playa Kobbe is a lovely spot. It is the closest beach to Panama City, less than 20 minutes from downtown. Since Kobbe Beach lies on the other side of the Canal, the water there is considerably cleaner than near Panama City, but it is still tinged with oil from the area's abundant ships, so it is hardly ideal for swimming or snorkeling. Once a popular picnic spot for locals, Playa Kobbe is now dominated by two all-inclusive resorts, the InterContinental Playa Bonita Resort and Spa, and the Westin Playa Bonita *(See Where to Stay)*, both of which restrict access to the beach, even though all beaches are public property under Panamanian law. The name Playa Bonita (beautiful beach) is a fairly recent PR invention, but it is rapidly replacing Playa Kobbe, named for the U.S. military base that once stood nearby, as the beach's moniker.

GETTING HERE AND AROUND

To drive to Kobbe from Panama City, take the Avenida de los Martires to the Bridge of the Americas and take the first exit after crossing the canal, turning left and following the signs to the Intercontinental Play Bonita Resort. A taxi should cost $25

WHERE TO EAT

It's not quite New York or Paris, but Panama City's restaurant scene is impressive. Panamanians like to eat out, and enough of them have incomes that allow for regular dining on the town, which has resulted in a growing cadre of restaurants. Many of the best restaurants are clustered in the Casco Viejo, El Cangrejo, Área Bancária, and nearby

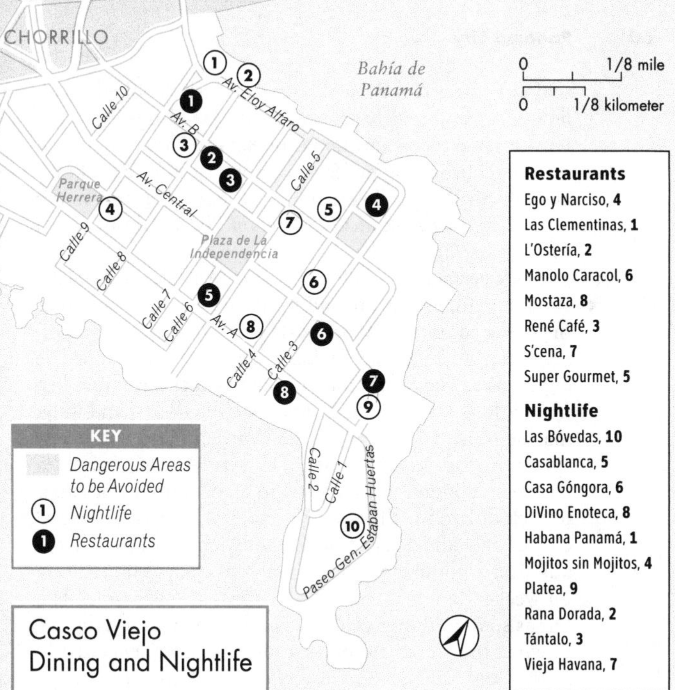

Casco Viejo Dining and Nightlife

Calle Uruguay, which is where you'll find most of the best hotels. Java junkies will rejoice over the fact that you can get a good cup of coffee just about anywhere; even the inexpensive restaurants have espresso machines.

CASCO VIEJO

Here you'll find some of Panama City's best restaurants, as well as the city's best ambience. Even if you stay downtown, you should head here for at least one meal, and a drink on Plaza Bolívar. TIP→ **Many restaurants here close between lunch and dinner, so call ahead if you want to eat between 2 and 7.**

$$$ ★ × **Ego y Narcisco.** *South American.* This small restaurant has tables on Plaza Bolívar, overlooking the Iglesia de San Francisco, making it one of Panama City's more charming dinner spots. If you can't handle the heat, though, you can always move into the air-conditioned dining room in the historic building across the street. The menu is a mix of Latin American and Italian cuisines, an example being chicken ravioli with a spicy Peruvian cream sauce called *ají de gallina.* They offer several other fresh pastas, as well as seafood and meat dishes. Popular starters include

seafood carpaccio, Peruvian *ceviche* (fish "cooked" with lime juice), and *mini brochetas*: try the breaded pork option with sesame seeds and tamarind sauce. Those *tapas* and the gorgeous setting make this a good spot for a cocktails and appetizers even if you dine elsewhere. *Average main: $19 ✉ Calle 3 Este and Av. Sucre, on Plaza Bolivar, Casco Viejo ☎ 507/262–2045.*

$$$ ★ ✕**Las Clementinas Café & Bar.** *Eclectic.* An eclectic blend of Panamanian, European, and Asian cuisines and the choice of dining in an Old-World café or on a distinctly tropical patio, make a meal at Las Clementinas a memorable experience. The bright dining room evokes a Parisian bistro, with its large, arched windows, tile floors, and long, marble-topped bar and the lush garden patio is a lovely spot for an intimate dinner. The menu ranges from sea bass with shiitake mushrooms in a coconut-ginger sauce to rack of lamb with grilled vegetables. They offer several cuts of beef and a selection of sandwiches, soups and salads, and a popular Sunday brunch. It can get quite lively on weekend nights, when reservations are recommended, but as soon as things calm down, the manager usually sits down at the piano and plays a song. *Average main: $20 ✉ Av. B and Calle 11, Casco Viejo ☎ 507/228–7617 www.lasclementinas.com Closed Mon.*

$$ ✕**L'Ostería.** *Italian.* Quality Italian cuisine served amid ancient walls make L'Ostería a popular dinner option. The restaurant is located under the Casa del Horno boutique hotel, in a restored colonial building, and the back patio, with its stone walls and small garden, is a lovely spot to spend a couple hours. The menu includes a small selection of pizzas, pastas, meat and seafood dishes. Try the pennette with a zucchini and almond pesto sauce, *corvina alla piastra* (sautéed sea bass served with grilled vegetables), or one of the excellent pizzas. *Average main: $14 ✉ Av. B between Calle 7 and Calle 8, Casco Viejo ☎ 507/212–0809 No lunch.*

★ $$$$ Fodor's Choice ✕**Manolo Caracol.** *Mediterranean.* Owned by Spanish chef Manolo Madueño, this restaurant-cum-art gallery in a restored colonial building is dedicated to the joy of dining, with a different prix-fixe menu consisting of 10 to 12 items offered each night. All you need to do is choose your beverage—perhaps a beer or a Spanish wine—and wait for the succession of succulent surprises that the waiters will deliver shortly after you scrape each plate clean. Meals tend to be strong on seafood, but there are always a couple of meat dishes. Manolo's is for people who like to eat big, so if you're a light eater, or are on a budget, you should head elsewhere. With its eclectic shrine to the Virgin Mary, and ancient, whitewashed walls hung with modern art, it's a charming spot to spend a few hours, which is how long dinner will take, especially when Manolo is there working the crowd. However, it get's noisy on weekend nights, when it can be hard to carry on a conversation, and it can get awfully hot at the tables near the cooking area, which is in the central back part of the dining area. *Average main: $35 Av. Central and Calle 3 Este, Casco Viejo 507/228–4640 www.manolocaracol.net Reservations essential.*

$$ × **Mostaza.** *Latin American.* Nestled in a restored colonial building across the street from the ruins of Santo Domingo, Mostaza offers a cozy and delicious dining experience in the heart of the historic quarter. Start with a drink on the plaza, then move into one of the two narrow dining rooms, one of which has a centuries-old exposed stone wall. The Argentine and Panamanian owners are usually in the kitchen, preparing an eclectic mix of local seafood and meat dishes that range from *lenguado* (sole) in a mushroom sauce to pork tenderloin in a *maracuya* (passion fruit) sauce. They offer some inventive fresh pastas, such as seafood ravioli in a vodka salmon sauce, and *langostinos* (prawns) sautéed with Gran Marnier, but meat lovers will want to try the classic Argentine *bife de chorizo* (a thick cut of tenderloin) with *chimichurri:* an olive oil, garlic, and parsley sauce. *Average main: $18 Av. A and Calle 3, Casco Viejo 507/228–3341 Closed Mon. No lunch weekends.*

$$ Fodor's Choice × **René Café.** *Latin American.* After managing Manolo Caracol for years, René opened his own place, while following Manolo's popular formula of offering a set menu that changes daily and consists of about a dozen items served in five or six courses. The difference is a more intimate setting, more Caribbean influence and lower prices. René is almost always there, making sure his guests are happy. The small restaurant is in a historic building on the northwest corner of Plaza Catedral, with a high ceiling and white walls that are invariably decorated with the work of local artists. There are also several tables on the sidewalk with cathedral views. The dining experience is a sort of culinary journey, in which fresh dishes appear every time you complete a course, and you happily chew your way forward, toward a light dessert. Simpler, inexpensive lunches are an alternative to René's seemingly endless dinners. *Average main: $22 Plaza Catedral, Calle Pedro J.*

Sossa, Casco Viejo ☎ *507/262–3487* 🌐 *www.renecafe.com* ✍ *Reservations essential* ⊗ *Closed Sun.*

$$$$ ✕ **S'cena.** *Mediterranean.* S'cena offers a good mix of ambiance and Mediterranean classics such as paella and original dishes such as *langosta en salsa mediterránea* (lobster in almond sauce), *filete a los tres hongos* (filet mignon with portobello, shiitake, and cremini mushrooms), and *atún rojo* (grilled tuna marinated in a cherry-soy sauce). It occupies the second floor of a restored colonial-era building, with patches of exposed stone walls and historic photos and paintings by local artists hanging on the plastered stretches. S'cena's location between Plaza Francia and Plaza Bolívar makes it a good spot to have lunch before, or dinner after, exploring the Casco Viejo. On a Thursday or Saturday, you can step downstairs afterward for the live music. $ *Average main: $25* ✉ *Calle 1 and Av. A, Casco Viejo* ☎ *507/228–4011* ⊗ *No dinner Sun.*

$ ✕ **Super Gourmet.** *Deli.* This American-owned deli, in a historic building behind the Palacio Municipal, is a popular ★ breakfast and lunch spot thanks to its selection of sandwiches, salads, and homemade soups. The ample breakfast menu includes several English muffin sandwiches and a house version of eggs Benedict, as well as excellent coffee. In addition to a dozen sandwiches, they offer a good selection of salads and such treats as homemade hummus and a brie and fruit plate. They also make good cookies and other desserts. The central location and free Wi-Fi make this a popular hangout for local expats. $ *Average main: $6* ✉ *Av. A and Calle 7, Casco Viejo* ☎ *507/212–3487* 🌐 *www.supergourmetcascoviejo.com* ⊗ *Open Mon.–Sat. 8 am–5 pm, Sun. 10–4 pm.*

$$ ✕ **Tántalo.** *International.* ★ This trendy tapas restaurant packs in the locals on weekend nights, but it's a fun place for a meal any time. Seating is at long, high tables, which different groups share under a tangle of wires and hanging lamps. The tapas are an international mix of flavors: from Greek salad to coconut cashew chicken to a selection of Panamanian *empanadas* (fried pastries stuffed with sausage and potato or beans and cheese). The portions vary in size, but the best thing is to start with two per person, and share. The atmosphere is hip, with house music on the stereo and original art on the walls. You may want to head up to the rooftop bar—a popular night spot with an impressive view—once you've had your fill of tapas. $ *Average main: $15* ✉ *Av. B and Calle 8, Casco Viejo* ☎ *507/262–4030* 🌐 *www.tantalohotel.com* ✍ *Reservations essential.*

CALZADA DE AMADOR

The best thing about eating on the Amador Causeway is that you usually get an ocean view with your meal. A great place for lunch, the Causeway is also a popular dinner destination, and its restaurants tend to serve food late.

$$ ★ × **Alberto's.** *Italian.* The best tables here are across the drive from the main restaurant, overlooking the Flamenco Marina and the city skyline beyond, but they are also the first ones to fill up. The other options are to sit on the large covered terrace, cooled by ceiling fans, or in the air-conditioned dining room. The food here is good, but the service can be leisurely. The menu has something for everyone, including a good selection of pizzas and pastas, but seafood is usually the best choice. You can start with *duo de mar* (corvina and lobster in béchamel sauce) or *mero* (grouper) carpaccio, and move on to pizza, salmon ravioli in a creamy tomato sauce, *corvina al cartucho* (sea bass and julienne vegetables broiled in tinfoil), or *langostinos provençal* (prawns sautéed with fine herbs and tomatoes). You may want to walk around the island a few times before visiting their Italian ice cream shop. *Average main: $16 ✉ Edificio Fuerte Amador, Isla Flamenco, Calzada de Amador ☎ 507/314–1134.*

$ × **Kayuco.** *Seafood.* This collection of simple tables shaded by umbrellas at the edge of the Flamenco Marina is the place to go for inexpensive dinner or a cold drink with a view. The food is basic but good—the Panamanian version of bar food—with dishes such as ceviche, sea bass fingers, hamburgers, and whole fried snapper, all served with *yuca* (fried cassava root) or *patacones* (plantain slices that have been fried and smashed). The relaxed atmosphere and low prices are a winning combination, and the place is packed on weekend nights. *Average main: $9 ✉ Isla Flamenco, Calzada de Amador ☎ 507/314–1998.*

$ × **Mi Ranchito.** *Latin American.* Topped by a giant thatch roof that has become an Amador Causeway landmark, Mi Ranchito has a great view of the city across the bay and is one of the best places in town to sample Panamanian cuisine. The food isn't gourmet, but it's authentic and inexpensive. House specialties include *corvina entera frita* (a whole fried sea bass), *crema de mariscos* (seafood chowder), *camarones a la criolla* (shrimp in a tomato and onion sauce), *corvina al ajillo* (sea bass in a garlic sauce), and a rib-eye steak *encebollado* (smothered in onions). They serve tasy *batidos* (frozen fruit drinks) made from papaya, *piña* (pineapple) and other tropical fruits; this is an excellent spot for a drink at sunset, when the skyline glows. At night, you can enjoy the live Latin music, often traditional Panamanian. *Average main: $10 Isla Naos, Calzada de Amador 507/228–4909 www.restaurantemiranchito.com.*

$$ ✕**Restaurante Barko.** *Seafood.* This open-air restaurant is known for serving large portions of fresh seafood, prepared a variety of ways, with an ocean breeze. The specialties are all from the surrounding sea, such as ceviche, *corvina con hongos* (sea bass with a mushroom sauce), and crispy *langostinos* (prawns) served with coconut rice and *guandú* (pigeon peas). The name is a misspelling of the word *barco* (boat), and you'll probably see a few as you dine, because most tables face the canal, whereas the rest overlook the bay and city, beyond the parking lot. The wine list has nearly 90 vintages from around the world. It's the first restaurant in the Brisas del Amador shopping center, on the left as you arrive at Isla Perico. *Average main: $18 Isla Perico, Calzada de Amador 507/314–0000.*

DOWNTOWN PANAMA CITY

Not only does the downtown area have a high concentration of restaurants, it also has the greatest variety of cuisines and prices. Many of these are within walking distance of hotels, and the area is very safe. It also has plenty of bars.

$$ ★ ✕**Beirut.** *Lebanese.* The interior of this Lebanese restaurant goes a bit overboard, with faux-stone columns and arches, but the food is consistently good, and the waitstaff is attentive. The extensive menu goes beyond the Middle East to include dishes such as grilled salmon and pizzas, but the best bets are the Lebanese dishes, which include an array of starters such as *falafel* (fried garbanzo balls), *baba ghanoush* (roasted eggplant), and a dozen salads that can make for an inexpensive, light meal. It's a good choice for vegetarians. Be sure to order some fresh flat bread to go with your meal. There is usually Arabic music playing, and they have belly dancing on Friday and Saturday nights. There is a collection of hookahs for smoking on the patio, which is a nice place to eat at night, as long as it isn't full of hookah smokers. The owner also has a restaurant on the Amador Causeway. *Average main: $15 Calles 52 and Ricardo Arias, across from Panama Marriott Hotel, Area Bancária 507/214–3815 www.beirutpanama.com.*

$ ★ ✕**Caffé Pomodoro.** *Italian.* Decent Italian food at reasonable prices served amidst tropical foliage make this restaurant

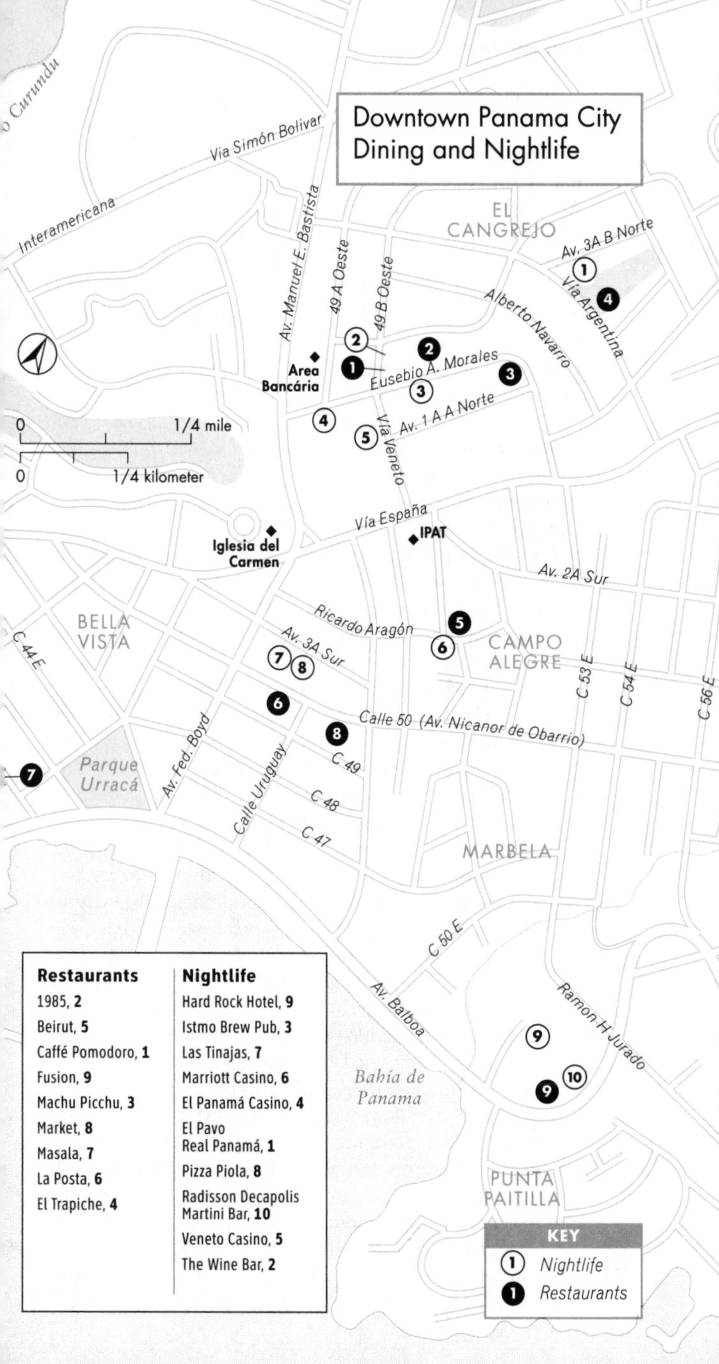

Downtown Panama City
Dining and Nightlife
Via Simón Bolivar
Interamericana
Av. Manuel E. Bastista
49 A Oeste
49 B Oeste
EL CANGREJO
Av. 3A B Norte
Vía Argentina
Alberto Navarro
Area Bancária
Eusebio A. Morales
Av. 1 A A Norte
Vía Veneto
0
1/4 mile
0
1/4 kilometer
Vía España
IPAT
Iglesia del Carmen
Av. 2A Sur
Ricardo Aragón
BELLA VISTA
Av. 3A Sur
CAMPO ALEGRE
C 44 E
C 53 E
C 54 E
C 56 E
Calle 50 (Av. Nicanor de Obarrio)
Av. Fed. Boyd
Calle Uruguay
Parque Urracá
C 49
C 48
C 47
MARBELA
C 50 E
Av. Balboa
Ramon H Jurado
Bahía de Panama
PUNTA PAITILLA
Restaurants
1985, 2
Beirut, 5
Caffé Pomodoro, 1
Fusion, 9
Machu Picchu, 3
Market, 8
Masala, 7
La Posta, 6
El Trapiche, 4
Nightlife
Hard Rock Hotel, 9
Istmo Brew Pub, 3
Las Tinajas, 7
Marriott Casino, 6
El Panamá Casino, 4
El Pavo Real Panamá, 1
Pizza Piola, 8
Radisson Decapolis Martini Bar, 10
Veneto Casino, 5
The Wine Bar, 2
KEY
Nightlife
Restaurants

in the Hotel Las Vegas a local favorite. Though there is a small air-conditioned dining room, the nicest tables are on the hotel's large interior patio, with its tropical trees, potted plants, and palms decorated with swirling Christmas lights. At lunch, it feels like a jungle oasis in the heart of the city, with birds singing in the branches above. The food is standard Italian, with eight varieties of homemade pastas served with any of a dozen different sauces, a variety of broiled meat and seafood dishes, personal pizzas, and focaccia sandwichess. For dessert, choose from chocolate cheesecake, tiramisu, and other treats. There is often a guitarist playing at dinnertime, and the Wine Bar next door has acoustic Latin music until late. *Average main: $9 Vía Veneto and Calle Eusebio A. Morales, El Cangrejo 507/269–5836 www.1985.com/restaurant_pomodoro.html.*

$$ × **Elephant Grill.** *Asian Fusion.* Although the low lighting and Chinese characters evoke an opium den, the pungent odors that waft through the air here are that of Asian spices such as ginger and lemongrass. Billed as a curry house, this is actually a pan-Asian restaurant with succulent dishes such as Misayaki marinated butterfish and Cambodian loc lac beef (beef marinated in lime juice) to complement such favorites as Massaman shrimp curry. The decor is subtle, with pastels, bamboo, and large fans hanging from the wooden rafters. You should make a reservation for dinner on weekends. *Average main: $16 Calle 47 at Calle Uruguay, Marbella 507/264–5652 www.elephantgrill.com Closed 2:30 pm–6:30 pm.*

$ × **El Trapiche.** *Latin American.* El Trapiche is a popular spot for traditional Panamanian food, thanks to its convenient location and reasonable prices. The menu includes all the local favorites, from *ropa vieja* (stewed beef, but literally "old clothes") to *cazuelo de mariscos* (seafood stew) and *sancocho* (chicken soup). They serve inexpensive set lunches, and typical Panamanian breakfasts, which include *bistec encebollado* (skirt steak smothered in onions), *tortillas* (thick deep-fried corn patties), and *carimañolas* (cassava croquets stuffed with ground beef). The decor is appropriately folksy, with drums, Carnaval masks and other handicrafts hanging on the walls, and a barrel-tile awning over the front terrace, at the end of which is the old *trapiche* (traditional sugarcane press) for which the place is named. *Average main: $8 Vía Argentina, 2 blocks off Vía España, El Cangrejo 507/269–4353.*

$$$ × **Fusion Restaurant.** *Eclectic.* This restaurant combines a wild decor with an inventive menu that melds the cuisines of

three continents. The central dining area looks like something out of a Hollywood adventure movie, dominated by a 20-foot bust reminiscent of the statues on Easter Island. By day, sunlight glistens down through portholes in the bottom of the pool on the roof. If the statue is a bit too much for you, look for a table in the other dining area, where the artistic decor includes giant vases and a wall of TVs broadcasting fire images. The menu matches the atmosphere with an inventive mix of Continental, Asian, and Latin American cuisines that is true to the restaurant's name. You can start your dinner with Peruvian ceviche or turkey ginger spring rolls, then dive into some shrimp and vegetables in a coconut curry, lamb ribs with a sweet and spicy sauce, or creamy lobster risotto with palm fruit. *Average main: $20* ✉ *Radisson Decapolis, Av. Balboa, next to Multicentro, Paitilla* ☎ *507/215–5000.*

★ $$$ Fodor's Choice ✕ **La Posta.** *Latin American.* An elegant ambience and innovative mix of Latin American and European flavors have kept La Posta one of Panama City's most popular restaurants. Located in a refurbished house just off Calle Uruguay, it has a classic Caribbean feel, with ceiling fans, cane chairs, colorful tile floors, and potted palms. There is usually Latin music playing, and the shiny hardwood bar stretching down one end of the dining room is the perfect place to sip a *mojito.* The menu changes regularly, but it always includes fresh seafood, USDA beef, and organic pork and chicken prepared in inventive ways, plus a few risottos and pastas. You can check its current offerings at the restaurant's Web site. Reserve a table in the back, overlooking the small, tropical garden, and try your best to save room for dessert. *Average main: $20* ✉ *Calle 49 and Calle Uruguay, Bella Vista* ☎ *507/269–1076* 🌐 *www.lapostapanama.com* ⊗ *Closed 2:30–6:30.*

★ $$ Fodor's Choice ✕ **Market.** *Steakhouse.* This trendy steak house a block off busy Calle Uruguay is the best option for a meat lover, whether you're in the mood for filet mignon, or a cheeseburger. You can get USDA Omaha beef here, but it costs considerably more than the Panamanian beef. The chicken and pork is organic and free-range from the restaurant's own farm. You can also get such American classics as a Cobb salad, or a side of macaroni and cheese, which are no doubt novelties for the predominantly Panamanian clientele. The steaks are excellent, but so is the Morrocan-style chicken with couscous, and the salmon *grille beurre d'hôtel.* There's an extensive wine list, and the service is excellent. You may want to reserve a table on weekends, when this place gets packed and noisy. They also serve brunch from 11:30 to 2:30 on weekends. *Average main: $17* *Calle 48 between Calle Uruguay and Aquino de La Guardia, Bella Vista* *507/226–9401* *www.marketpanama.com/Home.html* *Closed Mon.–Wed. 2:30–6:30.*

$$ ✕**Masala Indian Cuisine.** *North Indian.* Panama City's best Indian restaurant is also one of your surest bets for going vegetarian in a town short on options for herbivores. The shrine behind the bar shows a traditionally dressed Indian woman making the gesture meaning welcome, and owners Koreena Bajwa and César Marín certainly make guests feel that way. Their authentic north Indian cuisine is served in cozy, colorfully decorated dining rooms, which include an area for shoeless dining on the floor on plush cushions. Just about any of the dozens of vegetarian, chicken, and lamb options on the menu are guaranteed to make your taste buds smile. A great nonmeat option is the *thali*, a plate that includes four hefty samplers including beans or lentils and a yogurt-based dish. This popular restaurant is small, so reservations are essential. *Average main: $15* *Justo Arosemena between Calles 44 and 45, Bella Vista* *507/225–0105* *Reservations essential* *Closed Sun.*

$$$ ✕**1985.** *Swiss.* Named for the year it opened, this restaurant serves traditional French and Swiss cuisine in an eclectic mix of dining rooms. It holds the strange distinction of occupying the only building in Panama City that resembles a Swiss chalet. The owner, chef Willy Dingelman, trained in Lausanne then moved to Panama three decades ago, and has since developed a small restaurant and wine-importing empire. They consequently have an excellent wine cellar. When President Ricardo Martinelli was on the campaign trail, Dingelman promised he'd share a $15,000 bottle if he won the election; there's a photo of the post-election moment on the wall at the entrance. Dingelman's original Swiss restaurant, called the Rincón Suizo, is now a rustic dining room in the back of 1985—two menus under one roof. The decor is a bit of this and a bit of that, with a cluttered collection of chairs and couches in the long entrance, but people come here for the food, such as chicken *cordon bleu*, tenderloin in green peppercorn sauce, raclette, bratwurst, or *Zürcher Geschnetzeltes* (veal chunks in a mushroom cream sauce). *Average main: $20* *Calle Eusebio A. Morales, in front of Sevilla Suites hotel, El Cangrejo* *507/263–8541.*

$ ✕**Restaurante Machu Picchu.** *Peruvian.* This popular Peruvian restaurant named after that country's famous Inca ruins occupies an unassuming house a short walk from the hotels of El Cangrejo. Its relatively small dining room, decorated with paintings of Peruvian landscapes and colorful woven tablecloths, is often packed with Panamanians at night. The food they come for is traditional Peruvian, with a few inventions such as *corvina Hiroshima* (sea bass in a shrimp, bell pepper, ginger sauce) and *langostinos gratinados* (prawns au gratin). You can't go wrong with such Peruvian classics as ceviche, *ají de gallina* (shredded chicken in a chili-cream sauce), *seco de res* (Peruvian stewed beef with rice), and *sudado de mero* (grouper in a spicy soup). Be careful how you apply the *ají* hot sauce; it's practically caustic. *Average main: $12* ✉ *Calle Eusebio A Morales No. 16, El Cangrejo* ☎ *507/264–9308.*

WHERE TO STAY

Panama City has a good hotel selection, with something for every taste and budget. The Casco Viejo has boutique hotels in historic settings, but they lack the facilities of the bigger hotels and can be noisy on weekends. There are various large hotels scattered around the city, but most are clustered in El Cangrejo and the Area Bancária, which are busy, but have plenty of restaurants and nightlife. For a quieter alternative, head to Balboa, Cerro Ancón, or one of the areas just outside the city, such as Summit, or Playa Kobbe. TIP→ **Because of the cities oversupply of big hotels, you can often get a room for a fraction of the rack rate if you book online, especially on weekends.**

For expanded hotel reviews, visit Fodors.com.

CASCO VIEJO

The Casco Viejo has various small hotels in refurbished buildings dating from the early 20th or late 19th centuries, with great decors and views. They are an excellent option for those who want to experience life in the city's colorful historic quarter. ⚠ **The Casco Viejo has a critical mass of bars, and some hotels suffer party noise into the wee hours on weekends.**

$$$ ★ **Casa del Horno.** *B&B/Inn.* The impressive rooms in this restored 19th-century building two blocks from the Plaza Catedral are a seamless mix of old and new. **Pros:** gorgeous design; central location. **Cons:** loud music late night Thursday to Saturday. *Rooms from: $250* ✉ *Av. B between*

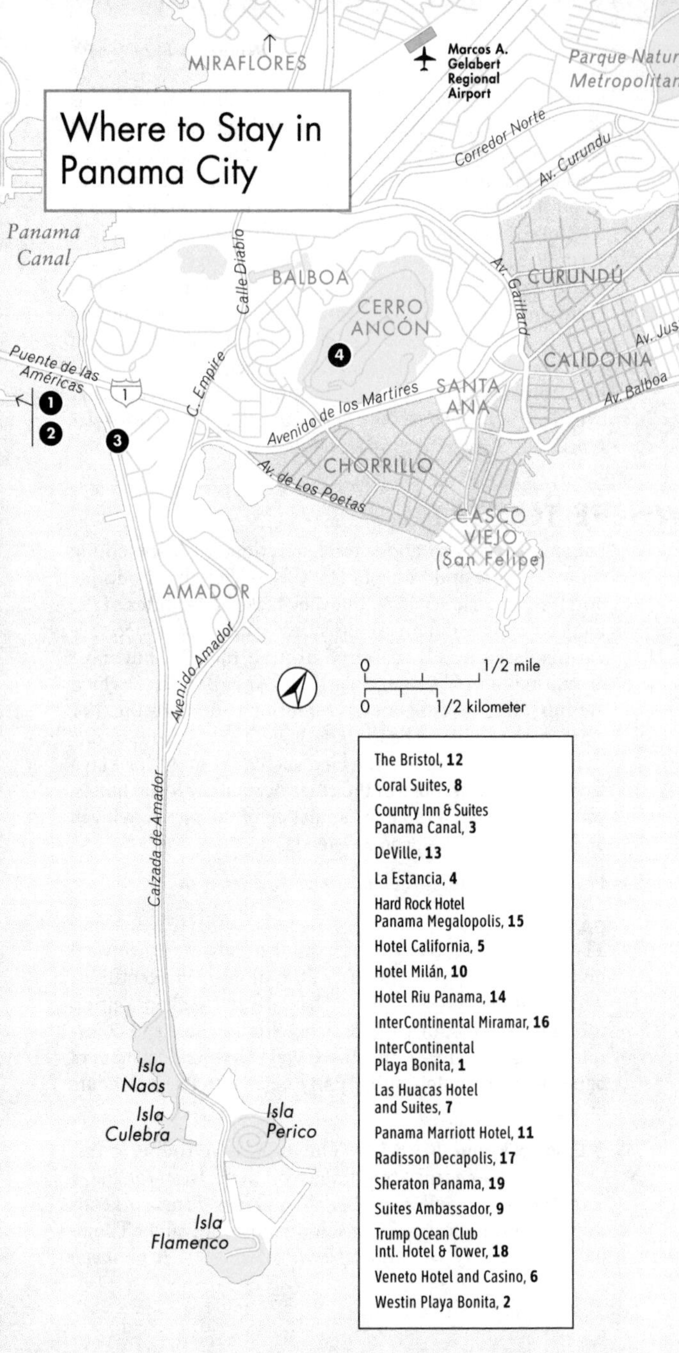
Where to Stay in Panama City
MIRAFLORES
Marcos A. Gelabert Regional Airport
Parque Natural Metropolitano
Corredor Norte
Av. Curundu
Panama Canal
Calle Diablo
BALBOA
CERRO ANCÓN
Av. Gaillard
CURUNDÚ
Av. Justo
CALIDONIA
Puente de las Américas
C. Empire
Avenido de los Martires
SANTA ANA
Av. Balboa
CHORRILLO
Av. de Los Poetas
CASCO VIEJO (San Felipe)
AMADOR
Avenido Amador
0
1/2 mile
0
1/2 kilometer
Calzada de Amador
Isla Naos
Isla Culebra
Isla Perico
Isla Flamenco
The Bristol, 12
Coral Suites, 8
Country Inn & Suites Panama Canal, 3
DeVille, 13
La Estancia, 4
Hard Rock Hotel Panama Megalopolis, 15
Hotel California, 5
Hotel Milán, 10
Hotel Riu Panama, 14
InterContinental Miramar, 16
InterContinental Playa Bonita, 1
Las Huacas Hotel and Suites, 7
Panama Marriott Hotel, 11
Radisson Decapolis, 17
Sheraton Panama, 19
Suites Ambassador, 9
Trump Ocean Club Intl. Hotel & Tower, 18
Veneto Hotel and Casino, 6
Westin Playa Bonita, 2

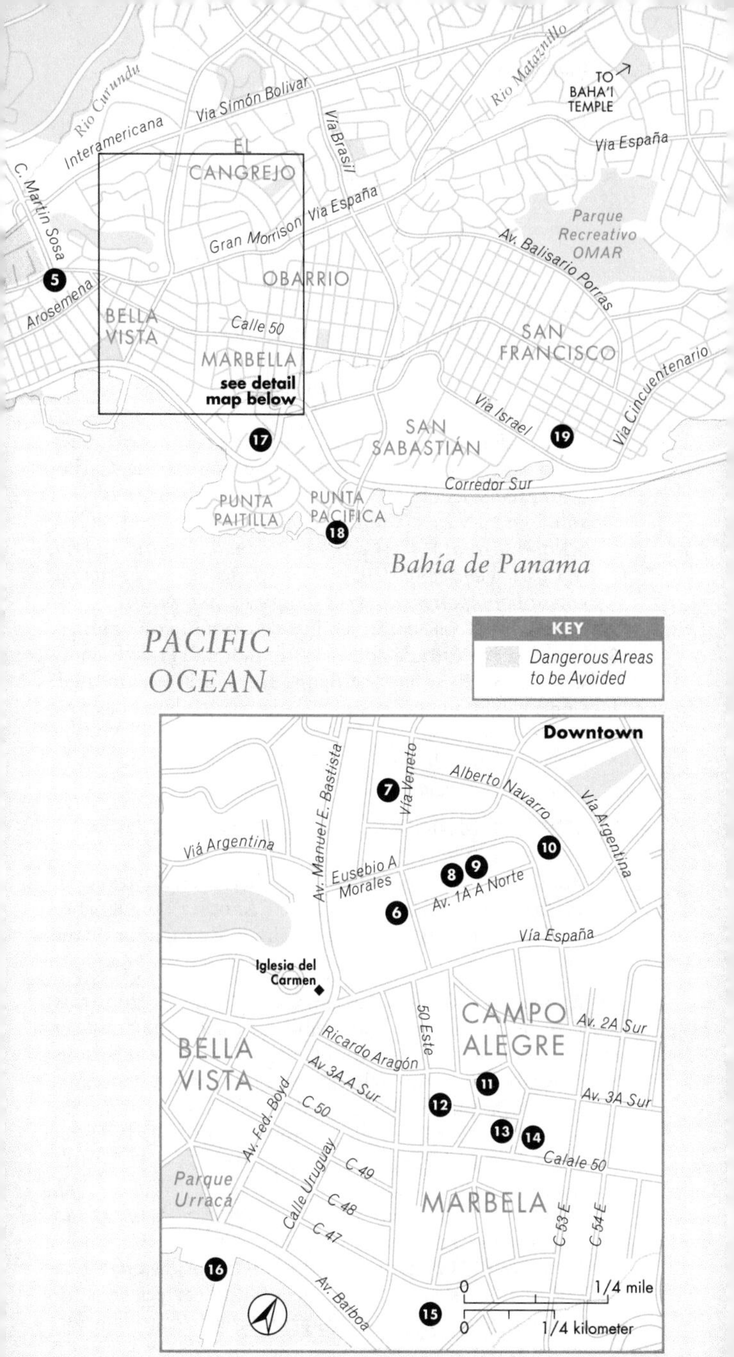

Rio Curundu
Interamericana
Via Simón Bolivar
Rio Matasnillo
TO BAHA'I TEMPLE
Via España
EL CANGREJO
Via Brasil
C. Martin Sosa
Gran Morrison Via España
Parque Recreativo OMAR
Av. Balisario Porras
5
Arosemena
OBARRIO
BELLA VISTA
Calle 50
MARBELLA
see detail map below
SAN FRANCISCO
Via Cincuentenario
Via Israel
19
SAN SABASTIÁN
17
Corredor Sur
PUNTA PAITILLA
PUNTA PACIFICA
18
Bahía de Panama
PACIFIC OCEAN
KEY
Dangerous Areas to be Avoided
Downtown
Av. Manuel E. Bastista
Vía Veneto
7
Alberto Navarro
Vía Argentina
10
Viá Argentina
Eusebio A Morales
8
9
Av. 1A A Norte
6
Vía España
Iglesia del Carmen
50 Este
CAMPO ALEGRE
Av. 2A Sur
Ricardo Aragón
BELLA VISTA
Av 3A A Sur
11
12
Av. 3A Sur
Av. Fed. Boyd
C 50
13
14
Calale 50
Calle Uruguay
C 49
Parque Urraca
C 48
MARBELA
C 53 E
C 54 E
C 47
16
Av. Balboa
15
0
1/4 mile
0
1/4 kilometer

Calle 7 and Calle 8, Casco Viejo ☎ *507/212–0052* 🌐 *www.casadelhorno.net* ⇒ *8 suites* 🍽 *Breakfast.*

★ **Fodor'sChoice** ▣ **Las Clementinas.** *B&B/Inn.* The six bright, **$$$$** spacious suites in this refurbished, early-20th-century apartment building are as charming as they are comfortable, which together with the friendly staff and an excellent restaurant make this a premier Casco Viejo lodging option. **Pros:** tasteful decor; friendly staff, conveniently located; great restaurant. **Cons:** noisy neighbors. $ *Rooms from: $270* ✉ *Calle 11 at Av. B, Casco Viejo* ☎ *507/228–7613, 877/889–0351* 🌐 *www.lasclementinas.com* ⇒ *6 suites* 🍽 *Breakfast.*

$ ▣ **Magnolia Inn.** *Hotel.* This American-run hotel is in a refurbished, 18th-century building behind the Cathedral. **Pros:** friendly owners; lovely historic building; good value; great views. **Cons:** very noisy on weekend nights. $ *Rooms from: $90* ✉ *Calle 8 between Av. Central and Av. B, Casco Viejo* ☎ *507/202–0872, 507/6551–9217* 🌐 *www.magnoliainnpanama.com* ⇒ *6 rooms* 🍽 *No meals.*

★ **Fodor'sChoice** ▣ **Tántalo.** *Hotel.* Eco-conscious luxury meets a **$$** hip, creative attitude at this 12-room hotel. **Pros:** friendly service; excellent bar and dining scene; centrally located. **Cons:** neighborhood gets a bit sketchy late-night; hot water can run out. $ *Rooms from: $280* ✉ *Ave. B and 8th St., Casco Viejo* ☎ *262–4030* 🌐 *www.tantalohotel.com* ⇒ *12 rooms* 🍽 *No meals.*

CERRO ANCÓN, BALBOA, AND THE CALZADA DE AMADOR

Hotels in the former Canal Zone offer clean air, tranquility, greenery, and priceless views. Another bonus: They are a short taxi trip from the Calzada de Amador or the Casco Viejo.

$$ ▣ **Country Inn & Suites Panama Canal.** *Hotel.* A front-row view of the Panama Canal and the peace and fresh air that come with an out-of-town location make this hotel a great option, especially for families. **Pros:** great canal views; peaceful; big pool; good value. **Cons:** public areas need work; "garden views" disappointing; could be better maintained and managed. $ *Rooms from: $135* ✉ *Calzada de Amador and Calle Pelícano, Balboa* ☎ *507/211–4500, 888/201–1746 in the U.S.* 🌐 *www.countryinns.com* ⇒ *185 rooms, 58 suites* 🍽 *Breakfast.*

★ **Fodor'sChoice** ▣ **La Estancia.** *B&B/Inn.* One of the city's best **$** bed-and-breakfasts, La Estancia is the perfect spot for nature lovers, because it sits at the edge of the rain forest high on Ancón Hill (Cerro Ancón). **Pros:** surrounded by nature; friendly, helpful staff; peaceful; inexpensive. **Cons:** far from restaurants and nightlife; rooms small and very basic. *Rooms from: $75 Quarry Heights, Casa No. 35; 50 yards south of ANCON office, Cerro Ancón 507/314–1417 www.bedandbreakfastpanama.com 15 rooms, 2 suites Breakfast.*

DOWNTOWN PANAMA CITY

Panama City's critical mass of accommodations is found in this amalgam of neighborhoods that extends from Bella Vista to Punta Paitilla. Many of them are found near the intersection of Vía España and Vía Veneto, the heart of El Cangrejo. Several are scattered through the nearby Área Bancária, the city's financial district, whereas a few more are on or near the coast, wither on the Cinta Costera, or Punta Paitilla. This area is safe for walking and is sprinkled with restaurants, shops, nightlife, and other diversions.

$$$$ ★ **The Bristol.** *Hotel.* Much like a European boutique hotel, the Bristol is gorgeous and classy, with personalized service and attention to detail to boot. **Pros:** excellent service; great rooms; convenient location; nice restaurant. **Cons:** no pool. *Rooms from: $265 Av. Aquilino de la Guardia, between Calle 50 and Vía España, Area Bancária 507/264–0000, 800/865–3570 in the U.S. www.thebristol.com 44 rooms, 12 suites Breakfast.*

$$ **Coral Suites.** *Hotel.* Popular with travelers on a budget, Coral Suites offers mini apartments with many of the same amenities you'll find in luxury hotels for less money. **Pros:** affordable; lots of amenities; great location. **Cons:** pool is small; no restaurant. *Rooms from: $140 Calle D, half a block east of Vía Veneto, El Cangrejo 507/269–3898 www.coralsuites.net 62 rooms Breakfast.*

$$$ **Hard Rock Hotel Panama Megapolis.** *Hotel.* Mega- is the right prefix for this 66-floor tower, starting with its expansive lobby and mezzanine of bars—a popular night spot—but the rooms are attractive, and the ocean views, impressive. **Pros:** hip vibe; abundant nightlife; attractive rooms; ocean views. **Cons:** service inconsistent; can be a zoo when full. *Rooms from: $209 Av. Balboa, next to Multicentro, Paitilla 507/380–1111 www.hardrockhotels.com 1,350 rooms, 150 suites.*

$$$$ ★ **Hotel DeVille.** *Hotel.* Tasteful, with an extremely friendly staff, the DeVille is popular with business travelers, and anyone else who feels that service and luxurious room are more important than a pool. **Pros:** handsome rooms; con-

venient location; excellent staff. **Cons:** no pool; no gym; noisy plumbing. *Rooms from: $270 Av. Beatriz Cabal, near Calle 50 Este, Area Bancária 507/206–3100 www.devillehotel.com.pa 33 rooms Breakfast.*

$ **Hotel Milán.** *Hotel.* With clean, reasonably priced rooms near some of the best restaurants in El Cangrejo, the Hotel Milán is one of the city's best options for budget travelers, especially considering its 15% discount if you pay cash. **Pros:** great location; decent rates. **Cons:** no pool; rooms lack personality. *Rooms from: $70 Calle Eusebio A. Morales No. 31, El Cangrejo 507/263–6130 www.hotelmilan.com.pa 90 rooms, 15 suites No meals.*

$$$ ★ **Hotel Riu Panama Plaza.** *Hotel.* Towering over busy Calle 50, this chic hotel caters to vacationers with its tropical decor, attractive rooms, large pool area, selection of bars and restaurants, and convenient location at the edge of the Area Bancária. **Pros:** attractive; nice pool area; often offer discounted rates. **Cons:** big; caters to tour groups. *Rooms from: $199 Calle 50 at Calle 53 Este, Marbella 507/378–9000, 507/269–1000, 888/748–4990 toll-free in U.S. www.riuplaza.com/en/hotel-riu-panama/ 610 rooms, 35 suites Breakfast.*

InterContinental Miramar. *Hotel.* Amazing ocean views, elegant rooms and an attractive pool area make this 25-story tower a good choice for business travelers and vacationers alike. **Pros:** amazing view; lovely pool; good breakfasts; good value. **Cons:** inconsistent service; slightly isolated; cold rooms. *Rooms from: $200 Miramar Plaza, Av. Balboa at Av. Federico Boyd, Bella Vista 507/206–8888 www.miramarpanama.com 165 rooms, 20 suites Breakfast.*

$$ **Las Huacas Hotel and Suites.** *Hotel.* Located on quiet street just a short walk from the bars and restaurants of El Cangrejo, Las Huacas is a good option if you're on a budget. **Pros:** bright rooms; convenient location, quiet neighborhood. **Cons:** service inconsistent; rooms can be musty. *Rooms from: $125 Calle 49, 1½ blocks north of Salsa's Bar and Grill, El Cangrejo 507/213–2222 www.lashuacashotel.com 72 rooms Breakfast.*

★ Fodor's Choice $$$ **Panama Marriott Hotel.** *Hotel.* From the airy lobby, with its marble floors and potted palms, to the sumptuous guest rooms, this 20-story hotel in the heart of the financial district is one of the city's best. **Pros:** good location; friendly staff; lovely rooms; some great views. **Cons:** small pool; some mediocre views; Wi-Fi is extra. *Rooms from: $225 Calle 52 and Calle Ricardo Arias,*

Area Bancária ☎ *507/210–9100, 888/236–2427 in the U.S.* 🌐 *www.marriott.com* ⇨ *290 rooms, 8 suites* 🍽 *No meals.*

$$$ ★ Fodor's Choice **Radisson Decapolis.** *Hotel.* Though most of the guests are business travelers, this modern, 29-story high-rise is a great place for vacationers, thanks to its circular pool, spa, chic lobby bar, and restaurant. **Pros:** hip atmosphere; friendly staff; some great views; good restaurant; close to shops and entertainment. **Cons:** some mediocre views; small pool. *Rooms from: $225* ✉ *Av. Balboa, next to Multicentro, Paitilla* ☎ *507/215–5000, 800/967–9033 in the U.S.* 🌐 *www.radisson.com* ⇨ *240 rooms* 🍽 *Breakfast.*

$ ★ **Suites Ambassador.** *Hotel.* Most rooms in this small, friendly hotel are extremely spacious, which combined with its great, but quiet, location near El Cangrejo's restaurants and bars, make it a good option for budget travelers. **Pros:** big suites; great location; friendly staff; lots of amenities. **Cons:** small pool. *Rooms from: $120* ✉ *Calle D, half a block east of Vía Veneto, El Cangrejo* ☎ *507/263–7274* 🌐 *www.suitesambassador-hotel.com* ⇨ *31 suites, 8 studios* 🍽 *Breakfast.*

$$$$ ★ **Trump Ocean Club International Hotel & Tower.** *Hotel.* The ocean views from the sleek guest rooms and 13th-floor pool terrace of this impressive skyscraper are the big selling points, but the restaurants, facilities, and friendly staff close the deal. **Pros:** first class service; great rooms; ocean views. **Cons:** far from most sites and restaurants. *Rooms from: $319* ✉ *Calle Punta Colón, Punta Pacífica* ☎ *507/215–8800, 885/225–9640 in U.S.* 🌐 *www.trumphotelcollection.com* ⇨ *350 rooms, 19 suites* 🍽 *No meals.*

$$$ **Veneto Hotel and Casino.** *Hotel.* The Veneto's massive marquee with flashing colored lights is Panama City's answer to Las Vegas, but its spacious rooms and competitve prices make it a good option for non-gamblers. **Pros:** centrally located; hopping casino. **Cons:** lobby may be too busy for some; indifferent service; definitely not a family-friendly atmosphere. *Rooms from: $190* ✉ *Vía Veneto and Av. Eusebio A. Morales, El Cangrejo* ☎ *507/340–8888, 888/611–9840 in the U.S.* 🌐 *www.venetocasino.com* ⇨ *300 rooms, 26 suites* 🍽 *No meals.*

SAN FRANCISCO

The predominantly residential neighborhood of San Francisco offers a decent supply of restaurants and one large hotel, the Sheraton, which is next door to the ATLAPA Convention Center.

$$$$ **Sheraton Panama.** *Hotel.* One of the city's original luxury hotels, the Sheraton Panama remains one of its best, in no small part thanks to is spacious pool area and lobby. **Pros:** quiet; nice pool; friendly staff; quick trip to the airport. **Cons:** far from many attractions; small bathrooms. *Rooms from: $250 Vía Israel and Calle 77, next to ATLAPA convention center, San Francisco 507/305–5100, 800/325–3535 in the U.S. www.sheratonpanama.com.pa 342 rooms, 19 suites No meals.*

PARQUE NATURAL METROPOLITANO, MIRAFLORES, AND SUMMIT

★ Fodor'sChoice $$ **Radisson Summit Hotel Panama Canal.** *Hotel.* This comfortable hotel has one of the country's best golf courses, making it a popular destination for golfers. **Pros:** 18-hole golf course; friendly staff; quiet; surrounded by nature; good value. **Cons:** 20–30 minutes from most restaurants and nightlife. *Rooms from: $175 Av. Omar Torrijos, 20 km (12 miles) northwest of Panama City Paraiso 507/232–3700, 800/395–7046 in U.S. and Canada www.radisson.com 103 rooms Breakfast.*

PLAYA KOBBE

$$$$ **InterContinental Playa Bonita Resort and Spa.** *Resort.* One of only two beach hotels near Panama City, this resort has extensve landscaped grounds, a long stretch of khaki sand, and great ocean views, all a short drive from most city sights. **Pros:** great views; nice beach; spa. **Cons:** large resort can feel impersonal at times; ocean slightly polluted. *Rooms from: $420 Road to Veracruz, Km 7, Playa Kobbe 507/211–8600, 888/424–6835 in U.S. www.ichotelsgroup.com/intercontinental 276 rooms, 27 suites.*

$$$ **Westin Playa Bonita.** *Resort.* Families, couples, and business travelers looking for the amenities of a full-service resort, the feel of a destination beach-retreat, and proximity to Panama City's best attractions will find that the Westin elegantly unites all these features in one towering complex. **Pros:** great beach getaway close to downtown Panama City; beautiful common areas with sea views; wide array of amenities/activities make it a great place for multigeneration vacation. **Cons:** guests who opt for all-inclusive have to wear a plastic bracelet; poolside snack fare is quite mediocre. *Rooms from: $250 Road to Veracruz, Km 6, Playa Kobbe 507/304–6600 www.westin.com/playabonita 611 rooms Multiple meal plans.*

NIGHTLIFE AND THE ARTS

There is plenty to do in Panama City once the sun sets, though it is much more of a party town than a cradle of the arts. Because it is so hot by day, the night is an especially inviting time to explore the city. The entertainment and nightlife centers are Casco Viejo, El Cangrejo, and the Calle Uruguay area. The entertainment tends more toward high culture in Casco Viejo, with its Teatro Nacional and jazz venues, while the scene in the other areas is more about casinos, drinking, and dancing the night away.

THE ARTS

Panama may be a commercial center, but its arts scene is lacking. There are occasional dance or classical music performances in Teatro Nacional and jazz or Latin music can be found at various bars and nightclubs. For information on concerts, plays, and other performances, check out the listings in the free tourist newspaper called *The Visitor* or the ATP website (🌐 *www.visitpanama.com*).

FOLK DANCING

Panamanians love their folk dancing, which forms an important part of regional festivals and other major celebrations. The typical folk dances have their roots in popular Spanish dances of the 18th century, but they also have African and indigenous influences. The easiest way to experience them is at Las Tinajas restaurant in the Area Bancária.

Las Tinajas. Las Tinajas is an attractive Panamanian restaurant with a convenient location in the financial district that offers a folk-dancing show every Tuesday, Thursday, Friday, and Saturday night. The hour-long show starts at 9 pm and costs $5—plus you need to consume $12 of food and drink. You should reserve ahead of time and get there early to choose a good table, since the stage is at the center of the room and not all tables have great views. ✉ *Calle 51, No. 22, near Av. Federico Boyd, Area Bancária* ☎ *507/269–3840.*

JAZZ

Panama has long had a jazz scene, especially in the Caribbean port of Colón, but its best musicians have always moved abroad. The city's prodigal son is Danilo Pérez, a celebrated pianist who has played with the best, lives in the States. Other notable Panamanian jazz musicians have included saxophonist Maurice Smith, who played with everyone from Charlie Mingus to Dizzy Gillespie, and pianist Victor Boa. Some very good musicians live in the city, though most have to play salsa and other popular genres to survive. The best time for jazz fans to visit the city is late January, during the **Panama Jazz Festival**, which features concerts by international stars. For information on the next festival, check the website (*www.panamajazzfestival.com*). Jazz fans have several opportunities per week to hear good music in the Casco Viejo.

Casa Góngora. Casa Góngora, a small cultural center in the Casco Viejo, offers occasional free jazz, usually Thursday at 7 pm, though sometimes the music is a Latin genre such as bolero or trova. TIP→ **Call ahead for schedule information.** *Calle 9 and Av. Central, Casco Viejo* *507/506–5836.*

Las Bóvedas. The bar at the French restaurant Las Bóvedas, on Plaza Francia, usually has live jazz on Friday nights. There's a mellower atmosphere than the Latin vibe at nearby Platea, and they play earlier, starting around 7 pm. Call to confirm that the band is playing. *Plaza Francia, Casco Viejo* *507/228–8068* *www.restaurantelasbovedas.net.*

Platea. Located on the ground floor of a restored colonial building, Platea usually has Latin jazz on Thursday nights. TIP→ **Call to confirm.** *Calle 1, in front of the old Club Union, Casco Viejo* *507/228–4011* *www.scenayplatea.com.*

NIGHTLIFE

Panama City's after-dark offerings range from a quiet drink on historic Plaza Bolívar to dancing until dawn at one of the clubs on Calle Uruguay, with plenty of options in between. Although there are bars everywhere, nightlife is concentrated in the Casco Viejo, El Cangrejo, and Calle Uruguay, though there are also a few options in the Area Bancária and Punta Paitilla.

The Casco Viejo is the city's night-life epicenter, with a variety of bars and clubs that rock into the wee hours on weekends. The Calzada de Amador is the place to head for a quiet drink with lovely ocean views. The streets around Calle Uruguay are packed on weekends, when a predominantly young crowd fills its bars and dance clubs. There are also a few night spots in El Cangrejo and Punta Paitilla, where a couple hotel bars have amazing views.

There are also strip clubs, locally called "nightclubs," scattered between the Área Bancária and El Cangrejo, which have traditionally catered to business travelers, but are becoming a bit of a tourist attraction in their own right. Prostitution is legal in Panama, but streetwalking is not, so representatives of the world's oldest profession gather at a few of its bars and casinos.

BARS AND MUSIC

CASCO VIEJO

Casablanca. Casablanca, on the ground floor of the old Hotel Colombia, has tables on beautiful Plaza Bolívar, which is a great spot for a drink and conversation at night. They have live Latin Music Thursday through Saturday, when this place really hops. ✉ *Calle 4 on Plaza Bolívar, Casco Viejo* ☎ *507/212–0040* 🌐 *www.restaurantecasablanca-panama.com.*

DiVino Enoteca. This corner restaurant and wine bar is a popular spot thanks to a cozy atmosphere, frequent live music, and an excellent selection of wine and light meals. ✉ *Av. A and Calle 4, Casco Viejo* ☎ *507/202–6867* 🌐 *www.enotecadivino.com.*

★ Fodor's Choice **Ego y Narciso.** This tapas restaurant has tables on Plaza Bolívar, with views of the illuminated Iglesia de San Francisco and other historic structures, making it one of the city's most romantic spots for a drink. ✉ *Calle 3 Este on Plaza Bolívar, Casco Viejo* ☎ *507/262–2045.*

La Rana Dorada. This popular microbrewery at the edge of the Casco Viejo offers half a dozen home brews and a small menu. You can sit indoors or on the front terrace, which has a view of the modern skyline across the bay. ✉ *Av. Eloy Alfaro and Calle 11, Casco Viejo* ☎ *507/212–2680.*

Las Bóvedas. This French restaurant on Plaza Francia has tables on the plaza and a bar inside one of the Bóvedas (arched, brick chambers dating from the Colonial era) that often features live jazz on Friday nights. ■ TIP→ **Call to confirm the evenings entertainment.** ✉ *Plaza Francia, Calle 1, Casco Viejo* ☎ *507/228–8058* 🌐 *www.restaurantelasbovedas.net.*

Mojitos Sin Mojitos. This funky little place on the southeast corner of Plaza Herrera looks like a construction site from the street, but at night, the ancient walls and tropical foliage create a very cool atmosphere, which is complemented by the music and young crowd. ✉ *Calle 9 and Av. A, Casco Viejo* ☎ *507/6855–4080.*

★ Fodor's Choice **Tántalo.** The rooftop bar of this hip hotel has a great view of the city's skyline beyond the ancient roofs of the Casco Viejo. Weekends vibrate with the boom-boom of deafening house music, though the quality of the DJs isn't always top. You can get a relatively quiet drink here Sunday through Wednesday. ✉ *Calle 8 and Av. B, Casco Viejo* ☎ *507/262–4030* 🌐 *www.tantalohotel.com.*

Vieja Havana. Cuban music, a massive, hardwood bar and walls covered with photos and piantings of Cuba make it easy to imagine you're in Havana's old quarter as you sip a mojito. ✉ *Av. B and Calle 5 Este, Casco Viejo* ☎ *507/212–3873.*

EL CANGREJO

El Pavo Real Panamá. El Pavo Real Panamá is an attractive, British-inspired pub on a quiet stretch of Via Argentina. It has a long bar, two pool tables, and serves bar food including fish-and-chips. They often have live music, mostly rock, on weekends, but you can always get a quiet drink on the front terrace. ✉ *Vía Argentina and Calle José Martí, across street from Angel Restaurante, El Cangrejo* ☎ *507/394–6853.*

The Wine Bar. The Wine Bar, located on the ground floor of the Las Vegas Hotel Suites, has live, Latin music nightly, mostly mellow duos, or a guitarist. They have a decent selection of wine by the glass and serve good pizza and other snacks till late. ✉ *Calle Eusebio Morales, east of Vía Veneto, El Cangrejo* ☎ *507/265–4701.*

MARBELLA

Altabar. The massive, open-air lounge on the second floor of a dance club is a hip spot to sip a cocktail beneath a ceiling fan, and perhaps nibble on an array of snacks. ✉ *Calle 49, half a block east of Calle Uruguay, Bella Vista* ☎ *507/390–2582* 🌐 *www.altabarpanama.com.*

Cielo. The pool bar on the roof of the Manrey Hotel is a popular weekend spot. DJs pump the crowd up and the danger of somebody falling into the pool increases with every martini served. The glowing-blue lap pool is surrounded by canopy couches, arm chairs and tables, beyond which twinkle the city lights, making it a splendid spot for a drink any night. ✉ *Calle Uruguay and Calle 48, Bella Vista* ☎ *507/203–0000.*

Pizza Piola. Pizza Piola is a small Argentinian restaurant serving an array of empanadas and pizza. It's usually dead, but it livens up on Thursday, which is tango night. Tango classes are offered on a small terrace in front at 7 pm, and the experienced dancers strut their stuff starting at 9 pm. ✉ *Calle 51, half a block up from The Bristol, Area Bancária* ☎ *507/263–4658.*

PUNTA PAITILLA

Azul. This pool bar and grill on the 13th floor of the Trump Hotel is a popular weekend spot, thanks to its impressive view of the sea and the skycrapers of Costa del Este. An elevator at the back of the building offers access to the bar for non-guests. ✉ *Calle Punta Colón, Paitilla* ☎ *507/215–8800.*

Radisson Decapolis Martini Bar. This large lounge, located in the Hotel Decapolis, was once one of the city's hottest lounges, but it's now a nice spot for a quiet drink. ✉ *Radisson Decapolis, Av. Balboa, next to Multicentro, Paitilla* ☎ *507/215–5000.*

Hard Rock Hotel Panama Megalopolis. The second floor of this massive hotel has several bars that are among the city's most popular, among them a Stage Bar that features live music Wednesday through Saturday and the tapas bar Mamie Lee. ✉ *Av. Balboa, behind the Radisson Decapolis Hotel, Paitilla* ☎ *294–4000.*

CASINOS

The nicest casinos are in, or next to, the city's big hotels, namely the Panama Marriott, Veneto, and El Panamá, which often have excellent bands performing Latin music in their bars.

El Panamá. The Hotel El Panamá has a large Fiesta Casino behind it that is popular with Panamanians. It includes a Salsas Bar that regularly hosts concerts by some of Panama's best salsa and *pindín* bands. ✉ *Vía Veneto and Calle Eusebio Morales, El Cangrejo* ☎ *507/213–1274.*

Panama Marriott. The Panama Marriott has a two-story Royal Casino next door that is quite popular with locals. It has live music most nights, and sometimes hosts concerts by the country's most popular groups. ✉ *Calle 52 and Calle Ricardo Arias, Area Bancária* ☎ *507/205–7777.*

Veneto Hotel and Casino. The Veneto Hotel and Casino has the city's biggest and most popular casino, which includes craps and poker, and a sea of slot machines. Expect live music, Panamanians and foreigners who simply come to party, and lots of Colombian prostitutes. ✉ *Vía Veneto and Calle Eusebio Morales, El Cangrejo* ☎ *507/340–8880.*

DANCE CLUBS

The city's dance clubs play a broad mix of music that includes pop, salsa, reggaetón, and house music. Cover charges run between $5 and $10, and sometimes include a drink.

CASCO VIEJO

★ **Habana Panamá.** This spacious, traditional dance hall is the best place in Panama to dance salsa, or to simply enjoy the live Latin music and watch the experts tear up the dance floor. The country's top salsa bands, and occasional international acts, perform on a large stage at the end of a long dance floor lined with plush booths, at the opposite end of which is a massive bar stocked with plentiful rum. ✉ *Eloy Alfaro and Calle 12 Este, Casco Viejo* ☎ *507/212–0152* 🌐 *www.habanapanama.com.*

Platea. Platea, the popular bar underneath S'cena restaurant, may not have much of a dance floor, but the club books hot salsa bands and is packed most Friday nights, when people dance in the aisles or wherever else there's room. The bartenders and waiters, dressed in black with Panama hats, are part of the show, as they dance while delivering *mojitos* and Cuba libres. ✉ *Calle 1, in front of the old Club Union, Casco Viejo* ☎ *507/228–4011.*

MARBELLA

Altabar. One of Panama's hottest dance clubs, Altabar has DJs from Wednesday to Saturday and a sleek decor of white sofas and a black tile floor. There's a mezzanine for those who prefer to watch the bodies moving to the techno beat from a safe distance. ✉ *Calle 49, half a block east of Calle Uruguay, Bella Vista* ☎ *507/390–2582.*

SHOPPING

Panama City has more shopping options than you can shake a credit card at. Because of the country's role as an international port, manufactured goods from all over the world are cheaper in Panama than in most countries. Merchants from South and Central America regularly travel here to shop, but Americans will find that the U.S. megastores often beat the local prices for cameras and other electronic goods—plus the stores back home are more convenient in terms of warranties. Busy Vía Veneto, in El Cangrejo, and the Casco Viejo have souvenir shops. The city also has several modern malls, where the selection ranges from the cheap to chic.

Panama also produces some lovely handicrafts. The famous Panama hat is misnamed, because it's actually made in Ecuador, but it has been associated with Panama since Teddy Roosevelt was photographed wearing one when he traveled to the country to check on canal construction. Panama does, however, produce its own distinctive hand-woven hats. The country's second most popular handicraft is the *mola,* a fabric picture sewn by Guna women and worn on their blouses as part of their traditional dress. The Guna are also known for their bead bracelets and necklaces, as well as simple jewelry made from seeds and shells. The Emberá and Wounaan are known for their animal figures carved out of dark cocobolo wood, or the seed of a rain-forest palm called *tagua*. They also produce attractive rattan baskets, bowls, and platters, which can take weeks to complete and are consequently expensive. The Ngöbe-Buglé Indians produce colorful dresses, jute shoulder bags, and intricate bead necklaces called *chaquiras*.

PANAMA HATS? They're actually from Ecuador. Teddy Roosevelt wore one of the wide-brimmed white hats when he came to Panama to inspect canal construction, and the apparel became forever associated with Panama, much to Ecuador's chagrin. Any such headwear you do find for sale here should be labeled "Genuine Panama Hat Made in Ecuador."

HANDICRAFT MARKETS

Even if you're not interested in buying, take a walk around one of the city's handicraft markets, all of which are open daily from 9 to 6. The rows of stalls filled with native handicrafts are great places to browse and learn a bit about the local cultures.

Centro Municipal de Artesanías Panameñas. A good place to shop for molas is the Centro Municipal de Artesanías Panameñas, a small market where most of the stands are owned by Kuna women, who are often sewing molas as they wait for customers. They also sell *chaquiras,* bags, hammocks, dresses, framed butterflies, T-shirts, and other souvenirs. ✉ *Av. Arnulfo Arias, three blocks up from old YMCA, Balboa.*

Mercado de Artesanía de Panamá Viejo. The Mercado de Artesanía de Panamá Viejo, next to the *Centro de Visitantes* (Visitor Center), is packed with small shops and stalls selling everything from indigenous handicrafts—many shop owners are indigenous—to woven hats, Carnaval masks, and other artisans' works from the country's interior. A number of Kuna families have shops here, making it a good place to buy *molas* (traditional fabric pictures). ✉ *Vía Cincuentenaria, Panamá Viejo* ☎ *507/560–0535.*

HANDICRAFT SHOPS

Though the selections aren't as impressive as those of the handicraft markets, the city's handicraft shops have more convenient locations.

Galería Arte Indígena. Galería Arte Indígena, just down the street from Plaza Francia, has indigenous handicrafts such as Emberá baskets, animal figures carved from *tagua* palm seeds, decorated gourds, hammocks, Panama hats (imported from Ecuador), and T-shirts. ✉ *Calle 1, No. 844, Casco Viejo* ☎ *507/228–9557.*

Papiro y Yo. Many of the bags, baskets, necklaces, and other items in this colorful shop are the product of recycling, made from magazine pages, flip tops, and other trash. Others are made from natural fibers, and almost everything is the work of families in the Panamanian countryside, so they're good for the environment, and people. ✉ *Calle 4 between Av. Central and Av. B, Casco Viejo* ☎ *507/391–3800* 🌐 *papyroyyo.com.*

JEWELRY

Reprosa. Reprosa sells elegant jewelry based on reproductions of pre-Columbian gold pieces and Spanish coins, as well as interesting modern designs in silver and high-quality indigenous *chaquira* beadwork, *cocobolo* wood carvings, paintings, and the ubiquitous *molas*. They have shops on Av. A, in the heart of the Casco Viejo, and on Av. Samuel Lewis, in Obarrio, near the Area Bancaría. ✉ *Art Deco Building, Av. A and Calle 4, Casco Viejo* ☎ *507/271–0033* 🌐 *www.reprosa.com* ✉ *Av. Samuel Lewis and Calle 54, Obarrio* ☎ *507/269–0457* 🌐 *www.reprosa.com.*

MALLS

Panama City has several modern shopping malls, and the more traditional Avenida Central pedestrian mall.

Albrook Mall. Albrook Mall is the people's mall, with more discount stores than the downtown malls. That, combined with its convenient location between the city's massive bus terminal and Albrook Airport, makes it the busiest mall. ✉ *In front of Terminal de Buses, Albrook* ☎ *507/303–6333* 🌐 *www.albrookmall.com.*

Avenida Central pedestrian mall. The Avenida Central pedestrian mall, a short walk from the Casco Viejo, is lined with shops selling imported electronics, jewelry, fabrics, and clothing. A stroll down this busy street can be quite entertaining, even if you don't buy anything. ■ TIP→ **Avoid the side streets.** ✉ *Between Plaza Santa Ana and Plaza Cinco de Mayo, Santa Ana.*

Multicentro. This modern, four-story mall, across from Punta Paitilla, holds dozens of shops, as well as a movie theater, food court, a casino, and a Hard Rock Cafe. ✉ *Av. Balboa, Punta Paitilla* ☎ *507/208–2500* 🌐 *www.multicentropanama.com.pa.*

Multiplaza. The city's high-end mall is just east of Punta Paitilla, on the road to ATLAPA and Panama Viejo. Its shops include the likes of Tiffany, Cartier, Luis Vuitton, and a Mac Store. It also has a movie theater, several restaurants, and an adjacent hotel. ✉ *Vía Israel, San Francisco* ☎ *507/302–5380* 🌐 *www.multiplaza.com.*

SOUVENIR SHOPS

Artesanías Panamá Bahía. This shop sells a mixture of Panamanian and Ecuadoran souvenirs, including an ample selection of Panama hats, from a convenient location on Busy Vía Veneto, across from the entrance to the El Panama hotel. ✉ *Via Veneto, El Cangrejo* ☎ *507/399–9012.*

La Ronda. La Ronda is an attractive little shop in a historic building near Plaza Francia that sells a mix of handicrafts and souvenirs: *molas,* Carnaval masks, wood carvings, paintings, Panama hats, and assorted knickknacks. ✉ *Calle 1 and Plaza Francia, Casco Viejo* ☎ *507/211–1001.*

SPAS

Spas at most Panama City hotels are open to nonguests; there are also spas on some of the country's beaches and in the mountains, so you'll have plenty of opportunities to rejuvenate during your travels.

IN THE CITY

Aquabella Sensory Spa by Clarins. Aquabella is a state-of-the-art, full-service spa with 15 treatment rooms and a vast menu of treatment options as well as holistic therapies such as Shiatsu and Reiki. It employs the latest technology in relaxation therapies, including Clarins' signature "Thermal Circuit Experience," which alternates hot, cold, and hydrotherapy experiences. ✉ *Westin Playa Bonita, Road to Veracruz, Km 6, Playa Kobbe* ☎ *877/800–1690* 🌐 *www.westinplayabonita.com/.*

Intercontinental Playa Bonita Resort and Spa. The Intercontinental Playa Bonita Resort and Spa, on the beach 8 km (5 miles) from Panama City, has a large spa offering an array of treatments for guests. ✉ *Playa Kobbe* ☎ *507/211–8600* 🌐 *www.ichotelsgroup.com.*

Radisson Decapolis. One of Panama City's best spas is located on the fourth floor of the Radisson Decapolis. If the treatments there don't leave you sufficiently relaxed, you can always top them off with a martini by the pool bar. ✉ *Av. Balboa, next to Multicentro, Paitilla* ☎ *507/215–5000* 🌐 *www.radisson.com/panamacitypan.*

Sheraton Panama. The Ygia Spa, in the Sheraton Panama, next to the ATLAPA convention center, offers an array of options ranging from the traditional massages and beauty treatments to "rejuvenation sessions" that can last anywhere from one to three hours. ✉ *Vía Israel and Calle 77, San Francisco* ☎ *507/305–5100* 🌐 *www.sheratonpanama.com.pa.*

Veneto Hotel and Casino. The flashy Veneto Hotel and Casino, on busy Vía Veneto, may seem like the last place you'd go to escape the hustle and bustle, but the large spa on the hotel's seventh floor is actually a very tranquil spot. ✉ *Vía Veneto and Av. Eusebio A. Morales, El Cangrejo* ☎ *507/340–8888* 🌐 *www.venetocasino.com.*

OUTSIDE OF PANAMA CITY

Esthetic Island Relax. Esthetic Island Relax is a small spa near the beaches and coral reefs of Bocas del Toro that provides various massages and skin treatments. ✉ *Calle 10, Av. G, Bocas del Toro* ☎ *6688–4303.*

Gamboa Rainforest Resort. The Gamboa Rainforest Resort's attractive Sensory Spa offers an extensive selection of massages, beauty treatments, and aromatherapy just steps away from the jungle. ✉ *Gamboa* ☎ *507/314–5000* 🌐 *www.gamboaresort.com.*

Los Mandarinos. Los Mandarinos is a peaceful and attractive hotel and spa at the edge of the forest in El Valle de Antón. It offers a long list of treatments ranging from massages to antiaging therapies. ✉ *El Valle de Antón* ☎ *507/983–6645* 🌐 *www.losmandarinos.com.*

SPORTS AND THE OUTDOORS

Thanks to its proximity to forest, canal, and ocean, Panama City offers plenty of options for enjoying the outdoors, which include hiking in the world's largest chunk of urban rain forest, biking down the causeway, navigating the Panama Canal, and white-water rafting in the jungle.

BEACHES

Because of the silt that the Panama Canal dumps into the ocean and the sewage from Panama City, the beaches near the city are not recommended for swimming. Some of the country's nicest Pacific beaches are on **Isla Contadora**, a 90-minute ferry ride, or 20-minute flight from the city *(⇨ Isla Contadora in "The Canal and Central Panama" chapter)*. For clear water nearer to Panama City, head to **Isla Taboga**, a 60-minute ferry ride from the Calzada de Amador, which is a popular day trip *(⇨ Isla Taboga in "The Canal and Central Panama" chapter)*. The closest beach to Panama City is **Playa Bonita** (Playa Kobbe; ⇨ *Exploring*), which is 8 km (5 miles) southwest of the city, across the canal. It is the site of the Intercontinental and Westin Playa Bonita resorts, where the only option for beach access for nonguests is to make lunch reservations at the hotels' beachfront restaurants.

BIKING

Bicicletas Moses. This bike shop rents an array of bikes for riding on Calzada de Amador. The shop is open Monday through Friday from 9 to 7:30, Saturday from 9 to 8, and Sunday from 8 to 7:30. ✉ *Behind Las Pencas, Calzada de Amador, Calzada de Amador* ☎ *507/211–3671.*

BIRD-WATCHING

Panama City has world-class bird-watching as close as the **Parque Natural Metropolitano,** which is home to more than 200 avian species and is 20 minutes from most hotels. There are several spots in nearby **Parque Nacional Soberanía,** which has more than 400 bird species, within 40 minutes of downtown, including **Pipeline Road,** where the Panama Audubon Society has held several world-record Christmas bird counts *(⇨ Parque Nacional Soberanía in "The Canal and Central Panama" chapter)*. Unless you're an expert, you're best off going with an experienced birding guide. Several local tour companies can set you up with a private guide or can book you onto an existing trip, which is less expensive. You may need to call several companies to find a trip for your dates, though.

Advantage Panama. This small nature tourism company offers early-morning tours of Parque Natural Metropolitano and day trips to Parque Nacional Soberanía. The company can also arrange custom trips to other protected areas. ✉ *Llanos de Curundú No. 2006, Curundú* ☎ *507/6676–2466* 🌐 *www.advantagepanama.com.*

★ Fodor'sChoice **Ancon Expeditions.** This company has excellent guides and offers day tours to protected areas near the capital, including exploration of the forest canopy of Parque Natural Metropolitano using a modified construction crane, bird watching in Parque Nacional Soberanía, and a popular boat trip on Gatún Lake that is great for families. ✉ *Calle Elvira Mendez, Edificio El Dorado No. 3, Area Bancária* ☎ *507/269–9415* 🌐 *www.anconexpeditions.com.*

Eco Circuitos Panama. Since 1999, this ecotourism company has been offering birding tours to Parque Nacional Soberanía, near the city, and the San Lorenzo area, on the Caribbean coast, and spots in between. ✉ *Albrook Plaza, No. 31, Urbanización Albrook, Albrook* ☎ *507/315–1305* 🌐 *www.ecocircuitos.com.*

Panama Audubon Society. The society runs one or two inexpensive bird walks, or overnight excursions per month. They require a bit of self-sufficiency, but can be a great way to meet local birders. ✉ *Casa #2006-B, Altos de Curundú* ☎ *507/232–5977* 🌐 *www.panamaaudubon.org.*

Panoramic Panama. This small company offers birding tours to areas in nearby Soberanía National Park, and can set up customized trips. ✉ *Quarry Heights, Casa #35, Cerro Ancón* ☎ *507/314–1417* 🌐 *www.panoramicpanama.com.*

Smithsonian Tropical Research Institute (STRI). This research institute offers full-day trips to Barro Colorado Island that combine bird-watching with general information on tropical ecology. ■ TIP→ **Tours should be booked a couple weeks ahead of time, either through the STRI office, or one of the other tour operators, which charge more, but will pick you up at your hotel.** ✉ *Tupper Center, Av. Roosevelt, Cerro Ancón* ☎ *507/228–8000* 🌐 *www.stri.org.*

CANAL TOURS

Although the canal is impressive when admired from any of the city's various viewing points, there's nothing quite like getting onto the water and navigating it amidst the giant cargo ships. People spend thousands of dollars on cruises that include a canal crossing, but you can have the same experience for $120 to $160, and spend the night in a spacious hotel room. Two companies offer partial transit tours, which travel through the canal's Pacific locks and Gaillard Cut, and occasional full transits, which take you from one ocean to the other. All transits are accompanied by an expert bilingual guide. Full transits include a Continental breakfast and a simple lunch. Partial transits travel between the islands at the end of the Amador Causeway and the port of Gamboa, on Gatún Lake, a trip that lasts 4–5 hours. Full transits take place once or twice a month and last 8–9 hours. Either trip is an unforgettable experience, fit for travelers of all ages.

Canal Bay Tours. This tour company offers partial and full transit tours on one of three ships: the 115-foot *Fantasía del Mar* has air-conditioned cabins and a large upper deck; the 85-foot *Isla Morada* has one large covered deck; and the 117-foot *Tuira II* has two covered decks. Partial transits cost $115 for adults and $60 for children; less frequent full transits, $165 adults and $75 children. ✉ *Bahía Balboa Building, next to Nunciatura, Punta Paitilla* ☎ *507/209–2009* 🌐 *www.canalandbaytours.com.*

Panama Marine Adventures. Panama Marine Adventures runs canal transits on the 119-foot *Pacific Queen*, a comfortable ship with air-conditioned cabins and two large decks. Partial transits cost $120 for adults and $65 for children; full transits, $175 adults and $75 children. ✉ *Villa Porras and Calle Belén, No. 106, San Francisco* ☎ *507/226–8917* 🌐 *www.pmatours.net.*

GOLF

Summit Golf Resort. The resort has an 18-hole, par-72 championship course designed by Jeff Myers that is hemmed by the rain forest of Camino de Cruces National Park. It's 30 minutes from most hotels, and is open to nonguests. Greens fees are $90, golf cart included, and club rentals cost $35. The course is open 6–6, and the earlier or later you play it, the less you'll sweat. ✉ *20 km (12 miles) northwest of town on road to Gamboa, Gaillard Rd.* ☎ *507/232–4653* 🌐 *www.summitgolfpanama.com.*

HIKING

The hiking options near Panama City range from the 40-minute trek to the top of Cerro Ancón to more demanding expeditions into the vast lowland forest of Parque Nacional Soberanía. The **Parque Natural Metropolitano** has five well-marked trails covering a total of about 5 km (3 miles), which range from flat stretches to a steep road up to a viewpoint. **Parque Nacional Soberanía** has several trails ranging from the historic **Camino de Cruces** to the shorter **Sendero el Charco**, which is on the right after Summit Botanical Gardens and Zoo (⇨ *Parque Nacional Soberanía in "The Canal and Central Panama" chapter*).

Advantage Panama. The company can arrange custom tours for hiking enthusiasts. ✉ *Llanos de Curundú No. 2006, Curundú* ☎ *507/6676–2466* 🌐 *www.advantagepanama.com.*

Eco Circuitos Panama. Half- and full-day tours are offered that include hiking in Parque Natural Metropolitano, Parque Nacional Soberanía, or the hills around El Valle de Antón. ✉ *Albrook Plaza, No. 31, Urbanización Albrook, Albrook* ☎ *507/315–1305* 🌐 *www.ecocircuitos.com.*

SPORTFISHING

The Bay of Panama has good sportfishing, but the best fishing is around and beyond the Pearl Islands, which are best fished out of **Isla Contadora**, a short flight, or ferry ride from the city (⇨ *Isla Contadora or Isla San José in "The Canal and Central Panama" chapter*). Day charters are available out of Panama City and usually head to the area around Isla Otoque and Isla Bono, which are about 90 minutes southwest of the city. You have a chance of hooking mackerel, jack, tuna, roosterfish, or wahoo in that area (billfish are less common there than in other parts of the country). A closer, less expensive option is light-tackle fishing for snook and peacock bass in **Gatún Lake,** the vast man-made lake in the middle of the Panama Canal. The lake is full of South

American peacock bass, which fight like a smallmouth bass but can reach 8–10 pounds *(⇨ Lago Gatún in "The Canal and Central Panama" chapter)*.

★ **Panama Canal Fishing.** This is the premier operator for freshwater fishing on Gatún Lake, which is famous for its peacock bass. Tours can be catered to serious anglers, beginners, or families, since they also include wildlife observation and views of ships on the canal. An all-inclusive day of fishing for two people costs $345 and $25 per extra angler, up to six per boat. They also offer snook and tarpon fishing on the Bayano River. ☎ *507/315–1905, 507/6678–2653* 🌐 *www.panamacanalfishing.com*.

Panama Fishing and Catching. Captain Tony offers bass and snook fishing on Gatún Lake ($450); snook and tarpon fishing on the Bayano River ($490); and deep-sea fishing charters in the Bay of Panama for mahimahi, jacks, wahoo, tuna, sailfish, and ocassionally marlin ($1,500–$2,000 per day). ☎ *507/6622–0212, 507/6505–9553* 🌐 *www.panamafishingandcatching.com*.

WHITE-WATER RAFTING

Aventuras Panama. Aventuras Panama runs white-water rafting trips on the Chagres River (Class II–III), which flows through the rain forests. The full-day trip requires no previous rafting experience, is available from May to late March, and costs $175 per person. A shorter, more challenging trip on the Mamoní River (Class III–IV), which flows through an agricultural area, is available from June to January, and costs $125. They also offer kayaking tours on Gatún Lake, the Chagres River, and alone the Caribbean coast near Portobelo. ✉ *Edif. Celma Of 3, Calle El Parcial, 1½ blocks west of Transístmica* ☎ *507/260–0044, 507/6679–4404* 🌐 *www.aventuraspanama.com*.

2

The Canal and Central Panama

3

WORD OF MOUTH

"We did a full transit of the canal. To be honest, it was a bit long. However, if you can arrange a partial transit, it would be perfect. Going through the locks is amazing."

—JeanH

www.fodors.com/forums

Updated by David Dudenhoefer

THE PANAMA CANAL BISECTS THE country just to the west of Panama City, which enjoys excellent views of the monumental waterway. Between the canal and the rain forest that covers its islands, banks, and adjacent national parks, there is enough to see and do to fill several days.

Central Panama stretches out from the canal across three provinces and into two oceans to comprise everything from the mountains of the Cordillera Central to the west, to the Caribbean coral reefs and colonial fortresses in the north, to the beaches of the Pearl Islands in the Bahía de Panamá (Bay of Panama) in the south. Most of this region can be visited on day trips from Panama City, but the hotels in gorgeous natural settings outside the city will make you want to do some overnights. You could easily limit your entire vacation to Central Panama; the region holds most of the nation's history and nearly all the things that draw people to the country—beaches, reefs, islands, mountains, rain forests, indigenous cultures, and, of course, the Panama Canal. Within hours of Panama City, in many cases a fraction of an hour, you can enjoy bird-watching, sportfishing, hiking, golf, scuba diving, white-water rafting, horseback riding, whale watching, or lazing on a palm-lined beach.

The Panama Canal can be explored from Panama City, Gamboa, or Colón, and its attractions range from the wildlife of Barro Colorado Island to the feisty peacock bass that abound in Gatún Lake. The coast on either side of the canal's Caribbean entrance offers the remains of colonial fortresses hemmed by jungle, half a dozen beaches, and mile upon mile of coral reef, most of it between one and two hours from Panama City. The mountains to the east of the canal hold flora and fauna that you won't find in the forests that flank it, plus there are indigenous Emberá villages and a white-water rafting route on the Chagres River. The Pacific islands offer idyllic beaches, sportfishing, decent dive sites, and seasonal whale watching, all within 90 minutes of the capital by boat or plane. The coast to the southwest of Panama City also has some nice beaches, whereas the nearby highland refuge of El Valle presents exuberant landscapes populated by a multitude of birds and an ample selection of outdoor activities.

TOP REASONS TO GO

The Panama Canal. History, technology, and nature combine like nowhere else in the world at the Panama Canal. The most popular way to explore is by taking one of the transit tours that ply its waters between the Calzada Amador (Amador Causeway) and Gamboa. You can get a different perspective on one of the nature or fishing tours available out of Gamboa.

The Rain Forest. Central Panama has some of the most accessible rain forest in the world, with roads, trails, and waterways leading into wilderness that's home to hundreds of bird species and other animals. Tropical nature can be experienced to the fullest in the forests along the canal, in the mountains to the east and west of it, or along the Caribbean coast.

The Oceans. With the Caribbean and Pacific just 50 miles apart at the canal, you can bathe or skin-dive in two oceans on the same day. The Caribbean coast has miles of coral reef, whereas the Pacific islands lie near good fishing, dive spots, and seasonal whale watching.

The Islands. Some of Panama's best beaches are on its islands, and Central Panama has isles where the sand is lined by coconut palms and other tropical foliage. These range from historic Isla Taboga to the uninhabited isles of the Pearl Archipelago, where three seasons of *Survivor* were based.

The Mountains. The hills of Central Panama are considerably lower than those in the country's western provinces, but they still provide a refreshing respite from the lowland heat, and their lush forests are home to hundreds of bird species.

ORIENTATION AND PLANNING

ORIENTATION

Central Panama's destinations are nearly all within a two-hour drive from Panama City, or in case of the islands to the southeast, within 90 minutes of the city by boat or plane. Most of the region's attractions can be visited on day trips from the capital, but a couple spots require overnights. Calle Omar Torrijos leads north from Panama City's Balboa neighborhood to the canal's Pacific locks, Summit, Gamboa, and Gatún Lake. If you go straight on that road past the left turn for Gamboa, you'll reach the Autopista Alfredo Motta, a toll road that leads to Sabanitas—where the road

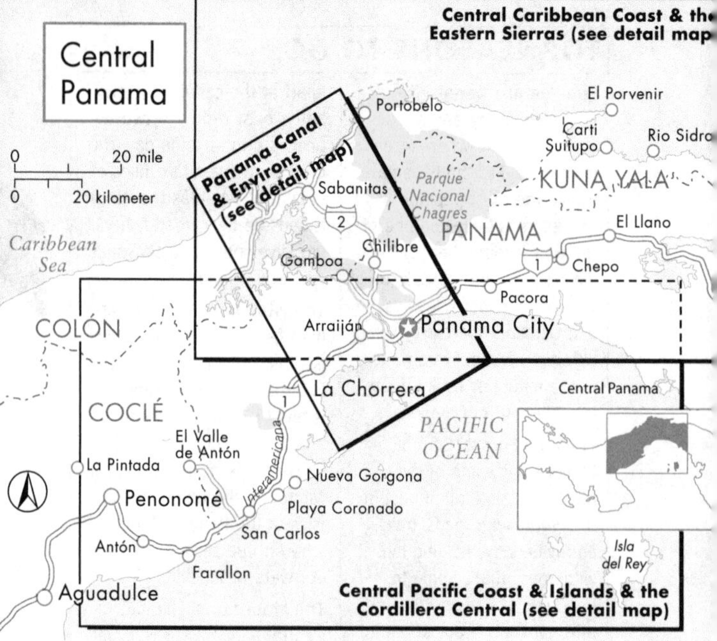

east to Portobelo and Santa Isabel begins—and Colón, and the turnoff for the Gatún Locks and San Lorenzo, shortly thereafter. The westbound Carretera Interamericana is reached by taking Avenida de los Mártires over the Bridge of the Americas. It becomes a two-lane highway and veers west before Chorrera, and winds over the mountains before reaching the Central Pacific beaches and El Valle de Antón, one to two hours from the city by car. The Pacific islands of Islas Taboga, and Contadora are reached by daily ferries or flights.

PLANNING

WHEN TO GO

Most of the canal and Central Pacific sites lie within 30 minutes to two hours of Panama City, so if you're based there, plenty of attractions can be visited on a spare morning or afternoon; others are amenable to spending an extra night or two. The best time to explore the area is the December to May dry season, or when rains let up in July and August. Note that Panamanians generally travel between Christmas and New Year's, during the weekend of Carnaval, in mid-February, or during Easter week; hotels fill up quickly at these times, and you will need to reserve rooms well in advance. Colorful Congo dances are performed in Portobelo for New Year's, Carnaval, and the Festival de Diablos y Congos (which takes place shortly after Carnaval).

GETTING HERE AND AROUND

You can visit most of the Central Pacific's sites on your own, but you have to join tours to do the canal transit, trips on Gatún Lake, visit indigenous communities, and white-water rafting in Chagres National Park. You can reach Summit, Parque Nacional Soberanía, and Gamboa by taxi, but you should rent a car to explore more distant areas such as Portobelo, the Pacific beaches, and El Valle de Antón. The Panama Canal Railway is an interesting trip, but the downside is getting dumped in Colón, which is why most people take the train as part of a tour that meets them at the Colón train station and takes them to nearby sites.

AIR TRAVEL

The domestic airline Air Panama has daily 25-minute flights to Isla Contadora, usually in the morning, though also on Friday and Sunday afternoons. Flights depart Panama City's Marcos A. Gelabert Airport (aka Aeropuerto de Albrook).

Contacts **Air Panama** ✉ *Marcos A. Gelabert Airport, Albrook, Panama City* ☎ *507/316–9000* 🌐 *www.flyairpanama.com.*

BOAT TRAVEL

Barcos Calypso Taboga. Barcos Calypso Taboga has a daily ferry service from Panama City to Isla Taboga departing from the Marina on Isla Naos, on the Amador Causeway, Monday through Thursday at 8:30, Friday at 8:30 and 3, and weekends and holidays at 8, 10:30, and 4. The ferry leaves Taboga Monday through Thursday at 4:30, Friday at 9:30 and 4:30, and weekends and holidays at 9, 3, and 5. On weekends and holidays, arrive at least 30 minutes before departure to buy your ticket. ✉ *Marina Isla Naos* ☎ *507/314–1730.*

BUS TRAVEL

Terminal de Transporte de Albrook. All regional buses depart from the massive Terminal de Transporte de Albrook. Buses to Gamboa leave every two hours from 6 am to 10 pm; the trip takes 40 minutes. Buses to Colón and Sabanitas, where you get off to catch the bus to Portobelo and Isla Grande, depart every 30 minutes, and the trip takes 90 minutes.

Buses to El Valle de Antón depart every 30 minutes. ✉ *Av. Gaillard, Albrook, Panama City* ☎ *507/303–3030.*

CAR TRAVEL

Renting a car is an easy way to visit many of the Central Pacific sites, because there are paved roads to just about everything but the islands. Cars can be rented in Panama City and Colón. Rentals usually cost $40 to $50 per day, whereas 4WD vehicles cost $60 to $70, plus insurance. Most major car-rental companies have offices in Panama City *(⇨ Essentials, in "Panama City" chapter)*; only Budget and Hertz have offices in Colón, both at the Colón 2000 cruise port.

Contacts **Budget** ✉ *Colón 2000, Paseo Gorgas Av., Colón* ☎ *507/441–7161* 🌐 *www.budget.com.* **Hertz** ✉ *Colón 2000, Paseo Gorgas Av., Colón* ☎ *507/441–3272* 🌐 *www.hertz.com.*

TRAIN TRAVEL

The Panama Canal Railway's commuter train to Colón departs from the train station in Panama City weekdays at 7:15 am and departs from Colón at 5:15 pm. The trip costs $25 one way, $50 round-trip.

Train Station Information **Atlantic Passenger Station** ✉ *Calle Mt. Hope, Mt Hope, Colón* 🌐 *www.panarail.com.* **Corozal Passenger Station** ✉ *Av. Omar Torrijos and Calle Corozal, Corozal, Panama City* ☎ *507/317–6070* 🌐 *www.panarail.com.* **Panama Canal Railway** ✉ *Estación de Corozal, Av. Omar Torrijos and Calle Corozal, Corozal, Panama City* ☎ *507/317–6070* 🌐 *www.panarail.com* ⊗ *No train weekends and holidays.*

THE COUNTRY? NO, THE CITY. **No matter where you travel in the central part of the country, you'll see highway signs directing you to "Panamá." Yes, you're already in the country of Panama, but that's the Spanish-language name for Panama City, too. In true developing-country fashion, all roads lead to the capital.**

ABOUT THE RESTAURANTS

Though Central Panama's restaurant selection is neither as impressive nor as varied as Panama City's, the region has some fun dining options. Rather than unforgettable food, you're likely to enjoy good food in unforgettable settings, which include the ocean views on the Caribbean coast and Pacific Islands and Chagres River views in Gamboa.

Prices in the reviews are the average cost of a main course at dinner or, if dinner is not served, at lunch.

ABOUT THE HOTELS

The accommodations in Central Panama range from big resorts to colorful bungalows in stunning natural surroundings. The region includes some comfortable nature lodges surrounded by rain forest, all-inclusive beach resorts where the bars stay open well past midnight, homey B&Bs, and boutique hotels in natural settings. Even in the cheapest hotels you can expect a private bathroom and air-conditioning. Although nearly all the hotels accept credit cards, some smaller places offer a discount if you pay in cash. Most hotels can book area tours for you, but tour companies will generally expect payment in cash. You can sometimes save a bundle (occasionally upward of $100) at some of the more expensive hotels and resorts by booking via their websites, especially for midweek or off-season stays.

Prices in the reviews are the lowest cost of a standard double room in high season. For expanded hotel reviews, facilities, and current deals, visit Fodors.com.

ESSENTIALS

EMERGENCIES

Ambulance service can be slow in rural areas. There are clinics in some of the rural communities, but they are good for little more than first aid. If you suffer an accident or have medical problems, get to the Hospital Punta Pacífica or Centro Médico Paitilla in Panama City as soon as possible.

Emergency Services **Ambulance** ☎ *911, 507/228–8127 in Cruz Roja.* **Fire department** ☎ *103.* **National police** ☎ *104.*

MONEY

Credit cards are widely accepted in this region, except for at the smaller restaurants and hotels. ATM distribution is less uniform outside of Panama City, so it is often a good idea to stock up on cash before exploring the Central Pacific's rural reaches. The only ATMs near the Caribbean Coast's attractions are in and around Colón, whereas the eastern sierras and Pacific islands have no ATMs, so get cash before driving east or boarding the ferry or plane to Islas Taboga or Contadora. There are ATMs in the Albrook Airport terminal and at the Brisas de Amador shopping center, near the Taboga ferry dock, as well as in the lobby of the Gamboa Rainforest Resort, the Gatún Locks, in the Super 99 supermarket in Colón 2000, and the El Rey supermarket in Sabanitas. To the west of Panama City, you can find ATMs in the El Rey Supermarket at the entrance to Coronado, one block north of the Royal Decameron Beach Resort, in the lobby of the Playa Blanca Resort, on the Avenida Principal of El Valle, and the shopping center by the Bristol Buenaventura.

SAFETY

There are certainly safety issues in Colón, which you shouldn't explore on foot. When hiking through the forest, always be careful where you put your hand and your feet, because there are poisonous snakes and stinging insects. If you slip on a muddy trail in the rain forest, resist the temptation to grab the nearest branch, because palms with spiny trunks are relatively common. If there are big waves at any beach you visit, don't go in unless you are an expert swimmer, because waves can create dangerous currents. The sun intensity at these latitudes means sunscreen and a brimmed hat are musts.

TOURS

Most of the major tour operators in Panama City *(⇨ Chapter 2 for details about these companies and their tours)* offer half- or full-day trips to attractions in this region, including the Panama Canal, trails in Parque Nacional Soberanía and Emberá villages in Parque Nacional Chagres. **Xtreme Adventures,** in Farallón, offers an array of outdoor and marine activities in the Playa Blanca area, including scuba diving, snorkeling, and sportfishing.

Contacts **Xtreme Adventures** ✉ *Marina Playa Blanca, Farallón* ☎ *507/993–2823* 🌐 *www.extremepanama.com.*

THE PANAMA CANAL AND ENVIRONS

The Panama Canal stretches across one of the narrowest parts of the isthmus to connect the Pacific Ocean and the Caribbean Sea. For much of that route it's bordered by tropical wilderness. About half of the waterway is made up of Lago Gatún (Gatún Lake), an enormous artificial lake created by damming the Río Chagres (Chagres River). In addition to forming an integral part of the waterway, the lake is notable for its sportfishing and for the wildlife of its islands and the surrounding mainland.

As much an attraction as the canal itself are the forests that line it, which for decades were protected within the Canal Zone. The Panamanian government has turned most

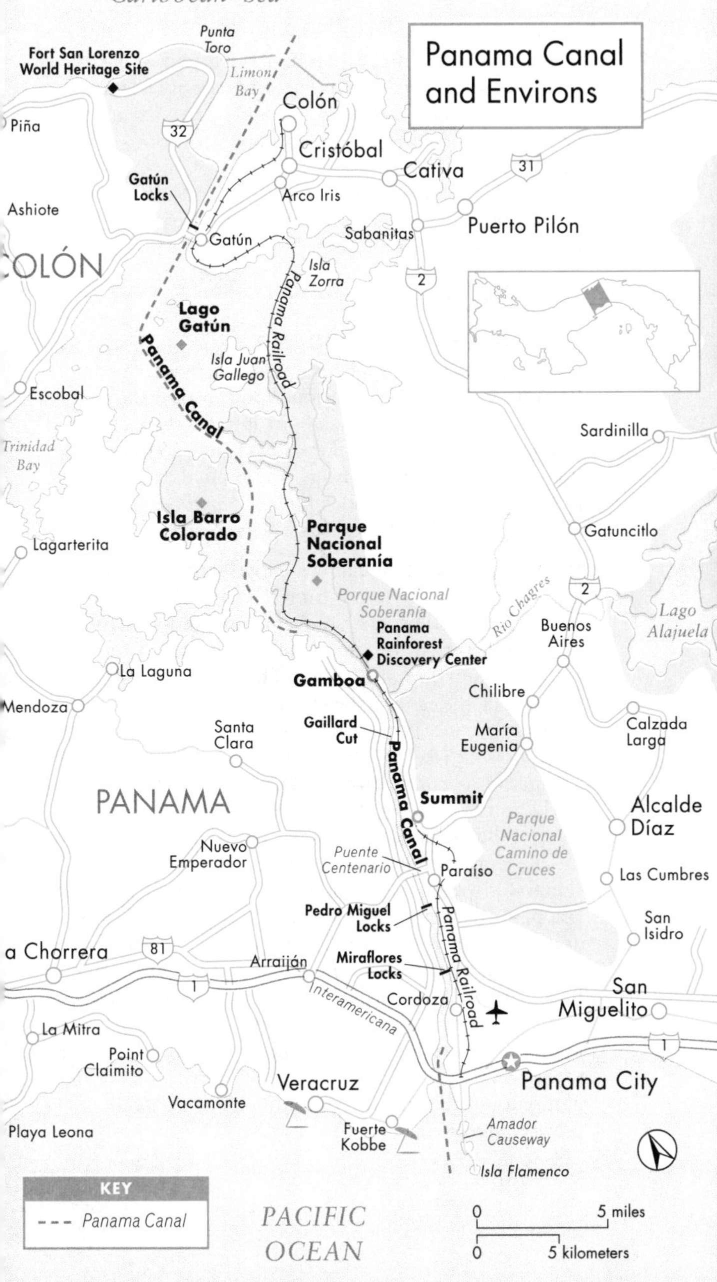

Panama Canal and Environs
Caribbean Sea
Punta Toro
Fort San Lorenzo World Heritage Site
Limon Bay
Colón
Cristóbal
Cativa
Piña
32
31
Gatún Locks
Arco Iris
Ashiote
Gatún
Sabanitas
Puerto Pilón
COLÓN
Isla Zorra
2
Panama Railroad
Lago Gatún
Panama Canal
Isla Juan Gallego
Escobal
Trinidad Bay
Sardinilla
Isla Barro Colorado
Lagarterita
Parque Nacional Soberanía
Gatuncitlo
Porque Nacional Soberanía
Río Chagres
Panama Rainforest Discovery Center
Buenos Aires
Lago Alajuela
La Laguna
Gamboa
Chilibre
Mendoza
Santa Clara
Gaillard Cut
María Eugenia
Calzada Larga
PANAMA
Summit
Parque Nacional Camino de Cruces
Alcalde Díaz
Nuevo Emperador
Puente Centenario
Paraíso
Las Cumbres
Pedro Miguel Locks
San Isidro
a Chorrera
81
Arraiján
Miraflores Locks
1
Interamericana
Cordoza
San Miguelito
La Mitra
Point Claimito
Veracruz
Panama City
Vacamonte
Fuerte Kobbe
Amador Causeway
Playa Leona
Isla Flamenco
KEY
Panama Canal
PACIFIC OCEAN
0
5 miles
0
5 kilometers

of those forests into national parks, whereas most of the former U.S. infrastructure has been privatized. Some of the former U.S. communities have become part of Panama City, while others, such as Gamboa, stand apart. The national parks have become increasingly important tourist attractions, and trails into the wilderness of Parque Nacional Soberanía and Monumento Natural Barro Colorado make the former Canal Zone one of the best places in the world to visit a tropical rain forest.

THE PANAMA CANAL

GETTING HERE AND AROUND

Since the Panama Canal runs along the western edge of Panama City, there are various spots within the metropolitan area from which to admire it *(⇨ Chapter 2)*. A taxi should charge $15 to Miraflores Locks and $25 to Gamboa. Buses to Gamboa depart from the Terminal de Transporte in Albrook about every other hour *(⇨ Gamboa, below)* and can drop you off at Miraflores Locks.

The Panama Canal. Panama's most famous landmark stretches 80 km (50 miles) from the edge of Panama City to the Caribbean port of Colón, and a paved road follows its route between the islands of the Amador Causeway and the inland port of Gamboa. The most interesting spot for viewing the canal is the visitor center at the Miraflores Locks *(⇨ Esclusas de Miraflores in Chapter 2)*. North of Miraflores the road to Gamboa heads inland but still passes a couple of spots with canal vistas, namely the Pedro Miguel Locks and the one-way bridge over the Chagres River. The bridge (and Gamboa in general) offers front-row views of the big ships as they pass though the canal. The Panama Canal Railway train to Colón continues north from Gamboa past other vantage points, which is much of that trip's draw. Two other spots with impressive views are the monument erected by the country's Chinese community on the Bridge of the Americas western side, and the Esclusas de Gatún (Gatún Locks), 10 km (6 miles) south of Colón. But nothing matches the experience of getting out onto the water, which can be done on a canal transit tour or on a nature tour or fishing trip on Gatún Lake. ✉ *Panama City* 🌐 *www.pancanal.com*.

CANAL FACTS

More than 14,000 vessels under the flags of some 70 countries use the canal each year.

Canal administration requires captains to turn over control of their ships to canal pilots for the duration of the transit.

A boat traveling from New York to San Francisco saves 7,872 miles by using the Panama Canal instead of going around Cape Horn.

Most ships take 8–10 hours to traverse the canal, but the U.S. Navy hydrofoil *Pegasus* has the record for the fastest transit at 2 hours and 41 minutes.

Each of the canal's locks is 1,000 feet long and 110 feet wide, dimensions that have governed shipbuilding since the canal's completion in 1914. The massive Panamax ships that move most cargo through the canal are designed to carry as much as possible while still fitting into the locks.

For each large ship that passes through the canal, 52 million gallons of fresh water are used by six locks, and more than one billion gallons of water flow from the canal into the sea every day. (It's a good thing the canal was built in a rain forest.)

At this writing the highest toll for Panama Canal passage is $375,600, paid by the cruise ship *Norwegian Pearl* in July 2011.

The lowest toll on record was the $0.36 paid by Richard Halliburton, who swam the canal in 1928. Halliburton's record is safe for posterity, since tolls have risen considerably since then.

Shipping companies may reserve transit slots up to one year in advance and must do so a minimum of four days ahead. Tolls—it's cash only, no credit—must be paid prior to arrival.

CANAL TRANSITS

Although the canal is impressive when admired from any of Panama City's various viewing points, there's nothing quite like getting onto the water and navigating it amid the giant cargo ships. People spend thousands of dollars on cruises that include a canal crossing, but you can have the same experience for $100 to $200 and be free to spend the night in a spacious hotel room. Two companies offer partial transit tours, which travel through the canal's Pacific locks and Gaillard Cut, and full transits, which take you from one ocean to the other. All transits are accompanied by an expert guide who tells a bit of the canal's history, and include a Continental breakfast, and, on full transits, a cold box lunch. Partial transits travel between the island marinas on the Amador Causeway and the port of Gamboa, on Gatún Lake, a trip that lasts four to five hours. Transits take place every Friday and Saturday, May–December, and Thursday–Saturday (with additional days per demand), during the January–April high season. Full transits take place once or twice a month, usually on Saturday, and last eight or nine hours. **TIP→ Departure times are fixed, but finishing times can be only approximate; the Panama Canal Authority always gives priority to larger cargo and cruise ships.** Either trip is an unforgettable experience, suitable for travelers of all ages.

Canal&Bay Tours. This company offers partial and full transit tours on one of three ships: the 115-foot *Fantasía del Mar*, which has air-conditioned cabins and a large upper deck, and the 85-foot *Isla Morada*, and the 85-foot *Tuira II*, both of which have one large covered deck. Partial transits are $115; full transits are $165. ✉ *Bahia Balboa Building, next to Nunciatura, Paitilla, Panama City* ☎ *507/209–2009* 🌐 *www.canalandbaytours.com*.

Panama Marine Adventures. Panama Marine Adventures runs canal transits on the 119-foot *Pacific Queen*, a comfortable ship with air-conditioned cabins and two large decks. Partial transits are $120; full transits are $175. ✉ *Villa Porras and Calle Belén, no. 106, San Francisco, Summit* ☎ *507/226–8917* 🌐 *www.pmatours.net*.

CANAL RAILWAY

Panama Canal Railway. The one-hour trip on the Panama Canal Railway from Corozal, just north of Albrook, to the Caribbean city of Colón, offers an interesting perspective of the rain forests of Soberanía National Park and the wetlands along Gatún Lake. The railway primarily moves freight, but it has a commuter service on weekdays that departs from Panama City at 7:15 am (returning from Colón at 5:15 pm, and costs $25 each way. Tourists ride in one of five air-conditioned cars (soon to be six) with curved windows on the roof that let you see the foliage overhead. The best views are from the left side of the train, and though the train moves too fast to see much wildlife, you may spot toucans, herons, and black snail kites fly-

CONFUSING DIRECTIONS

Though the Central American isthmus connects North and South America, the Panamanian portion of that land bridge actually runs west to east, with a slight S-shape. The canal itself runs northwest to southeast on the upward curve of the S, so a ship that crosses from the Atlantic to the Pacific actually travels 27 miles farther east, whereas an Atlantic-bound vessel ends up 27 miles farther west. To add to the compass behaving so counterintuitively, the sun rises over the Pacific on this slice of the isthmus and sets over the Atlantic.

ing over the lake. The downside: the trip passes a garbage dump and industrial zone near the end, and leaves you just outside the slums of Colón at 8:15 am, which is why you may want to take the trip as part of a tour that picks you up in Colón and takes you to either San Lorenzo or Portobelo. It is possible to do the trip on your own, in which case you should board one of the shuttle vans that await the train in Colón and have them take you to the Colón 2000 (pronounced coh-*loan* dose-*mill)* cruise-ship port, where you can pick up a rental car and drive to Portobelo, or hire a taxi for the day ($80–$100). The trains leave promptly, and it is complicated to pre-purchase tickets, so get to the station by 6:45 am to buy your tickets. ✉ *Av. Omar Torrijos, Corozal, Panama City* ☎ *507/317–6070* 🌐 *www.panarail.com.*

PARQUE NACIONAL SOBERANÍA

GETTING HERE AND AROUND

Soberanía is an easy drive from Panama City and is reached by following the same route for Summit and Gamboa. Shortly after the Summit Golf Club the road passes under the railroad and comes to an intersection where a left turn will put you on the road to Gamboa and most of the park's trails. If you want to hike the Camino Cruces trail, you should head straight at that intersection, toward Chilibre, and drive 6 km (3½ miles) to a parking area with picnic tables on your left, behind which is the trail. Turn left for the Plantation Road, which is on the right 3 km (1½ miles) past the Parque Natural Summit, at the entrance to the Canopy Tower. The dirt Plantation Road heads left from that entrance road almost immediately. The Sendero Los

CLOSE UP

Building the Panama Canal

Nearly a century after its completion, the Panama Canal remains an impressive feat of engineering. It took the U.S. government more than a decade and $352 million to dig the "Big Ditch," but its inauguration was the culmination of a human drama that spanned centuries and claimed thousands of lives. As early as 1524, King Carlos V of Spain envisioned an interoceanic canal, and he had Panama surveyed for routes where it might be dug, though it soon became clear that the task was too great to attempt. It wasn't until 1880 that the French tried to make that dream a reality, but the job turned out to be tougher than they'd imagined. The Frenchman Ferdinand de Lesseps, who'd recently overseen construction of the Suez Canal, intended to build a sea-level canal similar to the Suez, which would have been almost impossible given the mountain range running through Panama. But a different obstacle thwarted the French enterprise: Panama's swampy, tropical environment. More than 20,000 workers died of tropical diseases during the French attempt, which together with mismanagement of funds drove the project bankrupt by 1889.

The United States, whose canal-building enterprise was spearheaded by President Theodore Roosevelt, purchased the French rights for $40 million, and went to work in 1904. Using recent advances in medical knowledge, the Americans began their canal effort with a sanitation campaign led by Dr. William Gorgas that included draining of swamps and puddles, construction of potable water systems, and other efforts to combat disease. Another improvement over the French strategy was the decision to build locks and create a lake 85 feet above sea level. For the biggest construction effort since the building of the Great Wall of China, tens of thousands of laborers were brought in from the Caribbean islands, Asia, and Europe to supplement the local workforce. Some 6,000 workers lost their lives to disease and accidents during the American effort, which, when added to deaths during the French attempt, is more than 500 lives lost for each mile of canal.

The most difficult and dangerous stretch of the canal to complete was Gaillard Cut through the rocky continental divide. Thousands of workers spent seven years blasting and digging through that natural barrier, which consumed most of the 61 million pounds of dynamite detonated during canal construction. The countless tons of rock removed were used to build the Amador Causeway.

CLOSE UP

Building the Panama Canal

By the time the SS *Ancon* became the first ship to transit the Panama Canal in August 15, 1914, numerous records and engineering innovations had been accomplished. One of the biggest tasks was the damming of the Chagres River with the Gatún Dam, a massive earthen wall 1½ miles long and nearly a mile thick. It was the largest dam in the world when built, and the reservoir it created, Gatún Lake, was the largest man-made lake. The six sets of locks, which work like liquid elevators that raise and lower ships the 85 feet between Gatún Lake and the sea, were also major engineering feats.

Each lock chamber is 1,000 feet long and 110 feet wide—measurements that have governed shipbuilding ever since and gave the industry the term "Panamax"—and water flows in and out of them by gravity, so there are no pumps. Fears that the canal would fall into disrepair with the changing of the guard at the turn of the millennium never materialized, and experts have credited Panama for its forward-thinking administration and maintenance of the facility. Panama has also made the canal more tourist-friendly than it ever was during U.S. administration, a boon to you, dear visitor, as you view it in action. A $5.2-billion construction of new pairs of locks to complement Miraflores and Gatún began in 2007 and will allow larger post-Panamax ships, now 7% of the world's shipping fleet, to use the canal. As the canal approaches its 100th birthday, it remains an innovative and vital link in the global economy, and a monument to the ingenuity and industriousness of the people who built it.

Charcos is on the right 2 km (1 mile) after the Plantation Road. The Pipeline Road begins in Gamboa, at the end of the main road, past the dredging division and town. A taxi should charge $20–$25 to drop you off at any of these trails and buses to Gamboa depart from the terminal in Albrook every two hours. You're better off driving here, but you'll see and understand much more if you book a tour with an ecotourism company (⇨ *Sports and the Outdoors, below*).

★ **Parque Nacional Soberanía** (*Soberanía National Park*). One of the planet's most accessible rain-forest reserves, Parque Nacional Soberanía comprises 19,341 hectares (48,000 acres) of lowland rain forest along the canal's eastern edge that is home to everything from howler monkeys to chestnut-mandible toucans. Long preserved as part of the

U.S. Canal Zone, Soberanía was declared a national park, after being returned to Panama, as part of an effort to protect the canal's watershed. Trails into its wilderness can be reached by public bus, taxi, or by driving the mere 25 km (15 miles) from downtown Panama City, though you are best of visiting the park on a guided tour. Those trails wind past the trunks and buttress roots of massive kapok and strangler fig trees and the twisted stalks of lianas dangling from their high branches. Though visitors can expect to see only a small sampling of its wildlife, the park is home to more than 500 bird species and more than 100 different mammals, including such endangered species as the elusive jaguar and the ocelot.

If you hike some of the park's trails *(⇨ Hiking, below)*, you run a good chance of seeing white-faced capuchin monkeys, tamandua anteaters, raccoon-like *coatimundi*, or the large rodents called agouti. You may also see iridescent blue morpho butterflies, green iguanas, leafcutter ants, and other interesting critters. On any given morning here you might see dozens of spectacular birds, such as red-lored parrots, collared aracaris, violaceous trogons, and purple-throated fruit crows. From November to April the native bird population is augmented by the dozens of migrant species that winter in the park, among them the scarlet tanager, Kentucky warbler, and Louisiana water thrush. It is the combination of native and migrant bird species, plus the ocean birds along the nearby canal, that have enabled the Panama Audubon Society to set the Christmas bird count world record for two decades straight. ✉ *Ranger station on Av. Omar Torrijos, 25 km (15 miles) northwest of Panama City* ☎ *507/232–4192* *$5* ⏲ *Daily 7–5.*

WHERE TO STAY

For expanded hotel reviews, visit Fodors.com.

$$$$ ★ **Canopy Tower.** *B&B/Inn.* Occupying a former U.S. Army radar tower deep in the rain forest of Soberanía National Park, this lodge caters almost exclusively to serious bird-watchers and natural history enthusiasts. **Pros:** constant exposure to nature; excellent guides; good food, sustainable practices. **Cons:** basic rooms; lots of stairs; expensive. *Rooms from: $448* ✉ *Carretera Gamboa, 25 km (15 miles) northwest of Panama City* ☎ *507/264–5720, 800/930–3397 in the U.S.* 🌐 *www.canopytower.com* *10 rooms, 2 suites* *All meals.*

SPORTS AND THE OUTDOORS

BIRD-WATCHING

Soberanía has world-class bird-watching, especially from November to April, when the northern migrants boost the local population. Unless you're an expert, though, you're really better off joining a tour or hiring a guide through one of Panama City's nature-tour operators. Guests at the Canopy Tower *(⇨ above)* enjoy almost nonstop birding and tours led by the lodge's resident guides.

Advantage Panama. Advantage Panama has a day trip to Soberanía that combines a forest hike with a boat trip on Gatún Lake. ☎ *507/6676–2466* 🌐 *www.advantagepanama.com.*

Ancon Expeditions. This company has excellent guides that can take you bird-watching on Pipeline Road, or on Gatún Lake. They also have a tour that combines a hike through Soberanía National Park with boat trip on the Chagres River. ☎ *507/269–9415* 🌐 *www.anconexpeditions.com.*

Eco Circuitos Panama. A Soberanía birding tour is offered that starts with a hike and ends with a boat trip, birding on the Pipeline Road, a hiking tour on the Camino de Cruces trails, and a tour to Barro Colorado Island. ☎ *507/315–0315* 🌐 *www.ecocircuitos.com.*

Pesantez Tours. Pesantez Tours runs a half-day tour to Soberanía. ☎ *507/366–9100* 🌐 *www.pesantez-tours.com.*

HIKING

Soberanía's natural treasures can be discovered along miles and miles of trails and roads, whereas the western edge of the park can be explored on boat tours through local companies. The park also protects a significant portion of the old **Camino de las Cruces,** a cobbled road built by the Spanish that connected old Panama City with a small port on the Chagres River, near modern-day Gamboa. It's more than 10 km (6 miles) long and intersects with the Plantation Road before reaching the river, but you don't have to hike far to find cobbled patches that were restored a couple of decades ago.

The **Plantation Road** is a dirt road that heads east into the forest from the road to Gamboa for about 4 miles, to where it connects to the Camino de Cruces. That wide trail follows a creek called the Río Chico Masambi, and it's a great place to see water birds and forest birds. Two kilometers (1 mile) past the entrance to the Canopy Tower is the **Sendero el Charco** (Pool Trail), which forms a loop through the forest to the east of the road to Gamboa. The *charco* (pool) refers to a man-made pond near the beginning of the trail that was created by damming a stream. The trail follows that stream part of the way, which means you may spot waterbirds such as tiger herons, in addition to such forest birds as toucans and *chachalacas*. It is one of the park's most popular trails because it's a loop, it's short (less than a kilometer), and it's flat enough to be an easy hike.

The park's most famous trail is the **Camino del Oleoducto** (Pipeline Road), a paved road that follows an oil pipeline for 17 km (11 miles) into the forest parallel to the canal. One of the country's premier bird-watching spots, it is here that the Panama Audubon Society has had record-breaking Christmas bird counts year after year. The Pipeline Road is a great place to see trogons (five species have been logged there), motmots, forest falcons, and hundreds of other bird species as well as monkeys and agoutis. You can hike any of these on your own, but you'll see and learn more if you take a bird-watching tour.

KAYAKING

Aventuras Panama. This company offers kayaking tours on the Chagres River, or Gatún Lake, which allows you to watch ships navigating the canal. ☎ *507/260–0044* 🌐 *www.aventuraspanama.com*.

GAMBOA

32 km (20 miles) northwest of Panama City.

Though it lies a mere 40 minutes from downtown Panama City, the tiny community of Gamboa feels remote, no doubt due to the fact that it is surrounded by exuberant tropical nature. Its location on the north bank of the flooded Chagres River, nestled between the Panama Canal and rain forest of Soberanía National Park, makes Gamboa a world-class bird-watching destination and the departure point for boat trips on Gatún Lake. It is also a great place to stroll, have lunch amid nature, or kick back and admire the impressive tropical scenery. It is home to a massive nature resort that offers enough diversions to fill several days, but Gamboa's proximity to the capital also makes it a convenient day-trip from Panama City.

The town of Gamboa was built by Uncle Sam in the early 20th century to house workers at the Panama Canal dredging division, which is based here. The town's tiny port is full of canal maintenance equipment, but it's also the point of departure for the boat to Barro Colorado Island and for Pacific-bound partial canal transits. Private yachts sometimes spend a night near the port on the way through the canal, and a simple marina on the other side of the Chagres River holds the boats of local fishermen and tour companies that take groups onto the canal for wildlife watching along the forest's edge.

Over the years, biologists and bird-watchers have come to realize that Gamboa's combination of forests and wetlands make it home to an inordinate diversity of birds. The Panama Audubon Society has set world records for Christmas bird counts year after year on the **Camino del Oleoducto** (Pipleline Road), which heads into Parque Nacional Soberanía on the northwest end of town. That trail is the main destination for day visitors, but you can also see plenty of wildlife from the roads around town and the banks of the Chagres River.

GETTING HERE AND AROUND

Gamboa is an easy 40-minute drive from Panama City. Follow the signs from Avenida Balboa or Avenida Central to Albrook, veer right onto Avenida Omar Torrijos at the traffic circle and follow it north into the forest. Shortly after driving under a railroad bridge, turn left and stay on that road all the way to the one-way bridge over the Chagres River. Turn right just after the bridge for the Rainforest Resort and Los Lagartos restaurant, or continue straight ahead for the Pipeline Road and STRI dock. A taxi from Panama City should charge $20–$25 to drop you off here. SACSA buses depart from the Terminal de Transport in Albrook every two hours from 6 am to 6 pm.

EXPLORING

The massive **Gamboa Rainforest Resort** *(⇨ below)*, just east of town, is spread over a ridge with a panoramic view of the Chagres River. The resort has a 340-acre forest reserve that is contiguous with Soberanía National Park, within which is an aerial tram, a small orchid collection, a butterfly farm, an aquarium, and a serpentarium. The resort also has its own marina on the Chagres River; near it is the riverside restaurant Los Lagartos, which is a great spot for lunch and wildlife watching even if you don't stay at the hotel. The resort's owner even convinced a small indigenous Emberá community who were living in nearby Chagres National Park to rebuild their village across the Chagres River from the hotel, where they now receive tourists. (Realize the setup is artificial; it can't compare to a visit to an Emberá community in the Darién.)

Panama Rainforest Discovery Center. Just beyond Gamboa, adjacent to the Parque Nacional Soberanía and near the start of the Pipeline Road, lies the Panama Rainforest Discovery Center, operated by the local Eugene Eisenmann Avian Wildlife Foundation. Its centerpiece is a 32-meter (105-foot) steel observation tower giving ample opportunity for observation of life in the rain-forest canopy. Three other decks are positioned at about each of the quarter-way marks. A solar-powered visitor center contains exhibits about avian life in the Panamanian rain forest. Leading from the visitor center is 1.1 km (⅔ mile) of hiking trails. They open at 6 am, which is the best tme to see birds. Capacity is limited to 25 visitors at a time during the peak viewing hours, before 10 am, and to 50 people for the rest of the day, so you should reservations at least a day ahead from December to April. ✉ *3 km (2 miles) northwest of Gamboa* ☎ *507/6588–0697, 507/6450–6630 in Panama City* 🌐 *www.pipelineroad.org* 🎟 *$30 before 10 am; $20 after 10 am* ⏲ *Daily 6–4.*

WHERE TO EAT AND STAY

For expanded hotel reviews, visit Fodors.com.

$$ ✕ **Los Lagartos.** *Latin American.* Built out over the Chagres River, this open-air restaurant at the Gamboa Rainforest Resort is a great place to see turtles, fish, crocodiles, and waterfowl feeding in the hyacinth-laden water. If you travel with binoculars, you'll definitely want to bring them here, so that you can watch wildlife while you wait for your lunch. A small buffet is frequently available, but the à la carte selection is usually a better deal, with choices such as peacock bass in a mustard sauce, grouper topped with an avocado sauce and cheese, or the hearty, spicy fisherman's stew. Lighter items include Caesar salad, hamburgers, and quesadillas. It isn't Panama's best food, but it's good, and the view of the forest-hemmed Chagres River populated with grebes, jacanas, turtles, and other wildlife is worth the trip out here even if you have only a cup of tea. 💲 *Average main: $15* ✉ *Carretera Gamboa, right after bridge over Chagres River* ☎ *507/314–5000* ⏲ *Closed Mon.*

$$$ **Gamboa Rainforest Resort.** *Resort.* Panoramic views of the Chagres River and surrounding rainforest, abundant wildlife, a selection of outdoor excursions, and amenities such as a spa and massive pool make this hotel a great place to experience the rainforest without sacrificing comfort. **Pros:** amazing views; abundant wildlife; ample facilities and diversions; friendly staff. **Cons:** food can be disappointing; Wi-Fi access is expensive. *Rooms from: $185* *Av. Omar Torrijos, 32 km (19 miles) northwest of Panama City* *507/314–5000, 507/206–8888 in Panama City, 877/800–1690 in the U.S.* *www.gamboaresort.com* *160 rooms, 4 suites, 34 villas* *Breakfast.*

3

SPORTS AND THE OUTDOORS

BIRD-WATCHING

All the big nature tour operators offer bird-watching tours on Pipeline Road *(⇨ Parque Nacional Soberanía, above).*

HIKING

Ancon Expeditions. Ancon Expeditions has a three-hour hiking tour through the rain forest on the historic Camino de Cruces, followed by a boat trip on the Chagres River—it's an excellent trip for seeing wildlife. *Edificio Dorado #3, Calle Elvira Méndez, Area Bancária, Panama City* *507/269–9415* *www.anconexpeditions.com.*

SPORTFISHING

Gatún Lake is full of feisty peacock bass and also has snook and tarpon, adding up to excellent sportfishing. Charters depart from Gamboa's two marinas.

Panama Canal Fishing. Panama Canal Fishing is the best operator for fishing on Gatún Lake. An all-inclusive day of fishing on the Hurricane Fundeck with swivel chairs on the bow costs $445 per boat. *507/315–1905, 507/6678–2653* *www.panamacanalfishing.com.*

LAGO GATÚN (GATÚN LAKE)

GETTING HERE AND AROUND

Aside from seeing the entire canal on a complete transit tour, you can see a bit of the lake during the boat trip to Barro Colorado, or on one of the nature tours or sportfishing charters that leave from the marinas at Gamboa and the Meliá Resort, near Colón. You can also see parts of it from the Panama Railway.

Lago Gatún (Gatún Lake). Covering about 163 square miles, an area about the size of the island nation Barbados, Gatún Lake extends northwest from Parque Nacional Soberanía to the locks of Gatún, just south of Colón. The lake was created when the U.S. government dammed the Chagres River, between 1907 and 1910, so that boats could cross the isthmus at 85 feet above sea level. By creating the lake, the United States saved decades of digging that a sea-level canal would have required. It took several years for the rain to fill the convoluted valleys, turning hilltops into islands and killing much forest (some trunks still tower over the water nearly a century later). When it was completed, Gatún Lake was the largest man-made lake in the world. The canal route winds through its northern half, past several forest-covered islands (the largest is Barro Colorado, one of the world's first biological reserves). To the north of Barro Colorado are the Islas Brujas and Islas Tigres, which together hold a primate refuge—visitors aren't allowed. The lake itself is home to crocodiles—forego swimming here—manatees, and peacock bass, a species introduced from South America and popular with fishermen. Fishing charters for bass, snook, and tarpon are out of Gamboa Rainforest Resort (⇨ *Where to Eat and Stay in Gamboa*). ✉ *Gamboa.*

ISLA BARRO COLORADO

55 km (34 miles) northwest of Panama City, in the Panama Canal.

GETTING HERE AND AROUND

Barro Colorado can only be visited on tours run by the Smithsonian Tropical Research Institute (⇨ *above*). Tours leave from the STRI pier in Gamboa at 7:15 am on weekdays and 8 on weekends. The pier is on the left after the dredging division and has a parking lot. From Panama City, you can hire a taxi ($20–$30), or book through a tour operator, which will pick you up at your hotel.

EXPLORING

★ Fodor'sChoice **Isla Barro Colorado.** The island of Barro Colorado in Gatún Lake is a former hilltop that became an island when the Río Chagres was dammed during construction of the Panama Canal. It covers 1,500 hectares (3,700 acres) of virgin rain forest and forms part of the Barro Colorado Nature Monument, which includes five peninsulas on the mainland and protects an area several times that size. The reserve is home for more than 400 species of birds, 225 ant species, and 122 mammal species, including collared peccaries, ocelots, coatis, and five kinds of monkeys. Its forest has 1,200 plant species—more than are found in all of Europe—ranging from delicate orchids to massive strangler fig trees.

In 1923 the island was declared a biological reserve and a tropical research station was built there; it is now the oldest such facility in the world. The island is administered by the Smithsonian Tropical Research Institute (STRI), which facilitates research by 200 or so visiting scientists and students per year and runs several weekly educational tours. Those tours are not only one of the most informative introductions to tropical ecology you can get in Panama, they are excellent opportunities to see wildlife; after decades of living in a protected area full of scientists, the animals are hardly afraid of people.

Bring your passport, tour receipt, bottled water, insect repellent, binoculars, and a poncho or raincoat (May–December). Wear long pants, hiking shoes, and socks to protect against chiggers. You should be in decent shape, since the tour includes several hours of hiking on trails that are steep in places and can be slippery; children under 10 are not allowed, students pay a discounted rate. You can reserve and pay for tours at the STRI website, or through one of the city's tour companies that specialize in nature tours; the tour companies will charge extra to book the STRI tour and provide transportation between your hotel and the dock in Gamboa. 🌐 *www.stri.si.edu*.

Smithsonian Tropical Research Institute (*STRI*). Barro Colorado can be visited on full-day tours run by the Smithsonian Tropical Research Institute (STRI), which depart the STRI dock in Gamboa at 7:15 on Tuesday, Wednesday, and Friday, and 8 on Saturday, and Sunday. The $70 tour is well worth the money, since the English-speaking guides do an excellent job of pointing out flora and fauna and explaining the rain forest's complex ecology. Lunch in the research station's cafeteria and boat transportation to and from Gamboa are included. Tours should be booked and paid for a minimum of 15 days in advance, months ahead for weekends between December and April through the STRI website. Reservations that haven't been paid for 15 days before the tour will be canceled. If you failed to reserve, they sometimes have spaces available; it's worth calling

Tamara Castillo at the STRI office and asking whether there is a space. Last minute tours can be paid for at the Corotú Bookstore, in the Tupper Center, on Cerro Ancón ✉ *Av. Roosevelt, Cerro Ancón, Panama City* ☎ *507/212–8951* 🌐 *www.stri.si.edu* ⏲ *Open Mon.–Fri. 8 am–1 pm.*

THE CENTRAL CARIBBEAN COAST

Coral reefs, rain forests, colonial ruins, and a predominant Afro-Caribbean culture make Panama's Caribbean coast a fascinating place to visit. People from Panama City head to the Costa Arriba, the coast northeast of Colón, to enjoy its beaches and feast on fresh lobster, conch, or king crab. Scuba divers flock to Portobelo, a colonial town guarded by ancient fortresses and surrounded by rain forest, but the diving is even better to the northeast of there. The bird-watching is excellent around the colonial fortresses of San Lorenzo and Portobelo, and on the slopes of the Sierra Llorona.

COLÓN

79 km (49 miles) northwest of Panama City.

The provincial capital of Colón, beside the canal's Atlantic entrance, is named for the Spanish-language surname of Christopher Columbus, though the Americans called it Aspinwall in the 19th century. It was once a prosperous city, as the architecture of its older buildings attests, but it spent the second half of the 20th century in steady decay. Though the 21st century brought relief to the city's chronic unemployment problems, much of it remains a slum, and crime is endemic.

GETTING HERE AND AROUND

The easiest way to get to Colón from Panama City is to take the Panama Canal Railway commuter train that departs from Panama City at 7:15 am and returns at 5:15 pm. If you start your railway journey in Colón, you will need to purchase tickets from the conductor. Buses depart from Panama City's Albrook Terminal de Buses every 20 minutes, and the trip takes 90 minutes to two hours. Get directly into a taxi upon arrival at either the train or bus station; both are in unsafe neighborhoods. ⚠ **Take only licensed taxis in Colón—the license plate and number on the door should match. Robberies have been committed by unofficial cabbies.** You can rent a car at the Colón 2000 cruise

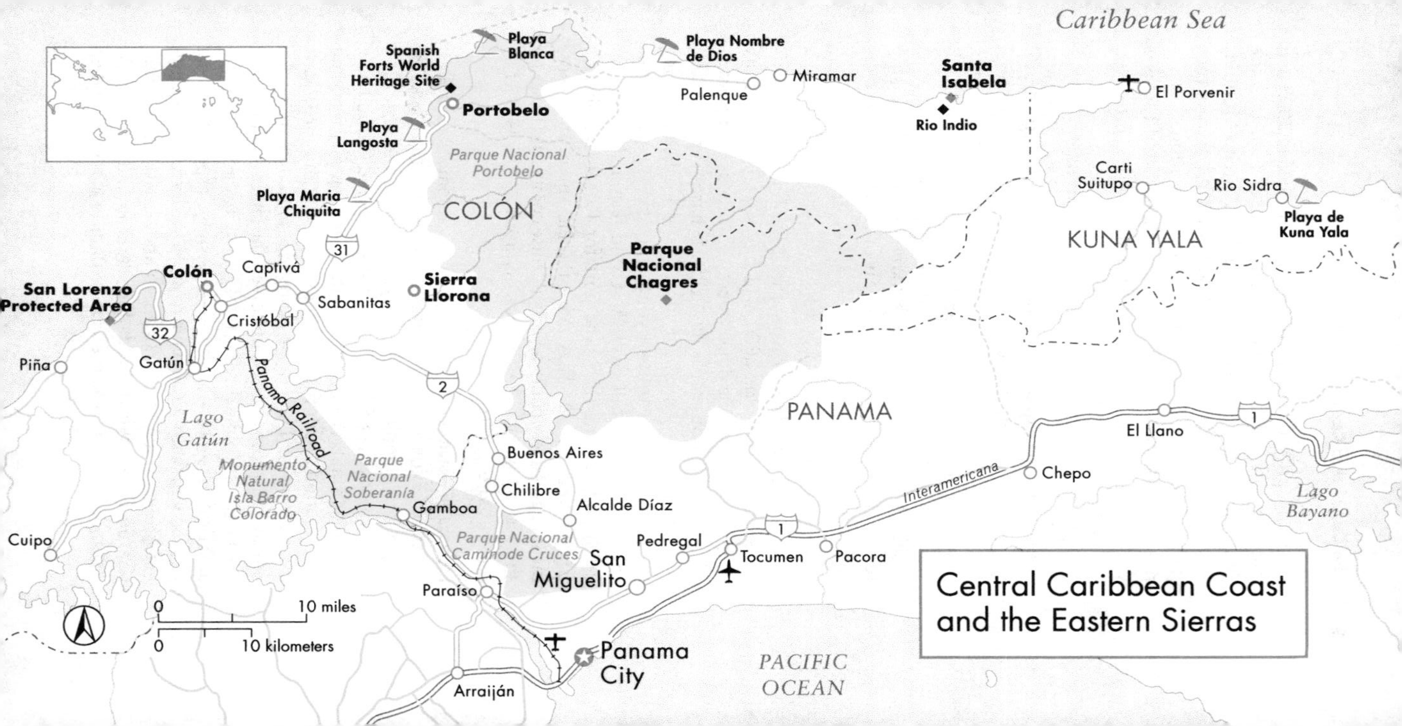
Central Caribbean Coast and the Eastern Sierras
Caribbean Sea
Playa Blanca
Spanish Forts World Heritage Site
Portobelo
Playa Nombre de Dios
Miramar
Palenque
Santa Isabela
Rio Indio
El Porvenir
Playa Langosta
Parque Nacional Portobelo
Carti Suitupo
Rio Sidra
Playa de Kuna Yala
Playa Maria Chiquita
COLÓN
KUNA YALA
31
Parque Nacional Chagres
Colón
Captivá
San Lorenzo Protected Area
Sierra Llorona
Sabanitas
Cristóbal
32
Piña
Gatún
Panama Railroad
2
PANAMA
Lago Gatún
1
El Llano
Buenos Aires
Monumento Natural Isla Barro Colorado
Parque Nacional Soberanía
Chilibre
Chepo
Interamericana
Alcalde Díaz
Lago Bayano
Gamboa
Parque Nacional Camino de Cruces
Pedregal
Cuipo
San Miguelito
Tocumen
Pacora
Paraíso
0
10 miles
10 kilometers
Panama City
Arraiján
PACIFIC OCEAN

center. A spiffy, four-lane toll highway opened in 2009 and puts Colón less than an hour from Panama City. Take the Avenida Omar Torrijo to the Autopista Alfredo Motta. If you are headed for the Gatún Locks, or San Lorenzo, turn left at the Centro Comercial Cuatro Altos, about 8 km (5 miles) before Colón, and follow the signs to and Esclusas de Gatún. (⇨ *See By Car and By Train, above, for rental car and train travel information.)*

SAFETY

⚠ **Travelers who explore Colón on foot risk being mugged,** and the route between the train station and the bus terminal is especially notorious. Do all your traveling in a taxi, rental car, or on a guided tour. If you do the Panama Railway trip on your own, take one of the shuttle vans to the Colón 2000 (pronounced coh-*loan* dose-*mill*) cruise-ship terminal, where you can rent a car or hire a taxi to see the sights near town.

EXPLORING

Colón 2000. Two blocks from the Zona Libre is the city's cruise-ship port, Colón 2000, which is basically a two-story strip mall next to the dock where ships tie up and passengers load onto buses for day trips. It has a supermarket, restaurants, two rental-car offices, and English-speaking taxi drivers who can take you on sightseeing excursions ($70–$100 for a full day). A second terminal opened in 2008 and became the home port for Royal Caribbean's *Enchantment of the Seas*, with the Panamanian government aggressively courting other cruise companies to set up shop here too. ✉ *Calle El Paseo Gorgas* ☎ *507/447–3197* 🌐 *www.colon2000.com.*

Esclusas de Gatún (*Gatún Locks*). Twelve kilometers (7 miles) south of Colón are the Esclusas de Gatún (Gatún Locks), a triple-lock complex that's nearly a mile long and raises and lowers ships the 85 feet between sea level and Gatún Lake. There's a small visitor center with a viewing platform and information about the boats passing through is broadcast over speakers. The visitor center doesn't compare to the one at Miraflores Locks, but given the sheer magnitude of the Gatún Locks—three sets of locks, as opposed to two at Miraflores—it is an impressive sight, especially when packed with ships. You have to cross the locks on a swinging bridge to get to San Lorenzo and the **Represa Gatún** (Gatún Dam), which holds the water in Gatún Lake. At 1½ miles long, it was the largest dam in the world when it was built, a title it held for several decades. Get there by taking the first left after crossing the locks. ✉ *12 km (7 miles) south of Colón* 🎟 *$5* ⏲ *Daily 8–4.*

WHERE TO STAY

For expanded hotel reviews, visit Fodors.com.

$ **Radisson Colón 2000.** *Hotel.* If you have to spend a night in Colón, this is your best option, since it's next to the Colón 2000 cruise port, with its shops and restaurants, in one of the safest parts of town. **Pros:** quiet; safe; business amenities. **Cons:** facilities can be overrun with cruise-ship passengers when ships are in port. *Rooms from: $120* ✉ *Paseo Gorgas, Calle 13* ☎ *507/446–2000, 800/830–5222 in the U.S. and Canada* 🌐 *www.radisson.com* *98 rooms, 4 suites* *Breakfast.*

3

SPORTS AND THE OUTDOORS

SPORTFISHING

Meliá Panama Canal. The Meliá Panama Canal runs inexpensive fishing tours on Gatún Lake that are open to nonguests. The fishing gear is basic, but you can be pretty much guaranteed that you'll catch some peacock bass. ✉ *Calle Principal, Res. Espinar* ☎ *507/470–1100.*

SAN LORENZO PROTECTED AREA

40 km (25 miles) west of Colón.

For information about San Lorenzo's park, fort, tours, and accommodations, visit 🌐 *www.sanlorenzo.org.pa.*

GETTING HERE AND AROUND

It usually takes two hours to drive to San Lorenzo from Panama City and 40 minutes from Colón, if it doesn't take too long to cross the Gatún Locks. Follow directions for Colón, but turn left at the Centro Comercial Cuatro Altos, 8 km (5 miles) before Colón, and follow the signs to Esclusas de Gatún. After crossing the locks, veer right and drive 12 km (7 miles) to Fort Sherman. Turn left onto a dirt road after the entrance to Fort Sherman and drive another 11 km (6 miles) to the fort. The Achiote Road is reached by turning left after crossing the locks and driving 12 km (7 miles)—over the Gatún Dam—to the second road on the right. The town of Achiote is 10 km (6 miles) up that dirt road.

EXPLORING

Fuerte San Lorenzo (*San Lorenzo Fort*). Perched on a cliff overlooking the mouth of the Chagres River are the ruins of the ancient Spanish Fuerte San Lorenzo, destroyed by pirate Henry Morgan in 1671 and rebuilt shortly after, then bombarded a century later. The Spaniards built Fort San Lorenzo in 1595 in an effort to protect the South American gold they were shipping down the Chagres River, which was first carried along the Camino de Cruces from Panamá Viejo. The gold was then shipped up the coast to the fortified city of Portobelo, where it was stored until the Spanish armada arrived to carry it to Spain. The fortress's commanding position and abundant cannons weren't enough of a deterrent for Morgan, whose men managed to shoot flaming arrows into the fort, causing a fire that set off stored gunpowder and forced the Spanish troops to surrender. Morgan then led his men up the river and across the isthmus to sack Panamá Viejo.

In the 1980s UNESCO restored the fort to its current condition, which is pretty sparse—it hardly compares to the extensive colonial ruins of Portobelo. Nevertheless, the setting is gorgeous, and the view from that promontory of the blue-green Caribbean, the coast, and the vast jungle behind it is breathtaking. ⚠ **Be careful walking around the edge outside the fort; there are some treacherous precipices, and guardrails are almost nonexistent. One visitor did have a fatal fall several years ago.** ✉ *23 km (14 miles) northwest of Gatún Locks* 🎟 *Free* ⏲ *Daily 8–4.*

Parque Nacional San Lorenzo. The wilderness just behind the Fuerte San Lorenzo is part of Parque Nacional San Lorenzo, a 23,843-acre (9,653-hectare) protected area that includes rain forest, wetlands, rivers, and coastline. For decades this was the U.S. Army's jungle training area, where tens of thousands of troops trained for warfare in the tropics. The army used parts of the park as a bombing range, and there may still be unexploded ordnance in its interior, though far from the roads and fortress. Today the park is the haunt of bird-watchers, who hope to focus their binoculars on some of the more than 400 bird species. Mammalian residents include spider monkey, armadillo, tamarin, and coati mundi. The lush forest here gets nearly twice as much rain as Panama City, and it doesn't lose as much of its foliage during the dry season. Most of that rain falls at night, so mornings are often sunny, even during the rainy season.

The most famous bird-watching area in Parque Nacional San Lorenzo is the **Achiote Road** (Camino a Achiote), which is about 25 km (15 miles) south of the fort. To reach it, turn left after crossing the locks and drive 15 km (9 miles) south. Members of the Panama Audubon Society once counted 340 bird species in one day on the Achiote Road during their Christmas bird count. The community of Achiote, about 4 km (2½ miles) northwest of the park on the Achiote Road, has trained birding guides and a visitor center with rustic accommodations. ✉ *15 km (9 miles) west of Gatún Locks* ☎ *507/226–4529* 🌐 *www.sanlorenzo.org.pa* 🎫 *$5* ⏲ *Daily 7–4.*

SPORTS AND THE OUTDOORS

BIRD-WATCHING

Ancon Expeditions. Panama City–based operator Ancon Expeditions offers a tour that combines bird-watching and forest exploration in San Lorenzo and Soberania National Parks, visits to the San Lorenzo fortress and Gatún Locks, and a one-way trip on the Panama Railway. ☎ *507/269–9415* 🌐 *www.anconexpeditions.com.*

Ecocircuitos Panama. Located in Panama City, this company offers a half-day birding tour to the Achiote Road, in San Lorenzo National Park, and a general interest tour that combines visits to the fortress and Gatún Locks. ✉ *Panama City* ☎ *507/315–1305* 🌐 *www.ecocircuitos.com.*

Nattur Panama. Colón-based Nattur Panama can put together à la carte birding tours of San Lorenzo, Portobelo National Park, and other areas. ✉ *Colón* ☎ *507/442–1340* 🌐 *www.natturpanama.com.*

PORTOBELO

99 km (62 miles) north of Panama City, 48 km (30 miles) northeast of Colón.

Portobelo has an inspiring mix of colonial fortresses, placid waters, and lushly forested hills. Christopher Columbus named it "beautiful port" in 1502 during his fourth and final voyage to the Americas. Unfortunately, cement-block houses crowded higgledy-piggledy amid the ancient walls detract from an otherwise lovely setting. Portobelo contains some of Panama's most interesting colonial ruins, with rusty cannons still lying in wait for an enemy assault, and is a UNESCO World Heritage Site, together with San Lorenzo. Depending on your timing, you could see congo dancing, or the annual Festival del Cristo Negro (⇨ *Black Christ Festival, below*). Between the history, turquoise sea, jungle, coral reefs (great for scuba diving or snorkeling), beaches, and local culture, its an enticing spot to spend a few days.

Once the sister city of Panamá Viejo, Portobelo was an affluent trading center during the 17th century, when countless tons of Spanish treasure passed through its customs house, and shiploads of European goods were unloaded on their way to South America. The Spaniards moved their Atlantic port in Panama from Nombre de Dios to Portobelo in 1597, since the deep bay was deemed an easier place to defend against pirates, who had raided Nombre de Dios repeatedly. During the next two centuries Portobelo was one of the most important ports in the Caribbean. Gold from South America was stored here after crossing the isthmus via the Camino de Cruces and Chagres River, awaiting semiannual *ferias,* or trade fairs, in which a fleet of galleons and merchant ships loaded with European goods arrived for several weeks of business and revelry before sailing home laden with gold and silver. That wealth attracted pirates, who repeatedly attacked Portobelo, despite the Spanish fortresses flanking the entrance to the bay and a larger fortress near the customs house. After a century and a half of attacks, Spain began shipping its South American gold around Cape Horn in 1740, marking the end of Portobelo's ferias, and turning the town into an insignificant Caribbean port. What remains today is a mix of historic and tacky, twentieth-century structures surrounded by spectacular natural scenery that looks much the same as it did in Columbus's day.

You can explore Portobelo's historic sites in a couple of hours, which leaves plenty of time for outdoor diversions. Several beaches in the area are worth visiting, half a dozen diving and snorkeling spots are nearby, there is decent fishing, and the bird-watching is excellent. It's also an ideal spot to kick back and unwind.

GETTING HERE AND AROUND

Portobelo is a 90-minute drive from Panama City and a mere 40 minutes from Colón. To drive there from Panama City, follow the directions to Colón but turn right after 60 km (37 miles), at the town of Sabanitas; from there it's 39 km (24 miles) to Portobelo. From Colón, head south toward Panama City for 15 km (9 miles) and turn left at Sabanitas. There is no reason to go to Colón on your way to Portobelo, unless you take the Panama Canal Railway, in which case hire a taxi or rent a car and drive to Portobelo.

EXPLORING

Iglesia de San Felipe. One block east of the Real Aduana is the Iglesia de San Felipe, a large white church dating from 1814 that's home to the country's most venerated religious figure: the **Cristo Negro** (Black Christ). According to legend, that statue of a dark-skinned Jesus carrying a cross arrived in Portobelo in the 17th century on a Spanish ship bound for Cartagena, Colombia. Each time the ship tried to leave, it encountered storms and had to return to port, convincing the captain to leave the statue in Portobelo. Another legend has it that in the midst of a cholera epidemic in 1821 parishioners prayed to the Cristo Negro, and the community was spared. The statue spends most of the year to the left of the church's altar, but once a year it's paraded through town in the Festival del Cristo Negro. Each year the Cristo Negro is clothed in a new purple robe, donated by somebody who's earned the honor. Many of the robes that have been created for the statue over the past century are on display in the Museo del Cristo Negro (Black Christ Museum) in the Iglesia de San Juan, a smaller, 17th-century church next to the Iglesia de San Felipe. ✉ *Calle Principal* 🎫 *$1* ⏲ *Daily 8–4.*

Parque Nacional Portobelo (*Portobelo National Park*). Parque Nacional Portobelo is a vast marine and rain-forest reserve contiguous with Chagres National Park that protects both natural and cultural treasures. It extends from the cloud forest atop 3,212-foot Cerro Brujo down to offshore islands and coral reefs, and comprises the bay and fortresses of Portobelo. It holds an array of ecosystems and a wealth of biodiversity that ranges from nurse sharks and sea turtles along the coast to toucans and spider monkeys in the mountains. There is no proper park entrance, but you can explore the rain forest and mangrove estuaries along the coast on hiking or boat trips from Portobelo.

You can't miss the remains of the three Spanish fortresses that once guarded Portobelo Bay. The first is **Fuerte Santiago de la Gloria,** which is on the left as you arrive at the bay. It has about a dozen cannons and sturdy battlements that were built out of blocks of coral, which were cut from the platform reefs that line the coast. Coral was more abundant and easier to cut than the igneous rock found inland, so the Spaniards used it for most construction in Portobelo.

Portobelo's largest and most impressive fort is **Fuerte San Jerónimo,** at the end of the bay. Surrounded by the "modern" town, it was built in the 1600s but was destroyed by Vernon and rebuilt to its current state in 1758. Its large interior courtyard was once a parade ground, but it's now the venue for annual celebrations such as New Year's, Carnaval, the Festival de Diablos y Congos (shortly after Carnaval), and the town's patron saint's day (March 20).

Fuerte San Fernando, across the bay from Fuerte Santiago, consists of two battlements—one near the water and one on the hill above. The upper fortress affords a great view of the bay and is a good place to see birds because of the surrounding forest.

■ TIP→ **Local boatmen who dock their boats next to Fuerte Santiago or Fuerte San Jerónimo can take you across the bay to explore Fuerte San Fernando for a few dollars.** They also offer tours to local beaches, or a trip into the estuary at the end of the bay, which is a good place to see birds. ✉ *Surrounding Portobelo* ☎ *507/448–2599 park office* *Free* ⏲ *Open 24 hrs.*

Real Aduana (*Royal Customs House*). Near the entrance to Fuerte San Jerónimo is the Real Aduana, where servants of the Spanish crown made sure that the king and queen got their cut from every ingot that rolled through town. Built in 1630, the Real Aduana was damaged during pirate attacks and then destroyed by an earthquake in 1882, only to be rebuilt in 1998. It is an interesting example of colonial architecture—note the carved coral columns on the ground floor—and it houses a simple museum with some old coins, cannonballs, and displays on Panamanian folklore. ✉ *Calle de la Aduana* *$1* ⏲ *Daily 8–4.*

WHERE TO EAT AND STAY

For expanded hotel reviews, visit Fodors.com.

$ ✕ **Restaurante Los Cañones.** *Seafood.* This rambling restaurant with tables among palm trees and Caribbean views is one of Panama's most attractive lunch spots. The food and service fall a little short of the setting, but not so far that you'd want to scratch it from your list. In good weather, dine at tables edging the sea surrounded by dark boulders and lush foliage. The other option is the open-air restaurant, decorated with shells, buoys, and driftwood, with a decent view of the bay and forested hills. House specialties include *pescado entero* (whole fried snapper), *langosta al* *ajillo* (lobster scampi), and *centolla al jengibre* (king crab in a ginger sauce). *Average main: $12* *2 km (1 mile) before Portobelo on left* *507/448–2980* *No credit cards* *Closes at 7 pm.*

★ Fodor's Choice **El Otro Lado.** *B&B/Inn.* This private retreat
$$$$ across the bay from Portobelo offers a splendid mix of ocean views, tropical nature, abundant art, friendly service, and fine dining. **Pros:** gorgeous atmosphere setting; intimate; great service. **Cons:** expensive. *Rooms from: $490* *Across bay from town, Portobelo* *507/202–0111* *www.elotrolado.com.pa* *3 suites, 4 houses* *Breakfast.*

$ **Sunset Cabins.** *Hotel.* This dive resort owned by Scuba Panama, the country's biggest dive company, has decent rooms in a lovely coastal setting at very low rates, making it a good option for budget travelers who can do without a lot of service. **Pros:** great location; inexpensive; scuba diving and snorkeling. **Cons:** basic rooms; limited service. *Rooms from: $55* *6 km (3 miles) before Portobelo on left* *507/448–2147, 507/261–3841 in Panama* *www.scubapanama.com* *6 rooms, 5 cabañas* *No meals.*

SPORTS AND THE OUTDOORS

BEACHES

Playa Blanca. Playa Blanca is a small, white-sand beach about 30 minutes by boat east of Portobelo. It has the nicest sand of any beach in the area, some shade trees, and there are reefs off shore for snorkelling. There are no roads there, nor are there restaurants or stores. The water is almost always calm, but if there are waves, don't go in deep. **Amenities:** none. **Best for:** solitude; snorkeling; swimming.

Playa Langosta. The easiest beach to visit in the vicinity is Playa Langosta, which is about 8 km (5 mi) south of Portobelo. The long, beige beach backed by coconut palms and other trees is quiet during the week, but on weekends and holidays, it can get packed with visitors from Colón and Panama City. There is a small charge for parking a car and renting tables on the beach with thatched sombrillas. Restaurant Mamani, on the beach, serves a small selection of seafood and cool drinks, and has the only bathrooms. **Amenities:** food and drink; parking; toilets. **Best for:** partiers, swimming, walking.

BIRD-WATCHING

The bird-watching is quite good at the edge of town and around the ruins. Bird-watchers may want to hire one of the boatmen who hang out around the docks near Batería

Santiago and Fuerte San Jerónimo to take them into the estuary behind town, which should cost $20.

SCUBA DIVING AND SNORKELING

Miles of coral reefs awash in rainbows of underwater wildlife lie within the northern reaches of **Portobelo National Park,** and dive centers on the road to Portobelo provide easy access to those marine wonders. Though they've suffered damage from fishermen, erosion, and climate change, the reefs in the Portobelo area consist of nearly 50 coral species and are inhabited by more than 250 fish species. The underwater fauna ranges from moray eels to colorful butterfly fish, damselfish, trumpet fish, and other reef dwellers. Popular spots include Buffet Reef, a plane wreck, a shipwreck, and the distant Escribano Bank, east of Isla Grande. Visibility varies according to the sea conditions, but tends to be low from December to April, when high seas can hamper dives. The best conditions are between July and December. PADI certification courses are also available.

Aventuras Panama. The Panama City–based outfitter Aventuras Panama runs a day tour to Portobelo that combines kayaking and snorkeling. ✉ *Portobelo* ☎ *507/260–0044* 🌐 *www.aventuraspanama.com.*

Scuba Panama. The country's oldest dive operator, Scuba Panama has a dive center at the Sunset Cabins hotel, where it operates day and overnight dive tours to reefs near Portobelo. ✉ *6 km (3 miles) before Portobelo on the left* ☎ *507/448–2147, 507/261–3841* 🌐 *www.scubapanama.com.*

SANTA ISABELA

44 km (27 miles) east of Isla Grande, 26 km (16 miles) west of El Porvenir (Guna Yala).

To the east of Portobelo, the coast becomes wilder, and the ocean more pristine. Nestled in a remote cove about two-thirds of the way between Isla Grande and the Guna enclave of El Porvenir (⇨ *Chapter 6)*, is one of the country's best eco-lodges, Coral Lodge, which provides access to miles of coral reefs that few divers have seen. The lodge is near the fishing village of Santa Isabela, which is 16 km (10 miles) from the nearest road, in Miramar, and 29 km (18 miles) by water from the island of El Porvenir.

WHERE TO STAY

For expanded hotel reviews, visit Fodors.com.

$$$$ **Coral Lodge.** *Hotel.* Nestled in an idyllic cove on the ★ remote coast between Portobelo and Guna Yala, Coral Lodge's bungalows and restaurant are perched over the sea and surrounded by amazing scenery—emerald waters, mangroves, and a golden beach backed by jungle. **Pros:** gorgeous scenery; snorkeling; kayaking. **Cons:** remote location; no-see-ums can be a problem; boat ride can be rough. *Rooms from: $386 Santa Isabela, 16 km (10 miles) east of Mirimar. 507/836–5434, 888/499–2497 in U.S. www.corallodge.com 7 bungalows All meals.*

3

THE EASTERN SIERRAS

A large mass of mountains rises up to the northeast of the Panama Canal, which collect much of the rainwater used by the locks. The Panamanian government consequently protected that vast watershed within Parque Nacional Chagres. Chagres is contiguous with Portobelo National Park—the relatively small Sierra Llorona defines the border between the two parks.

SIERRA LLORONA

80 km (50 miles) north of Panama City, 22 km (14 miles) southeast of Colón.

Sierra Llorona is a small but steep mountain range east of Gatún Lake and southwest of Portobelo that spends much of the year enveloped in clouds, and the abundant waterfalls that result from that rain are the origin of the range's name, which translates as "crybaby sierra." The sierra stretches southwestward from Portobelo and Chagres national parks to a sparsely populated area where you'll find the family-run Sierra Llorona Lodge, on a 500-acre private reserve that is home to an array of wildlife. The lodge is worth spending a night or two at, but day visitors get lunch and a local guide for $35.

GETTING HERE AND AROUND

It's an easy one-hour drive to Sierra Llorona from Panama City. Follow directions for Colón and turn right where the toll road ends, at a sign for Santa Arriba and Sierra Llorona, from where it's a 4½-km (3-mile) drive up a narrow, windy road. In the rainy season a four-wheel-drive vehicle is recommended for the last stretch. The Sierra Llorona Lodge has detailed instructions on its website and can arrange transportation for guests.

WHERE TO STAY

For expanded hotel reviews, visit Fodors.com.

$ **Sierra Llorona Panama Lodge.** *B&B/Inn.* Birdsong is the ★ Muzak at this small lodge in the rain forest, making it an ideal place for bird watchers and other nature lovers. **Pros:** lovely forest setting; good bird-watching; monkeys; hiking. **Cons:** basic meals. *Rooms from: $80* ✉ *Santa Rita Arriba, 4½ km (3 miles) east of Transístmica* ☎ *507/6574–0083* ⊕ *www.sierrallorona.com* *6 rooms, 1 suite* 🍽 *Breakfast.*

PARQUE NACIONAL CHAGRES (CHAGRES NATIONAL PARK)

40 km (24 miles) north of Panama City.

GETTING HERE AND AROUND

There is no easy access to Parque Nacional Chagres, so you have to take a tour—hiking, white-water rafting—to visit it.

Parque Nacional Chagres (*Chagres National Park*). The mountains to the northeast of the canal form a vast watershed that feeds the Chagres River, which was one of the country's principal waterways until it was damned to create the canal, and is now the source of nearly half of the water used in the locks. To protect the forests that help water percolate into the ground and keep the river running through the dry season, the Panamanian government declared the entire watershed a national park in 1985. It is one of the country's largest parks, covering more than 320,000 acres, and it holds an array of ecosystems and expanses of inaccessible wilderness that is home to spider monkeys, harpy eagles, toucans, tapirs, and other endangered species. The park's northern border, defined by Sierra Llorona, and its southern extreme, in Cerro Azul, are the easiest areas to visit, thanks to paved roads. Most people visit the national park on day tours from Panama City to one of several Emberá villages, but you can see more of its forests on a white-water rafting trip down the Chagres River or by hiking on the trails of Cerro Azul.

All the major tour operators in Panama City offer day trips to **Emberá villages** in the park (⇨ *"Tours," in Panama City Essentials, Chapter 2)*. Visiting the villages—relocated here from Alto Bayano three decades ago, when their land was flooded by a hydroelectric project—is an interesting cultural experience, but most itineraries aren't great for seeing wildlife. The Emberá's traditional territory stretches from eastern Panama to northwest Colombia, but the relocated communities live much as their relatives to the east do, in thatched huts with elevated floors. They wear their traditional dress for tour groups—men wear loincloths and women wrap themselves in bright-color cloth skirts, with no tops, sometimes covering their breasts with large necklaces. Men and women paint their upper bodies with a dye made from mixing the sap of the *jagua* fruit with ashes. The tours are a bit of a show, but they provide an interesting introduction to Emberá culture. Tours usually include demonstrations of how the Emberá live, a traditional dance, handicraft sales, and optional painting of visitors' arms with *jagua*. (Note the *jagua* tattoos take more than a week to wash off.) Communities that receive visitors include Parara Puru and San Juan de Pequiní, but the best trip for nature lovers or adventurers is to Emberá Drua, since it entails a boat trip deep into the park and a tough hike. ✉ *Transístmica, Km. 40* ☎ *507/260–8575* 🎫 *$5* ⏲ *Daily 7–5.*

SPORTS AND THE OUTDOORS

HIKING

Camino Real. Serious hikers can trek deep into the jungles of Parque Nacional Chagres by following the old Camino Real across the mountains to the Caribbean coast. Spanish colonists built the "Royal Road" in the 16th century to carry gold and other goods between Panamá Viejo and the Caribbean port of Nombre de Dios, and most of that route remains surrounded by lush rain forest. Weeklong trips organized by **Ancon Expeditions** (☎ *507/269–9415* 🌐 *www.anconexpeditions.com*) include visits to colonial ruins and an Emberá village and several nights in tent camps in the national park.

WHITE-WATER RAFTING

Aventuras Panama. Aventuras Panama runs white-water rafting trips on the Chagres River (Class II–III), which flows through the heart of Parque Nacional Chagres. The full-day trip requires no previous rafting experience, but is available only from June to February; it costs $175, which includes lunch and breakfast. ☎ *507/260–0044* 🌐 *www.aventuraspanama.com.*

SHOPPING

A big part of a visit to an Emberá village is the opportunity to buy authentic indigenous handicrafts from the artisans themselves. Among the items usually sold are tightly woven baskets and platters, and animal figures carved from *tagua* palm seeds, or *cocobolo* wood.

THE CENTRAL PACIFIC ISLANDS

The Gulf of Panama holds more than a dozen islands and countless rocky islets, which include Isla Taboga, a mere 20 km (12 miles) south of Panama City, and the Archipelago de las Perlas (Pearl Islands), which are scattered across the gulf between 60 and 90 km (about 40 to 60 miles) southeast of the city. Isla Taboga has a historic town lined with vacation homes, whereas the Pearl Islands remain largely undeveloped, with a few fishing villages and vast expanses of rain forest. The aquamarine waters that wash against the islands hold varied and abundant marine life, providing opportunities for sportfishing, scuba diving, and whale watching (June to October).

The islands were inhabited when the Spaniards arrived in Panama, Isla Taboga became a Spanish stronghold from the start due to its deep bay, ideal for mooring ships close to shore. The Spanish conquistador Francisco Pizarro defeated the indigenous leader of the Pearl Islands, King Toe, in 1515. Pizarro stole plenty of pearls from Toe's people, and the Spanish government continued to exploit the archipelago's pearl beds for the next two centuries, first with indigenous labor, and later, with African slaves, after disease decimated the indigenous population. Overexploitation exhausted the pearl supply in the 19th century, and since then the archipelago's inhabitants have survived on fishing, tourism, and building vacation homes.

Because the Pearl Archipelago is so extensive, its islands were often the haunt of pirates, who used them as bases from which to attack Spanish galleons carrying South American gold to Panama during the 16th and 17th centuries. More recently, the archipelago has been exploited by a new breed of opportunist: the producers of the *Survivor* reality television series, who based three seasons here (2003, 2004, and 2006). Modern-day invaders have discovered that the islands' true treasures are their beaches and ocean views.

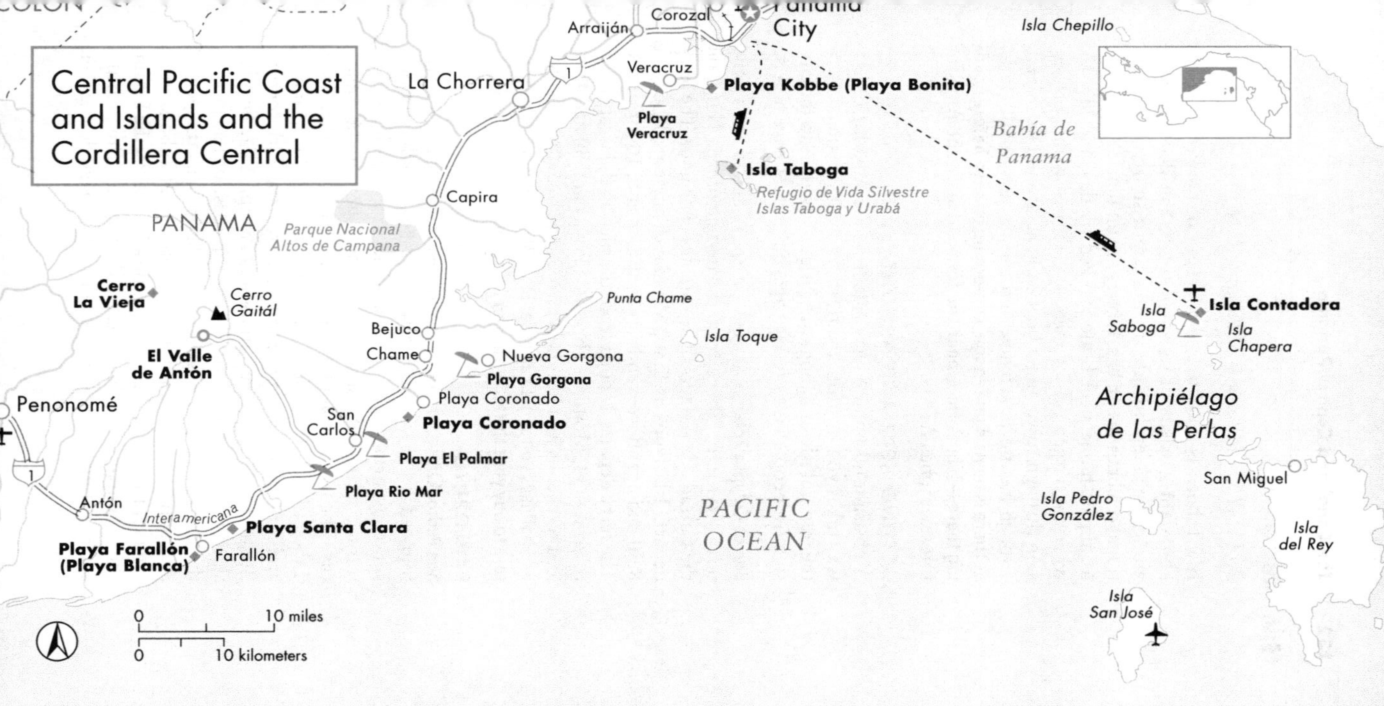
Central Pacific Coast and Islands and the Cordillera Central
PANAMA
Parque Nacional Altos de Campana
Arraiján
Corozal
City
La Chorrera
Veracruz
Playa Veracruz
Playa Kobbe (Playa Bonita)
Isla Taboga
Refugio de Vida Silvestre Islas Taboga y Urabá
Isla Chepillo
Bahía de Panama
Capira
Cerro La Vieja
Cerro Gaitál
El Valle de Antón
Bejuco
Chame
Punta Chame
Isla Toque
Nueva Gorgona
Playa Gorgona
Playa Coronado
Playa Coronado
Penonomé
San Carlos
Playa El Palmar
Playa Rio Mar
Antón
Interamericana
Playa Santa Clara
Playa Farallón (Playa Blanca)
Farallón
PACIFIC OCEAN
Isla Saboga
Isla Contadora
Isla Chapera
Archipiélago de las Perlas
San Miguel
Isla Pedro González
Isla del Rey
Isla San José
0
10 miles
0
10 kilometers

ISLA TABOGA

20 km (12 miles) south of Panama City.

Isla Taboga is known as the "Island of Flowers" for the abundant gardens of its small town, San Pedro, spread along the steep hillside of its eastern shore. The traditional celebrations on Isla Taboga are on June 29, when the local parishioners celebrate San Pedro's day, and July 16, when the Virgen del Carmen is celebrated with a procession through town and a boat caravan around the island. Taboga has no pharmacy, and only a very small clinic. ⚠ **There is no ATM on Taboga, so stock up on cash before heading there**—Isla Perico, near the ferry dock on the Amador Causeway, has ATMs.

GETTING HERE AND AROUND

A pleasant 60-minute ferry ride from the Amador Causeway takes you far from the traffic jams of Panama City to the tranquil isle of Taboga. The island lies close to the city, so most people visit on day trips, but it does have hotels.

Barcos Calypso Taboga. Barcos Calypso Taboga has a daily ferry service to Taboga from the marina on Isla Naos, on the Calzada de Amador. The trip takes one hour. The ferry departs Isla Naos at 8:30, Monday–Thursday; Friday at 8:30 and 3; and weekends and holidays at 8, 10:30, and 4. The ferry departs Taboga from the pier on the west end of town at 4:30, Monday–Thrusday; Friday at 9:30 and 4:30; and weekends and holidays at 9, 3, and 5. ⚠ **On weekends and holidays you should arrive at least 30 minutes before departure to buy your ticket.** ✉ *Marina Isla Naos* ☎ *507/314–1730.*

EXPLORING

San Pedro. One of the country's oldest towns, San Pedro was founded in 1524, though its whitewashed church is the only surviving structure from the colonial era; folks here claim it is the second-oldest still-operating church in the Americas. The conquistador Francisco Pizarro embarked from Taboga in 1530 on his voyage to crush the Inca Empire, and it remained an important port until the 20th century. Because of the extreme variation of Panama's Pacific tides, ships were unable to moor near the coast of Panama, so the deep bay on Taboga's eastern shore was the perfect alternative. The Spanish built a fortress on Taboga in an attempt to defend the bay from pirates, the Pacific Steamship Company was based there during the 19th century, and the French built a sanatorium on the island during their attempt to build a canal. Upon completion of the canal, with its various docks and marinas, Taboga became what it is today, a sleepy fishing village that wakes up on weekends and holidays, when visitors from the capital arrive en masse.

There are few vehicles on the island, and most of its streets resemble extra-wide sidewalks. The main road runs along the town beach, Playa Honda, which lines a small bay holding dozens of fishing boats. Many of the bougainvillea-lined streets pass shrines to the Virgen del Carmen, considered the protector of fishermen throughout Latin America, who is celebrated every July 16 here. ✉ *Isla Taboga.*

BEACHES

Isla Taboga has two beaches: **Playa Honda,** the beach in front of town, and **Playa Restinga,** a spit of sand that connects Taboga with the tiny island of El Morro, just north of town. At low- or mid-tide, Playa Restinga is a gorgeous swath of golden sand flanked by calm waters, but at high tide, it disappears. It's often packed on weekends and holidays, when the radios and screaming kids can be a bit too much, but it is practically deserted on most weekdays. The ruins of the Hotel Taboga, which was demolished in 2005, stand behind the beach. Playa Honda, the beach in front of town, is unattractive, a bit rocky, and dirty—you are as likely to see vultures on it as seagulls—though it does retain a bit of sand at high tide. ⚠ **San Pedro's sewage flows untreated into the bay, so swimming at Playa Honda, or even on the south side of Playa Restinga, is not recommended.**

WHERE TO STAY

For expanded hotel reviews, visit Fodors.com.

$ **Hotel Vereda Tropical.** *B&B/Inn.* Isla Taboga's best hotel, the Vereda Tropical is perched on the hillside overlooking the Bay of Panama. **Pros:** great views; decent restaurant; short walk to beach. **Cons:** service inconsistent; noisy neighborhood. *Rooms from: $75* ✉ *100 meters south of ferry dock* ☎ *507/250–2154* ⊕ *www.veredatropicalhotel.com* *10 rooms* *Breakfast.*

SPORTS AND THE OUTDOORS

Aside from swimming and sunbathing, Taboga's outdoor options include snorkeling, hiking, fishing, or a boat trip around the island. Trails lead to the island's two highest points: Cerro de la Cruz, a hill south of town that is topped with a 20-foot cross, and Cerro Vigia, the mountain behind town. A **wildlife refuge** covers the western half of

Isla Taboga and the nearby island of Urabá, which is the best dive spot in the area. One of the best parts of going to Isla Taboga is actually the trip itself, since the ferry passes dozens of massive ships and provides great views of the islands and the city.

SNORKELING

The snorkeling is pretty good around El Morro, where the visibility is best when the tide is high. Serious divers head to Isla Urubá, a protected island just south of Taboga.

Scuba Panama. Taboga lacks a dive center, but the Panama City–based operator Scuba Panama can arrange a diving day trip to Isla Morro, which includes a stop at Isla Taboga. ☎ *507/261–3841* 🌐 *www.scubapanama.com.*

ISLA CONTADORA

70 km (43 miles) southeast of Panama City.

★ Fodor'sChoice The island of Contadora, a mere 20 minutes from Panama City by plane, has some of the country's loveliest beaches. Half a dozen swaths of beige sand backed by exuberant foliage line Contadora's coves, and they lie within walking distance of affordable accommodations. It is a small island, covering less than a square mile, but it can serve as a base for day trips to nearby isles with deserted beaches and snorkeling sites, as well as deep-sea fishing, scuba diving, and whale watching.

The Pearl Archipelago's indigenous inhabitants undoubtedly had another name for Isla Contadora, but its current name, which translates as "counting isle," was given to it nearly five centuries ago, when it held the offices of the Spanish crown's pearl-diving enterprise. The island was deserted for years after the pearl harvest diminished. Contadora gained its current status as a vacation destination in the 1970s, when wealthy Panamanians began to buy coastal property here. The government built the massive Hotel Contadora—now in ruins—and the island developed a vibrant weekend party scene. The island's most famous temporary resident was the deposed Shah of Iran, on the heels of the Tehran embassy takeover in 1979, who recovered from heart surgery there. Contadora's star has since faded, and it isn't the haunt of the glitterati it once was, but it can be a fun, mid-range place for a vacation.

The island's tiny town center is just to the west of the airstrip, next to which sits its largest hotel. Nearly everything to the west is residential. A series of narrow roads winds through the forests that cover most of the island to the stately vacation homes scattered along its coastline, and an inland neighborhood that has some smaller houses. In the center of the island are a soccer field, a pond, and a small church; to the north lies Playa Ejecutiva, and to the south, Playa Cacique, two of the island's nicest beaches. Contadora is small enough to walk everywhere, but given the heat you may want to rent a golf cart, or scooter.

Isla Contadora's main attraction is its selection of beaches, but there is decent snorkeling around its many rocky points, and better snorkeling at several nearby islands. Though the water is warm most of the year, high winds from December to April cool it down, and decrease visibility. Boat tours to the surrounding islands are recommended, and from June to October, you may see humpback whales. The Contadora Welcome Center, across from the airstrip, can arrange boat tours.

GETTING HERE AND AROUND

Sea Las Perlas runs a daily ferry between Panama City and Contadora, departing the Calzada de Amador at 8 am, and returning at 2:45. The trip takes 90 minutes. Panama's domestic airline, Air Panama, has daily flights to Contadora (OTD) from Aeropuerto Marcos A. Gelabert (Aeropuerto Albrook). The flight takes 25 minutes.

Contacts **Air Panama.** Air Panama has an 8:30 am flight from the Albrook airport to Contadora every day except Sunday, returning at 9, and a 4:30 pm flight on Friday and Sunday, returning at 5. ☎ *507/316-900, 507/250-4009 on Contadora* 🌐 *www.flyairpanama.com.*

Sea Las Perlas. This catamaran ferry makes the trip between Isla Perico, on the Amador Causeway, to Isla Contadora in 90 minutes. The ferry departs from the Brisas del Amador parking lot, on Isla Perico, daily at 8 am (you should arrive between 7 and 7:30), and returns at 3 pm. From July to October, you may see whales during the trip. ✉ *Brisas de Amador, Isla Perico, Calzada de Amador, Panama City* ☎ *507/391-1424, 507/6780-8000* 🌐 *www.sealasperlas.com.*

EXPLORING

Isla Mogo Mogo (*Isla Pájaros*). Isla Mogo Mogo, 4 mi south of Contadora, on the other side of Isla Chapera, has a sugar-sand beach in a deep cove where snorkelers may find sea stars. Tiny **Isla Boyarena,** just to the south, has a pale sandbar that becomes a beach at low tide.

Isla Pacheca. Isla Pacheca, 3 mi north of Contadora, has a lovely white-sand beach and a brown pelican rookery where about 8,000 birds nest, whereas the nearby islets of Pachequilla and Bartolomé have good scuba-diving and snorkeling spots.

WHERE TO EAT

$$ ✕ **Gerald's.** *German.* This restaurant is a short walk from the beach, serves some of the best food on the island, and rents basic rooms. The rooms are in a two-story building behind the restaurant, with high ceilings, TVs, and air-conditioning. The restaurant is a rustic, open-air affair under a high-thached roof, which means it picks up the breeze, if one is blowing. The menu is a mix of fresh fish and seafood dishes, and German standards such as Wiener schnitzel and goulash. They also make a decent pizza. *Average main: $15 ✉ On ridge above landing strip, Isla Contadora ☎ 507/6560–3824 ⊕ www.island-contadora.com.*

WHERE TO STAY

For expanded hotel reviews, visit Fodors.com.

$ **Contadora Island Inn.** *B&B/Inn.* This small B&B occupies a ranch house in a quiet residential neighborhood, just a 10-minute walk from the beach. **Pros:** affordable; quiet; clean. **Cons:** not on the beach. *Rooms from: $85 ✉ Paseo Urraca ☎ 507/6699–4614 ⊕ www.contadoraislandinn.com ⇨ 5 rooms 🍽 Breakfast.*

$$$ **Hotel Punta Galeón.** *Hotel.* Spread along a rocky point, the hotel has a premier location, with captivating ocean views, but it isn't very well maintained. **Pros:** great views; steps away from the beach. **Cons:** needs refurbishing; overpriced. *Rooms from: $180 ✉ North of airstrip, next to Playa Galeón ☎ 507/214–7869, 507/250–4221 ⊕ www.puntagaleonhotel.com ⇨ 48 rooms 🍽 No meals.*

$ ★ **Perla Real Inn.** *B&B/Inn.* This attractive B&B was designed to resemble a Spanish mission, and the owners paid great attention to the details, importing hand-painted tiles and sinks and getting a local carpenter to make replicas of furniture found in southern California missions. **Pros:** tasteful; friendly staff. **Cons:** not on the beach. *Rooms from: $99*

Paseo Urraca 50 507/250–4095, 949/228–8851 in North America www.perlareal.com 4 rooms, 2 suites, 1 villa Breakfast.

$ ★ **Villa Romántica.** *B&B/Inn.* You can't top this small hotel's location, on a ridge overlooking stunning Playa Cacique, just steps away from the beige sand and turquoise waters, but the "romantic" decor of guest rooms—giant hearts, or bas-relief Grecian nudes—may be too much for some travelers. **Pros:** beachfront; good restaurant. **Cons:** some rooms have tacky decor. *Rooms from: $96 Playa Cacique, 200 meters southwest of church 507/250–4067 www.contadora-villa-romantica.com 15 rooms, 2 suites Breakfast.*

SPORTS AND THE OUTDOORS

Contadora Welcome Center. The welcome center across from the air strip rents golf carts, scooters, and bikes for getting around the island. They also rent jet skis, kayaks, and snorkeling equipment, and can arrange boat tours, to explore its marine surroundings. *Across from air strip, Isla Contadora 507/6544–8962 www.contadorapanama.com.*

BEACHES

Because Panama's Pacific tides are extreme, beaches change considerably through the course of the day; what is a wide swath of sand at low tide is reduced to a sliver at high tide. All beaches in Panama are public property, so you can use any of them, no matter what hotel you stay in.

★ **Playa Cacique.** Stretched along a small cove on the south side of the island, Playa Cacique is Contadora's loveliest beach, with pale beige sand backed by tropical trees and vacation homes. The water is calm and clear, making it a decent snorkeling spot, and a popular area for people to moor their boats. You can see Isla Chapera beyond those boats. The Villa Romántica hotel sits on the ridge behind the beach, and its restaurant is a good spot for lunch or a sunset drink. At low tide, you can walk west, around a small bluff, to a smaller beach called **Playa Camarón. Amenities:** food and drink. **Best for:** snorkeling, swimming, sunset.

Playa Ejecutiva. One of Contadora's quietest beaches is Playa Ejecutiva, a few hundred yards north of the church and soccer field. It's a tiny beach that practically disappears at high tide, but the water is calm and safe for swimming, and you can snorkel around the point to the west of it. Its backed by a small forest, which provides convenient shade, and several vacation homes, the owners of which have built a attractive shelter behind the beach for parties. If you visit Contadora on a busy weekend, or holiday, this is a good spot to escape the crowd. **Amenities:** none. **Best for:** solitude, swimming.

★ **Playa Galeón.** Just north of the airstrip and east of the Hotel Punta Galeón, this small beach is one of Contadora's most popular spots. It's where the ferry arrives and departs from, so it can get crowded during the high season. But, it's a good swimming beach, with calm, blue-green water, and it has decent snorkeling. This is a pretty convenient spot to hang out: the hotel's restaurant is next to the beach, Gerald's is just up the hill, and the welcome center, across from the air strip, rents everything from towels and beach umbrellas to jet skis. **Amenities:** food and drink, toilets, water sports. **Best for:** snorkeling, swimming.

Playa Larga. Contadora's longest beach, Playa Larga, stretches along the island's eastern end, in front of the now-demolished Hotel Contadora—the island's original resort. Its a lovely strip of ivory sand, backed by coconut palms, Indian almonds, and other trees, but the ruins of the hotel and the abandoned boat at one end give it a forlorn feel. At high tide, it's a mere sliver of sand, whereas at low tide, massive black rocks are exposed. The water can be murky, so it usually isn't good for snorkeling. **Amenities:** none. **Best for:** solitude, swimming, walking.

Playa Suecas. Hidden in the island's southeast corner, at the end of the road that runs east from Villa Romantica, Playa Sueca (Swedish Beach) is Contadora's officially sanctioned nude beach. It is realatively small, backed by forest, with tan sand sloping into calm, aquamarine waters. At low tide, there are some exposed rocks in front of the beach. Be sure to use plenty of sunscreen on those pale parts! **Amenities:** none. **Best for:** solitude, nudists, swimming.

SCUBA DIVING

The reefs around Contadora have much less coral than you find in the Caribbean, but you can see a lot of fish there, some of which gather in big schools. Isla Pachequilla is one of the area's best dive spots, where you might see rays, moray eels, white-tipped reef sharks, and large schools of jacks. The only problem is visibility, which averages 15 to 30 feet, but sometimes tops 45 feet, especially from June to August, though there is less marine life in the area then.

The best diving is in December and January, when there is decent visibility and large numbers of fish; the worst visibility is from February to April.

Coral Dreams. Coral Dreams offers scuba diving at various dive spots, as well as certification courses and snorkeling excursions. ✉ *Main road, across from airstrip* ☎ *507/6536–1776* 🌐 *coral-dreams.com.*

SPORTFISHING

The fishing around Contadora is quite good, which means you can go out for half a day and stand a decent chance of hooking something. The most common fish in the area are dolphin, jack, tuna, wahoo, roosterfish, and—in deeper water—snapper and grouper. The Contadora Welcome Center can arrange light-tackle fishing charters.

THE CENTRAL PACIFIC COAST

The Central Pacific Coast has Panama's most popular beaches, if not its most beautiful. Due to the organic matter that washes out of rivers along the coast, its beaches tend to have salt-and-pepper sand. The sea is usually calm, but in the rare event that there are significant waves, swimming can be dangerous. The beaches are popular weekend destinations for city folk from December to May, but you may have them to yourself if you visit during the week, especially between May and November.

The Central Pacific beaches range from Coronado, lined with vacation homes and with little access for tourists, to Farallón (aka Playa Blanca), which has the country's largest beach resorts.

PLAYA CORONADO

84 km (52 miles) southwest of Panama City.

Playa Coronado began to develop as a weekend destination for wealthy Panamanians decades ago, and today the coast is almost completely lined with condos and weekend homes, leaving few spots for nonresidents to get onto the beach. The sand here is pale gray with swaths of fine black dirt, which gives it a sort of marbled appearance. It is usually safe for swimming. The big attraction is the 18-hole golf course that is part of the Coronado Golf & Beach Club *(⇨ below)*. One of the country's best golf destinations, the resort gets packed with Panamanian families on weekends and holidays, but is practically dead most weekdays.

GETTING HERE AND AROUND

There is no public transportation to Coronado, but the Coronado Golf & Beach Club provides a shuttle for guests from Panama City. It is also an easy drive; take the Carretera Interamericana west from Panama City one hour, and look for the turnoff next to a large shopping center on the left, just after the town of Chame. You'll have to stop at a guardhouse, then look for the golf resort on the left.

WHERE TO EAT AND STAY

$ × **El Rincón del Chef.** *Latin American.* In colonial-style building on the road to Playa Coronado, this attractive restaurant serves a good variety of quality dishes. The menu changes daily, but always offers a good mix of meat and seafood dishes that feature a mix of Panamanian and international fare. There is invariably *corvina* (sea bass), *langostinos* (prawns), and grilled (rather expensive) USDA-certified beef, including a good burger. The ambience—terra-cotta floors, ocher walls, and a high wooden beams ceiling—is right out of the 19th century, except for the TV and ceiling fans. *Average main: $12* ✉ *Beginning of road to Playa Coronado, on right* ☎ *507/345–2072.*

$$$$ **Coronado Golf & Beach Club.** *Resort.* Both a hotel and a private club, this resort has an 18-hole golf course, tennis courts, a large pool, an equestrian center, and a small beach club a 10-minute drive away. **Pros:** golf course; spacious rooms; ample facilities. **Cons:** not on a beach; very busy on weekends. *Rooms from: $305* ✉ *Playa Coronado, Av. Punta Prieta, left at Brigada de Bomberos, Playa Coronado* ☎ *507/264–3134, 507/264–3164 in Panama City, 866/465–3207 in the U.S.* *www.coronadoresort.com* *78 suites* *No meals.*

SPORTS AND THE OUTDOORS

GOLF

Coronado Golf Course. This 18-hole, par-72 golf course was designed by Tom and George Fazio. Hotel guests pay $98 to play 18 holes on weekends, and $77 on weekdays, golf cart rental included. The course is also open to nonguests, who pay $127 on weekends and $117 on weekdays, golf-cart included. Clubs can be rented and there is a par-27, 9-hole course for beginners and younger golfers. ✉ *Coronado Golf & Beach Club, Av. Punta Prieta Coronado* ☎ *507/240–3137* *www.coronadoresort.com.*

HORSEBACK RIDING

Club Ecuestre Coronado. The Equestrian Club offers guided rides on several breeds of horses. Horseback tour rates range from $30 for half hour on the club's grounds to $155 for a three-hour tour that includes riding on the beach. ✉ *Av. Punta Prieta, Coronado* ☎ *507/240–1434.*

PLAYA SANTA CLARA

115 km (71 miles) southwest of Panama City.

The small beach town of Santa Clara lies just to the east of Playa Blanca. For years, it consisted of a tiny fishing enclave, a handful of vacation homes, and a few budget hotels. It now has the large Sheraton Bijao Beach Resort and surrounding residential development, just to the east of town.

WHERE TO STAY

For expanded hotel reviews, visit Fodors.com.

$$ **Las Sirenas.** *Rental.* An alternative to the all-inclusive resorts that dominate this area, Las Sirenas's beachfront cottages have well-equipped kitchens, making them a good option for a family on a tight budget, or anyone who wants to do it themeselves, and can speak a little Spanish. **Pros:** nice beach; good value; self-catering options. **Cons:** no English spoken; weekend and holidays are packed. $ *Rooms from: $130* ✉ *110 km (66 miles) west of Panama City on Careterra Interamericana, turn left at Santa Clara and bear left at Y, Playa Santa Clara* ☎ *507/993–3235* 🌐 *www.lasirenas.com* *11 bungalows* *No meals.*

$$$$ **Sheraton Bijao Beach Resort.** *All-Inclusive. Resort.* Rooms in the upper floors of this stately resort are steps away from the beach, and have great views of a cascading series of pools and the glistening Pacific, but it suffers the service problems common to the country's all-inclusive resorts. **Pros:** nice rooms; on beach. **Cons:** service inconsistent; food may disappoint. $ *Rooms from: $355* ✉ *109 km (68 miles) west of Panama City on Carretera Interamericana, Playa Santa Clara* ☎ *507/908–3600* 🌐 *www.starwoodhotels.com* *254 rooms, 40 suites* *All-inclusive.*

SPORTS AND THE OUTDOORS

BEACHES

Playa Santa Clara. Playa Santa Clara has the same pale sand with swaths of gray dirt as the adjacent, and more famous, Playa Blanca. The sea here is usually calm enough for swimming, but isn't a good spot for snorkeling. On those rare occasions when there are waves, you shouldn't go in any deeper than your waist, due to the danger of rip currents. Much of the beach is lined with vacation homes, but the Sheraton Bijao Beach Resort towers sits over its eastern end and the rambling Las Veraneras Restaurant sits behind its western end. The western end can get packed, and littered, on holidays and dry-season weekends, but this beach is quiet most of the year. **Amenities:** food and drink; parking ($2); toilets. **Best for:** partiers, swimming, walking. ✉ *111 km (69 miles) west of Panama City on CA 1, Santa Clara.*

PLAYA FARALLÓN (PLAYA BLANCA)

115 km (71 miles) southwest of Panama City.

For years, few people visited this lovely, long stretch of white beach because it lay behind a military base used by Panama's national guard and was restricted. The base saw heavy fighting during the 1989 U.S. invasion, and for much of the 1990s its buildings, pockmarked with bullet holes, were slowly being covered with jungle. Everything changed at the beginning of the 21st century, when the Colombian hotel chain Decameron opened a massive resort here and began promoting it as "Playa Blanca" (White Beach). Panamanians still use the Farallón (*fahr-ah-YOHN*) name. Now the area is the epicenter of beach development in Panama, with several new resorts, two 18-hole golf courses, and a growing number of homes and condos.

GETTING HERE AND AROUND

To drive to Playa Blanca, take the Carretera Interamericana west from Panama City for about 90 minutes and look for the hotel entrances on the left after Santa Clara—the entrance to the Playa Blanca Beach Resort is 2 km (1 mile) after the entrance to the Royal Decameron, and the Buenaventura Beach Resort is several kilometers farther down the same road. All resorts provide shuttle services from Tocumen Airport and Panama City hotels. An international airport was under construction at Farallón in 2012.

WHERE TO STAY

For expanded hotel reviews, visit Fodors.com.

$$$$ **Bristol Buenaventura.** *Resort.* Panama's loveliest beach resort combines elegant rooms and Spanish colonial architecture with an 18-hole golf course and a splendid stretch of sand. **Pros:** gorgeous design and beach; golf course; good restaurants. **Cons:** service inconsistent. $ *Rooms*

RIP-CURRENT KNOW-HOW

Though Central Pacific beaches are usually safe for swimming, rip currents (riptides) are a danger on any beach with waves. Even the strongest swimmer can't fight these currents, but almost anyone can escape one. Swim parallel to shore until you feel that you are no longer heading out to sea, then head toward shore. Rip currents aren't wide, and it is always possible to swim out of them; however, you may be far from shore by the time you do. Don't waste energy swimming against the current. Only swim toward shore when you are free of the rip current.

3

from: $395 ✉ 121 km (75 miles) west of Panama City on CA 1, Playa Blanca ☎ 507/908–3333, 507/264–0000 🌐 www.thebristol.com/buenaventura ⇨ 109 rooms, 5 suites, 4 villas.

$$$ **Royal Decameron Beach Resort, Golf and Casino.** *All-Inclusive. Resort.* Panama's largest, and one of its most attractive, beach resort offers good deals outside of the peak season, but also the food and service problems typical of all-inclusive resorts. **Pros:** great beach and grounds; lots of activities; competitive rates. **Cons:** droves of guests; inconsistent service and food. *$ Rooms from: $212 ✉ 155 west of Panama City on CA 1 ☎ 507/993–2255, 507/294–1900 Panama City sales office 🌐 www.decameron.com ⇨ 852 rooms 🍴 All-inclusive.*

SPORTS AND THE OUTDOORS

GOLF

Mantaraya Golf Club. The club is near the Royal Decameron Beach Resort, but guests at any hotel can play its 18-hole, par-72 golf course, which was designed by Randall Thompson. The greens fee for 18 holes is $58 on weekdays and $79 on weekends and holidays. The greens fee for 9 holes is $42 weekdays and $53 weekends. Cart rental costs $10 for 9 holes and $19 for 18. Club rentals range from $15 to $25, according to their condition. *☎ 507/986–1915 🌐 www.decameron.com.*

WATER SPORTS

Xtreme Adventures. Farallón-based Xtreme Adventures offers all manner of guided beachy activities here and at adjoining Playa Coronado, including horseback riding, jet skiing, parasailing, and waterskiing. ☎*507/993–2823* ⊕*www.extremetourspanama.com.*

THE CORDILLERA CENTRAL

Mountains to the north of the Central Pacific coast offer a refreshing alternative to the hot and deforested lowlands a short drive from the beaches. The massif to the southwest of Panama City, an extinct volcano that was in eruption 5 million years ago, forms the eastern extreme of the Cordillera Central, the country's longest mountain range. On the eastern slope of that verdant mountain is Parque Nacional Altos de Campana; its western slope holds Cerro de la Vieja. The highest point of the range is Cerro Gaital, a forested hill more than 3,500 feet above sea level that towers over El Valle de Antón. Both Cerro de la Vieja and El Valle de Antón are cool and verdant refuges where you can take a break from the lowland heat, explore the mountain forests, and do a bit of bird-watching and hiking. El Valle is a well-established destination with an array of hotels and restaurants, but Cerro la Vieja, to the northeast of Penonomé, has just one eco-lodge.

EL VALLE DE ANTÓN

125 km (78 miles) southwest of Panama City, 28 km (17 miles) north of Las Uvas: the turnoff from Carretera Interamericana.

A serpentine road winds north from the town of Las Uvas, on the Carretera Interamericana between Playa Coronado and Playa Farallón, to a small, lush mountain valley and the town that is sheltered in it, both called El Valle de Antón, commonly referred to as El Valle (The Valley). That verdant valley has a refreshing climate, an abundance of trees and birds, and an array of outdoor activities. Thanks to its altitude of approximately 2,000 feet above sea level, the temperature usually hovers in the 70sF, and at night it often dips down into the 60s. El Valle has long been a popular weekend and holiday destination for Panama City's wealthier citizens, and its roads are lined with comfortable vacation homes with large lawns and gardens. In fact, one of those streets is called *Calle de los Milionarios* (millionaires' row).

The town's Avenida Principal belies the beauty of El Valle's remote corners, with ugly supermarkets and other uninspiring cement-block structures. The attractions for travelers are the flora and fauna of the protected forests north and west of town center, the varied hiking and horseback-riding routes, and the Sunday handicraft market. Since El Valle has long been popular with Panamanian tourists, it has developed some touted but tepid attractions that can be skipped, such as its tiny hot springs, Pozos Termales, and the "square trees," or *arboles cuadrados,* behind the old Hotel Campestre.

GETTING HERE AND AROUND

El Valle is 125 km (75 miles) southwest from Panama City, about two hours by car, on good roads. To drive, take the Carretera Interamericana west for 98 km (59 miles) to Las Uvas, where you turn right and drive 28 km (17 miles) north on a narrow, winding road. Buses to El Valle depart from the Terminal de Buses in Albrook every hour and cost $4, but they take almost three hours. Taxis hang out at the Mercado during the day, and charge $1–$2 for most trips within the valley.

EXPLORING

NORTH AND WEST OF TOWN

★ **Monumento Natural Cerro Gaital** (*Cerro Gaital Natural Monument*). El Valle's northern edge is protected within the 827-acre (335-hectare) nature reserve Monumento Natural Cerro Gaital, which covers the hills of Cerro Gaital, Cerro Pajita, and Cerro Caracoral. Cerro Gaital is a steep, forest-draped hill that towers over the valley's northern edge, rising to a summit of more than 3,500 feet above sea level. The lush wilderness that covers it is home to more than 300 bird species, including such spectacular creatures as the red-legged honeycreeper, bay-headed tanager, and blue-crowned motmot. It also protects the habitat of the rare golden toad (*Atelopus zeteki*), which has almost been wiped out in the wild by a fungal disease. The bird-watching is best along the edges of that protected area, since its lush foliage provides too many hiding places for those feathered creatures, and the terrain is dangerously steep. The areas around El Nispero, Los Mandarinos hotel, and the old Hotel Campestre are excellent for bird-watching. There is a trail into the forest by the ranger post on the right, above the Refugio Ecológico Chorro Macho, approximately 10 kilometers from the church. It requires good shoes and decent physical condition and is best done with a guide.

✉ *Turn right at end of Av. Principal, continue past Canopy Tour, trail on the right* ☎ *507/983–6411* 🎫 *$5* ⏲ *Daily 6–6.*

Piedra Pintada. A short drive to the west of the Mercado, at the end of a rough road and trail, is a simple remnant of El Valle's pre-Columbian culture called Piedra Pintada, a 15-foot boulder, the underside of which is covered with a bizarre collection of ancient petroglyphs. To get there, turn right at the end of the Avenida Principal and left onto the second road after the bridge, then drive to the end of that road, where a foot path heads to the nearby boulder. ⚠ **Cars left at the trailhead have been broken into, so don't leave any valuables in your vehicle, and leave the doors unlocked to avoid broken windows.** ✉ *End of Calle La Pintada* 🎫 *Free* ⏲ *24 hrs.*

★ Fodor'sChoice **Refugio Ecológico del Chorro Macho** (*Chorro el Macho Ecological Reserve*). El Valle's most user-friendly forest experience is available at the small, private Refugio Ecológico del Chorro Macho, west of Cerro Gaital. The reserve has well-kept trails, walking sticks, and the option of hiring a guide at the gate. It belongs to Raúl Arias, who also owns the adjacent Canopy Lodge, and it contains one of El Valle's major landmarks, **El Chorro Macho,** a 115-foot cascade surrounded by lush foliage. You're not allowed to swim beneath the waterfall, but there is a lovely swimming pool fed by river water to the left upon entering the reserve, so bring your bathing suit and a towel. Enter the gate to the left of the main entrance to reach the pool. The refuge has a tour called **Canopy Adventure** (⇨ *Sports and Outdoors, below*), which can take you flying through the treetops and over the waterfall on zip lines strung between platforms high in trees. Most visitors are happy simply to explore the trails that loop through the lush forest past the waterfall and over a small suspension bridge that spans a rocky stream. ✉ *2½ km (1½ miles) northwest of church, at west end of Av. Principal, on left* ☎ *507/983–6547* 🎫 *$3.75, guided hike $37* ⏲ *Daily 8–5.*

IN TOWN

El Nispero. El Nispero (named after a native fruit tree) is a private zoo and plant nursery hidden at the end of a rough dirt road. It covers nearly seven acres at the foot of Cerro Gaital, and its forested grounds are attractive, but most of the animals are in small cages. This is one of the few places you can see the extremely rare golden toad, which has been wiped out in the wild by a fungal disease. Those little yellow-and-black anurans—often mistakenly called frogs—are on display at the **El Valle Amphibian Research Center,** funded by several U.S. zoos. Biologists at the center are studying the fungus that is killing the species (*Batrachochytrium dendrobatidis*), while facilitating the toad's reproduction in a fungus-free environment. The zoo has many other Panamanian species that you are unlikely to see in the wild, such as jaguars, tapirs, collared peccaries (wild pigs), white-faced capuchin monkeys, and various macaw species. Exotic species such as Asian golden pheasants and white peacocks run the grounds. Most of the animals at El Nispero are former pets that were donated, or confiscated from their owners by government authorities. The tapirs, for example, belonged to former dictator Manuel Noriega. ✉ *Calle Carlos Arosemena, 1½ km (1 mile) north of cell tower on Av. Principal* ☎ *507/983–6142* 🎫 *$3, kids $2* ⏲ *Daily 7–5.*

3

Mercado. One traditional tourist attraction worth checking out is the Mercado, an open-air bazaar under a high red roof on the left side of the Avenida Principal, two blocks before the church. The market is most interesting on weekends, especially Sunday mornings, when vendors and shoppers arrive from far and wide. Locals go to the market to buy fresh fruit, vegetables, baked goods, and plants. Handicrafts sold here include the *sombrero pintao* (a traditional straw hat), handmade jewelry, soapstone sculptures, and knickknacks such as the various renditions of El Valle's emblematic golden toad. Even if you don't want to buy anything, it's a colorful, festive affair. Some Panama City tour operators offer a day trip—a long day trip—to the market on Sundays. ✉ *Av. Prinicpal, on left two blocks before church* 🎫 *Free* ⏲ *Daily 8–6.*

WHERE TO EAT

$ **Bruchetta.** *Italian.* This small Italian restaurant next to the lobby of the Anton Valley Hotel has a covered terrace where you can watch the townsfolk roll by. The food is quite good and the menu includes an ample selection of salads and pastas, half a dozen different bruschetta, *corvina* (sea bass), salmon, and beef tenderloin. The nicest seating is on the front terrace, which has a view of the main road and the church, and access to Wi-Fi. $ *Average main: $9* ✉ *Av. Prinicpal* ☎ *507/983–5118* ▭ *No credit cards* ⏲ *Closed Tues.*

★ $$ **Fodor's Choice** ✕ **La Casa de Lourdes.** *Eclectic.* After years of running one of Panama City's most popular restaurants, Lourdes Fabrega de Ward built this elegant place across from her retirement home so that she wouldn't get bored.

It now seems unlikely that she'll ever retire, since old clients and a growing list of new fans pack the place on weekends, drawn by Lourdes' inventive menu and the magical ambience of her Tuscan-style *casa.* Meals are served on a back terrace with views of her garden and Cerro Gaital framed by high columns, arches, and an elegant pool. It is truly a house, and you enter through a spacious living room with couches, a piano, and family photos. She changes her menu frequently, but it always has a good mix of seafood and meat dishes, as well as amazing desserts. Reservations are essential on weekends. *Average main: $17 ✉ Calle El Ciclo, behind Hotel Los Mandarinos, 1.2 (½ mile) km north and 800 meters west of Supermercado Hong Kong ☎ 507/983–6450.*

$ **Restaurante Rincón Vallero.** *Latin American.* This open-air restaurant, a short drive from the main road, is like something out of a fairy tale. There are stone floors, plants everywhere, gold-fish ponds and a stream running between the tables; the food is pretty good, too. The ample menu ranges from traditional Panamanian dishes such as *sancocho* (chicken soup with tropical tubers) and *corvina* (sea bass) prepared various ways, to filet mgnon and chicken cordon bleu—they spell it "gordon blue." There's a playground and a tiny menagerie in the back garden. They also rent rooms, but they're cramped, dark, and musty. *Average main: $10 ✉ Calle Espavel, 1 km (½ mile) south of main road, near Park Eden B&B, El Valle ☎ 507/397–1393.*

WHERE TO STAY

For expanded hotel reviews, visit Fodors.com.

$$$$ **Canopy Lodge.** *B&B/Inn.* Nestled in the forest overlooking the boulder-strewn Guayabo River, this lovely lodge is a mecca for bird watchers, and other nature enthusiasts. **Pros:** gorgeous setting; abundant birds; good guides; friendly staff; quiet setting. **Cons:** expensive; early breakfasts. *Rooms from: $484 ✉ 2 km (1 mile) past church, turn right on road to El Chorro Macho, on left ☎ 507/264–5720 Panama City, 507/983–6837, 800/930–3397 in the U.S. www.canopylodge.com 12 rooms All meals.*

$ **The Golden Frog Inn.** *Rental.* One of the best deals in El Valle, this vacation rental near Cerro Gaital consists of just three suites with kitchenettes and two standard rooms surrounded by 2½ acres of gardens and lovely views. **Pros:** friendly owners; lovely grounds; great views; quiet. **Cons:** no bar or restaurant; 2 km (1 mile) from town. *Rooms from: $95 ✉ 1½ km (1 mile) north of Texaco Station, dirt* *road on right* ☎ *507/983–6117* 🌐 *www.goldenfroginn.com* *2 rooms, 3 suites* ☰ *No credit cards* 🍽 *No meals.*

$$ ★ **Los Mandarinos Boutique Spa and Hotel.** *Hotel.* This attractive hotel and spa, built in the Tuscan style—stone walls, arched doorways, and barrel-tile roofs—has some of the nicest rooms in El Valle. **Pros:** great location; lovely architecture; well-equipped rooms; friendly staff. **Cons:** standard rooms lack views. *Rooms from: $150* ✉ *Calle El Ciclo* ☎ *507/983–6645* ☎ *888/281–8413 toll free in U.S.* 🌐 *www.losmandarinos.com* *25 rooms, 6 suites* 🍽 *Breakfast.*

Park Eden. *B&B/Inn.* This lovely collection of houses and rooms surrounded by manicured gardens, great trees, and a babbling brook has a tranquil, homey feel. **Pros:** friendly owners; nice gardens. **Cons:** far from center of town. *Rooms from: $110* ✉ *Calle Espave, 100 meters south of Rincón Vallero* ☎ *507/983–6167* 🌐 *www.parkeden.com* *6 rooms, 2 suites, 1 cottage* 🍽 *Breakfast.*

SPORTS AND THE OUTDOORS

BIRD-WATCHING

From tiny green hermits to elegant swallow-tailed kites, a remarkable diversity of birds inhabits El Valle's sky and forests. More than 350 bird species have been spotted in the area—compared with 426 species in all of Canada. The best viewing season is October to March, when northern migrants such as the yellow warbler and northern waterthrush boost El Valle's bird diversity. The migrants are especially common in the gardens of the valley's hotels and homes, whereas the forests of Cerro Gaital and surroundings hold such tropical species as the tody motmot and sun bittern. El Valle's avian rainbow includes 5 kinds of toucans, 6 parrot species, and 25 hummingbird species. Though you can only hope to see a fraction of those birds, your chances will be greatly increased if you hire an experienced guide.

Canopy Lodge. Guests at the Canopy Lodge enjoy the services of the area's best birding guides. ☎ *507/983–6837* 🌐 *www.canopylodge.com.*

Mario Bernal. El Valle's most experienced guide is Mario Bernal, who has written a guide to the birds of El Valle. But he is often on the road guiding groups during the dry season. ☎ *507/6693–8213.*

Mario Urriola. The nature guide Mario Urriola, a biologist who owns the Serpentario (a reptile zoo), has trained a cadre of local guides and can arrange bird-watching, general nature, or hiking tours, for surprisingly low rates. ✉ *Serpentario, Calle el Hato* ☎ *507/6569–2676.*

CANOPY TOUR

Canopy Adventure. Adventure seekers will want to try the Canopy Adventure, an installation affiliated with the Canopy Tower Ecolodge in Parque Nacional Soberanía. It takes you—you're strapped in with a very secure harness—flying through the forest canopy and over a 115-foot waterfall via zip-line cables strung between four platforms high in trees. The tour ($54) is in the **Refugio Ecológico del Chorro Macho**, a private reserve a few kilometers northwest of El Valle. This is more adrenaline rush than nature tour, though you do pass through some gorgeous rain forest scenery. The tour takes about 90 minutes and begins with a 30-minute hike to the first platform. ☎ *507/983–6547* 🌐 *www.canopytower.com.*

HIKING

El Valle has enough hiking routes to keep you trekking for days. ■ TIP→ **Hikes are best done early in the morning, when the air is clearer and the birds are more active.** One of the best hiking trips in El Valle is the two- to three-hour hike up **Cerro Gaital,** which passes through lush forest and includes a mirador (lookout point) affording a view of the valley, the Pacific coast, and, on clear days, the Caribbean coast. Another impressive view of El Valle is the one from the **Monte de la Cruz,** a deforested mountain ridge topped by a cement cross on the northwest end of the valley. Both of these trails are reached by heading up the road to El Chorro Macho, with the Cerro Gaital trail on the right, and the Monte de la Cruz trail a continuation of the road itself.

The popular hiking route up and along the **India Dormida** ridge, on the western end of the valley combines treks through patches of forest with scenic views. The trail up the ridge is reached by heading west of town, turning right after the baseball stadium, and left again at the first road.

Because El Valle's trails are not well marked, you should hire a guide for these hikes. Nature guide Mario Urriola (☎ *507/6569–2676*) is the contact person for a group of local guides who can lead you up Cerro Gaital, the India Dormida, and other hiking routes.

HORSEBACK RIDING

Alquiler de Caballos Mitzila. An inexpensive horseback adventure is available from Alquiler de Caballos Mitzila, across from the small church on Calle El Hato, a few blocks before the Hotel Campestre. A horse costs $12 per hour, and each group has to pay an additional $12 per hour for the guide. The most popular ride is around the back of Cerro Gaital, a loop that takes about four hours to complete, though you can also ride for an hour and then come back on the same route. Neither the owner, Mitzila, nor her guides speak English. ⊠ *Calle El Hato* ☎ *507/6646–5813.*

SHOPPING

Artesanía Don Pedro. A handicrafts selection to rival that at the weekly Mercado is available at Artesanía Don Pedro, open seven days a week. ⊠ *Av. Prinicpal, on left 1 block before Mercado* ☎ *507/983–6425.*

Mercado. El Valle is known for its Sunday-morning handicrafts market at the Mercado, a festive affair that brings together vendors and shoppers from far and wide. ⊠ *Av. Prinicpal, on left two blocks before church.*

Chiriquí Province

4

WORD OF MOUTH

"We headed to Boquete. That place is gorgeous. We did a coffee plantation tour and loved learning about the biz."

—Marissa_FoxJensen

www.fodors.com/forums

Updated by Jeffrey Van Fleet

PANAMA'S SOUTHWEST PROVINCE OF CHIRIQUÍ contains the country's most varied scenery. Landscapes that evoke different continents—from alpine peaks to palm-lined beaches—lie mere hours apart. The diverse environments provide conditions for world-class sportfishing, bird-watching, scuba diving, river rafting, horseback riding, hiking, and surfing, making Chiriquí an ideal destination for nature lovers.

Lush cloud forest covers the northern sector of the province. The valleys that flank Volcán Barú—an extinct volcano and Panama's highest peak—have cool mountain climates and unforgettable scenery. Boquete, Bambito, and Cerro Punta are popular with bird-watchers, rafters, and hikers, and have captivating landscapes and charming restaurants and inns. The southern lowlands are less impressive—hot and mostly deforested—and become brown and dusty in the dry season. To the south lies the Golfo de Chiriquí, with dozens of pristine islands and countless acres of coral reef awash with rainbows of marine life, and an opportunity to sample world-class, but little-known, surfing and sportfishing.

ORIENTATION AND PLANNING

GETTING ORIENTED

The provincial capital of David sits centrally located in the lowlands and is no more than two hours from most of Chiriquí's attractions. The Carretera Interamericana skirts David's northern edge, as a four-lane highway. It becomes a two-lane road east of town, where it leads to the town of Chiriquí and to the turnoff for Boca Chica, the gateway to Parque Nacional Marino Golfo de Chiriquí. A 30-minute drive southwest of David takes you to Playa Barqueta; a 40-minute drive north takes you to Boquete. Concepción is a short drive west of David on the Interamericana, and there the road veers north to Volcán, Bambito, and Cerro Punta, bases from which to explore the Barú Volcano. The Costa Rican border at Paso Canoas lies about 20 minutes west on the Interamericana.

PLANNING

WHEN TO GO

The December-to-May dry season is the most popular time to visit Chiriquí since days tend to be sunny in the lowlands. From December to March the valleys of Cerro Punta and Boquete can be cool and windy and may get light rain. In

TOP REASONS TO GO

Misty Mountains. The upper slopes of the Cordillera de Talamanca are draped with lush cloud forest and are usually enveloped in mist. Much of that forest is protected within La Amistad and Barú Volcano National Parks, home to a wealth of wildlife, which can be explored via hiking trails.

Teeming Sea. The Golfo de Chiriquí is home to an amazing array of fish, ranging from colorful king angelfish to the mighty black marlin, making the province an ideal destination for scuba divers and sport fishers alike.

Birds in the Bush. The mountains of Chiriquí are a must-visit for bird-watchers because they hold species found nowhere else in Panama, such as the resplendent quetzal and long-tailed silky flycatcher. From November to April, northern migrants push the bird count to more than 500 species.

Pristine Islands. Between Parque Nacional Marino Golfo de Chiriquí and the Islas Secas, the sea here brims with uninhabited islands: think palm-lined beaches, crystalline waters, and coral reefs a short swim from shore.

Farming Communities. The mountain communities of Boquete, Bambito, and Cerro Punta are surrounded by gorgeous scenery and are distinguished by charming wooden houses, exuberant flower gardens, cozy restaurants, and hotels that combine all of the above.

March and April the mountain valleys are warm and sunny, whereas the lowlands become increasingly dry and brown. It rains just about every day from May to mid-July, but from mid-July to mid-September you can get several sunny days in a row. Again, from mid-September to mid-December it rains almost daily. The water in the Golfo de Chiriquí is clearest for scuba diving and snorkeling from December to July, whereas the surf is best from July to December.

GETTING HERE AND AROUND

AIR TRAVEL

Air Panama flies daily between Panama City and David's Aeropuerto Enrique Malek (DAV). Air Panama has direct flights between David and San José, Costa Rica, three days a week. The airport was undergoing a major expansion in 2012, with the hope of attracting nonstop flights from the United States.

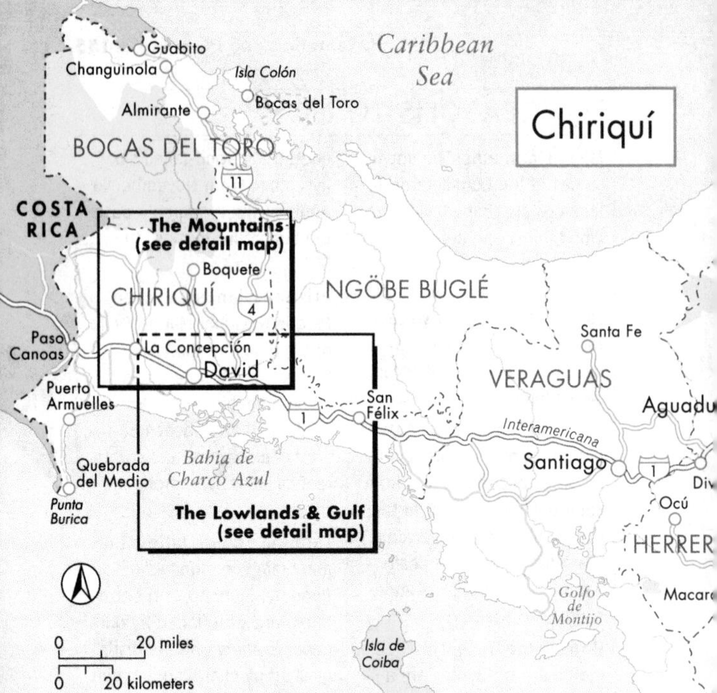

Contacts **Aeropuerto Enrique Malek** ✉ *Av. Reed Gray, 5 km (3 miles) south of David* ☎ *507/721–1072.* **Air Panama** ☎ *507/316–9000* 🌐 *www.flyairpanama.com.*

BUS TRAVEL

Padafont has hourly buses between Panama City's Albrook Terminal and David from 6 am to 8 pm and direct buses at 10:45 pm and midnight. The trip takes about eight hours, with a meal stop in Santiago. Small buses to Boquete, Volcán, Cerro Punta, and Paso Canoas (the border post with Costa Rica) depart every 30 minutes during the day.

Contacts **Padafont** ☎ *507/774–2974.* **Terminal de Buses** ✉ *Av. del Estudiante, one block east of Av. Obaldía, David.*

CAR TRAVEL

A car is the best way to explore Chiriquí as roads are in good repair and well-marked. Avenida Obaldía heads straight north out of David to Boquete as a four-lane highway, no turns required. All other areas are reached via the Carretera Interamericana, which skirts David to the north and east. Most major rental agencies have offices in David and offer 4WD vehicles as well as less expensive standards (sufficient for most trips).

Car-Rental Agencies **Alamo** ✉ *Aeropuerto Enrique Malek, David* ☎ *507/721-0101* 🌐 *www.alamopanama.com.* **Avis** ✉ *Aeropuerto Enrique Malek, David* ☎ *507/721-0884* 🌐 *www.avis.com.pa.* **Budget** ✉ *Aeropuerto Enrique Malek, David* ☎ *507/721-0845* 🌐 *www.budgetpanama.com.* **Hertz** ✉ *Aeropuerto Enrique Malek, David* ☎ *507/721-3345* 🌐 *www.hertzpanama.com.pa.* **National** ✉ *Aeropuerto Enrique Malek, David* ☎ *507/721-0974* 🌐 *www.nationalpanama.com.* **Thrifty** ✉ *Aeropuerto Enrique Malek, David* ☎ *507/721-2477* 🌐 *www.thrifty.com.*

TAXI TRAVEL

It is possible, if a little less convenient, to explore this region without a car. Yellow taxis ply the streets of major tourist centers. Your hotel or restaurant will be happy to arrange transportation for you. In fact, if you want to hike the Sendero los Quetzales, it's best to hire a taxi in Cerro Punta to take you to the trailhead. It only takes about 90 minutes to drive from David to Boca Chica. If you spend a few nights there, you may want to have your hotel arrange a taxi transfer from David.

ABOUT THE RESTAURANTS

You can get a good meal almost anywhere in the province, but Boquete has its best restaurant selection. The specialty in the mountains is local farm-raised trout, but because the Gulf of Chiriquí has such great fishing, seafood is also a good bet. Chiriquí is cattle country, so you'll also find plenty of beef on the menu.

Prices in the reviews are the average cost of a main course at dinner or, if dinner is not served, at lunch.

ABOUT THE HOTELS

Accommodation in Chiriquí ranges from Boquete's affordable B&Bs to the luxurious eco-lodge on the Islas Secas, where the rates approach twice those of any other hotel in the country. The province has some of Panama's best small lodges, many surrounded by tropical nature.

Prices in the reviews are the lowest cost of a standard double room in high season. For expanded hotel reviews, facilities, and current deals, visit Fodors.com.

ESSENTIALS

EMERGENCIES

If you have a medical emergency in Chiriquí, head straight to David, which has a modern hospital. In 2012, plans were underway to open a branch of that hospital in Boquete. Boquete and Volcán have ambulances, and there are police stations in every town.

Emergency Services **Ambulance** ☎ *911.* **Fire** ☎ *911.* **Police** ☎ *911.*

Hospital Chiriquí ✉ *Calle Central and Av. 3 Oeste, David* ☎ *507/774-0128* 🌐 *www.hospitalchiriqui.com.*

MONEY MATTERS

There are ATMs all over David, in front of banks and in the big supermarkets, pharmacies, and gas stations, though they tend to be concentrated around the central plaza and along the Interamericana. There are also ATMs at the banks in the centers of Boquete and Volcán.

SAFETY

Aside from the usual dangers associated with scuba diving and surfing, the province's biggest health concerns are sunburn and hypothermia on the heights of Volcán Barú. If you hike to the summit of Barú, take warm, waterproof clothing, even in the dry season, because the weather can change radically near the peak within an hour.

VISITOR INFORMATION

People at the ATP's regional office (open weekdays 8:30–4:30) in David are amiable but not very helpful. The CEFATI Visitor Center (open daily 9–3:30), on the southern end of Boquete, does a better job. ANAM (the Autoridad Nacional del Ambiente, or the National Environment Authority) is the government entity charged with administering Panama's national parks. Individual park offices are helpful in providing information for your visit.

Tourist Information **ANAM** (*National Environment Authority*). ☎ *507/500-0855 in Panama City* 🌐 *www.anam.gob.pa.* **ATP** ✉ *Av. Domingo Díaz, across from Cable and Wireless, David* ☎ *507/775-2839* 🌐 *www.visitpanama.com.* **CEFATI** ✉ *Av. Central, Av. Central, at south entrance to town, Boquete* ☎ *507/720-4060.*

THE LOWLANDS AND GULF

The torrid lowlands that spread out around David are almost all pasture, and the small towns there are home to the province's traditional Chiricano cowboy culture. The vast Golfo de Chiriquí holds dozens of islands, coral reefs, world-class surf breaks and sportfishing. Although David can serve as a base for gulf trips, it's more easily explored from Boca Chica, Boca Brava, the Islas Secas, or Morro Negrito.

DAVID

440 km (274 miles) west of Panama City, 53 km (33 miles) east of Paso Canoas.

The province's bustling, sweltering capital won't be the Chiriquí you came to see. All services are here, however—at 80,000 inhabitants, lowland David clocks in as Panama's third largest city. With the vagaries of transportation in this region, you may find yourself spending the night here, so we list a few lodgings and services. Whether staying or just passing through, pronounce the city's name the Spanish

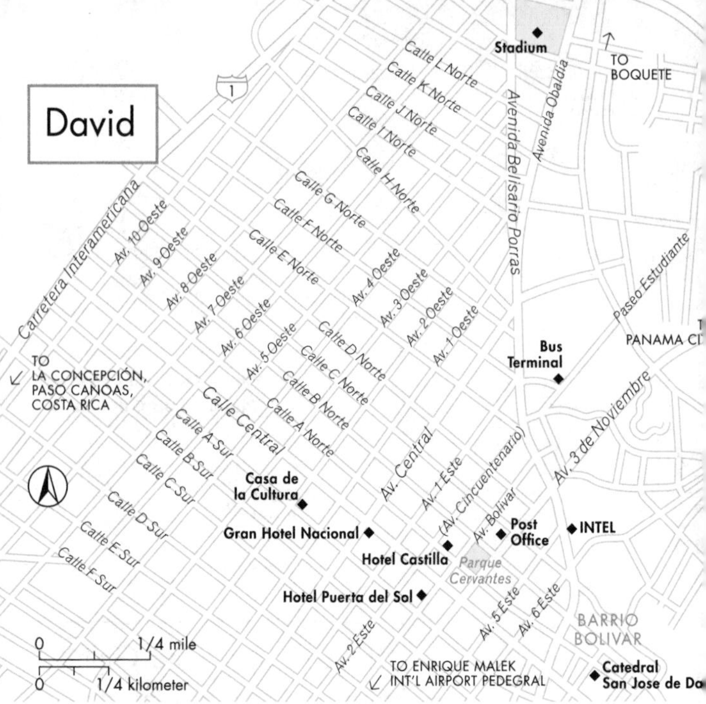

way (Dah-VEED), so that people understand what you're talking about.

GETTING HERE AND AROUND

The 440-km (274-mile) drive between David and Panama City takes about six hours—an easy trip on the Carretera Interamericana that can be done in a day. However, because there are plenty of flights and rental-car companies in David, it isn't worth doing unless you visit destinations such as Santa Catalina en route, because the scenery consists primarily of pastures and unattractive towns.

WHERE TO EAT

$ ✕ **Pizzería Gran Hotel Nacional.** *Italian.* This simple restaurant serves 17 varieties of good pizza, as well as mediocre pastas, many meat and seafood dishes, and inexpensive, three-course lunch specials. The decor is limited to vibrant tablecloths and tacky art, but the place is clean, bright, air-conditioned, and very popular. *Average main: $12* ✉ *Gran Hotel Nacional, Calle Pérez Balladares (Calle Central) at Av. 9 de Enero (Av. Central)* ☎ *507/775–1042.*

$ ✕ **Restaurante Steakhouse.** *Chinese.* Despite the name, this popular place at the edge of town across from the *estadio* (stadium) is really a Chinese restaurant. The spacious dining room has a high ceiling, huge chandeliers, big Chinese prints on the walls, and a flat-screen TV. Locals pack in to feast on *chiau jiam ja* (spicy shrimp in fried noodles), *king tung* (pork ribs with sweet-and-sour sauce), and *langosta estilo cantonés* (lobster medallions stir-fried with vegetables). It's worth the $2 taxi ride to get here. *Average main: $9 Calle Alberto Osorio at Av. 7 Oeste 507/775–8490.*

WHERE TO STAY

For expanded hotel reviews, visit Fodors.com.

4

$ **Gran Hotel Nacional.** *Hotel.* Rooms are spacious, but the decor is dated in David's old standby hotel, popular with foreigners who pass through. **Pros:** pool; spacious rooms; central location; decent restaurants. **Cons:** brusque receptionists at times; rooms facing the street have poor views. *Rooms from: $85 Calle Pérez Balladares (Calle Central) and Av. 9 de Enero (Av. Central) 507/775–2221 507/775–7729 www.hotelnacionalpanama.com 112 rooms, 5 suites Breakfast.*

$ **Hotel Castilla.** *Hotel.* This three-story building located kitty-corner from Parque Cervantes has basic rooms with good beds and small desks at reasonable prices. **Pros:** central location; competitive rates. **Cons:** interior rooms dark; junior suites can be noisy. *Rooms from: $40 Calle Aristides Romero (Calle A Norte) at Calle Bolívar (Calle 3 Este) 507/774–5260 castilladavi@cwpanama.net 62 rooms, 7 suites No meals.*

$$ **Hotel Puerta del Sol.** *Hotel.* Just a five-minute drive from David's Enrique Malek Airport, this clean hotel has rooms that can sleep up to four people, each with cable TV and private bath. **Pros:** large rooms; central location **Cons:** poor views. *Rooms from: $86 Between Av. 3 and Calle Central 507/774–8422 507/775–1662 www.hotelpuertadelsol.com.pa 80 rooms, 6 suites No meals.*

PLAYA LA BARQUETA

26 km (16 miles) southwest of David.

Playa La Barqueta, the closest beach to David, is a long ribbon of dark-gray sand that's popular with local surfers. The area behind the beach is deforested, and the sea is often murky due to a nearby mangrove estuary. Nonetheless, it's a pleasant spot to spend a day or two, and you can stroll for miles without seeing a soul (except during holidays). The beach is public, but a day pass ($10) from the resort,

Hotel Las Olas, includes pool, gym, and bar access. There are also several simple restaurants with inexpensive Panamanian fare. ⚠ **La Barqueta's sand can get hot enough to burn your feet. If the sea is rough there's a risk of rip currents, so don't go in any farther than waist-deep.**

GETTING HERE AND AROUND

The 26-km (16-mile) drive southwest from David to Playa La Barqueta is well marked with signs for Las Olas. Every two hours, buses leave for Playa La Barqueta from the main bus terminal in David.

EXPLORING

Refugio de Vida Silvestre Playa de la Barqueta Agrícola (*Playa La Barqueta Agricultural Wildlife Refuge*). Five sea-turtle species nest on Playa la Barqueta, and 14 km (8½ miles) of the beach's eastern half lies within this wildlife refuge. From June to November, olive ridley, hawksbill, loggerhead, and green sea turtles nest on the beach; massive leatherback turtles and olive ridleys nest from November to March. The turtles crawl onto the beach at night and bury their eggs in the sand; two months later eggs hatch and baby turtles dig their way out and scurry to the sea. The best time to look for nesting turtles is high tide, preferably when the moon is a mere crescent, though you may find hatchlings on the beach any afternoon from August to January. To look for nesting turtles, you must pay an admission fee ($5) and get a permit during the day at the Ranger Station just east of the Las Olas Beach Resort. ☎ *507/6716–8301, 507/6524–9421.*

WHERE TO STAY

For expanded hotel reviews, visit Fodors.com.

$ **Las Olas Beach Resort.** *Resort.* Ample diversions are yours at this small beach resort, including four pools, massages, and surfing lessons, as well as volleyball and tennis courts, boogie boards, and horseback riding. **Pros:** beachfront; wildlife refuge; ample facilities. **Cons:** mediocre beach; can be dead during low season. *Rooms from: $75* ☎ *507/772–3000, 831/920–4866 in U.S.* ⊕ *www.lasolasresort.com* *47 rooms* *No meals.*

SPORTS AND THE OUTDOORS

SURFING

Playa La Barqueta has the best surf near David, with various beach breaks.

Playa Sandía. Serious surfers will want to go west of La Barqueta to Playa Sandía, which has a beach break and a long right in front of the estuary at the west end of the beach.

Punta Burica. Few surfers get to isolated Punta Burica, a three-hour trip down the beach south from Puerto Armuelles. It's accessible only at low tide and with a 4WD vehicle.

BOCA CHICA AND ISLA BOCA BRAVA

54 km (32 miles) southeast of David.

Long a sleepy fishing port at the end of a bone-rattling road, Boca Chica now has a paved road and a small selection of hotels that serve the islands of Parque Nacional Marino Golfo de Chiriquí. The town is on a peninsula overlooking the nearby island of Boca Brava. Together, they define the eastern edge of a mangrove estuary that extends all the way to Playa La Barqueta. Neither the island nor the mainland has great beaches. The attractions are beyond Boca Brava on the uninhabited islands of the Parque Nacional Marino Golfo de Chiriquí (⇨ *below*), a 40-minute boat ride away. Beyond them lie world-class sportfishing and diving around the Islas Ladrones and Islas Secas.

GETTING HERE AND AROUND

The Panama Big Game Fishing Club and Cala Mia have boat transport (60 minutes) for guests from the Pedregal marina near David. It's more expensive than by land, but more pleasant and takes half the time. It takes about 90 minutes to drive from David to Boca Chica; go east on the Carretera Interamericana for 39 km (24 miles), then turn right at the intersection for Horconcitos. Most hotels arrange transfers from the David airport.

WHERE TO STAY

For expanded hotel reviews, visit Fodors.com.

★ Fodor'sChoice **Cala Mia.** *B&B/Inn.* Bungalows at this Boca
$$$ Brava eco-lodge are tastefully decorated and have terraces with couches, hammocks, and tree-shrouded water views. **Pros:** gorgeous design and location; trips to islands; natural food; friendly staff. **Cons:** isolated; no-see-ums can be a problem. *Rooms from: $240* ✉ *Isla Boca Brava* ☎ *507/851–0059* ⊕ *www.boutiquehotelcalamia.com* *11 bungalows* *Closed Oct.* *Breakfast.*

$$ **Gone Fishing.** *Resort.* Though fishing is an option here, this is really a waterfront hotel that offers various activities. **Pros:** great view; nice pool. **Cons:** bugs can be a problem; occasional noise from common areas. *Rooms from: $115* *On left before town* *507/851–0104, 786/393–5882 in U.S.* *www.gonefishingpanama.com* *5 rooms* *No meals.*

$$$$ **Panama Big Game Fishing Club.** *All-Inclusive. Hotel.* This small lodge on Boca Brava, just across the channel from Boca Chica, is all about sportfishing, and it's some of the country's best. **Pros:** small and intimate setting; great fishing; good food. **Cons:** no pool; nothing for nonfishers, although get break in rates; bugs can be a problem; four-night minimum. *Rooms from: $1420* *Isla Boca Brava* *507/6674–4824, 866/281–1225 in U.S.* *www.panamabiggamefishingclub.com* *4 bungalows* *All-inclusive.*

$$$ ★ **Seagullcove Lodge.** *B&B/Inn.* This hillside hotel sports Mediterranean decor with its arched doorways, terra-cotta flooring, and manicured gardens. **Pros:** great views of the bay; good food; friendly service. **Cons:** steep stairs; small grounds; bugs can be a problem. *Rooms from: $180* *On left just before town* *507/851–0036, 786/735–1475 in the U.S.* *www.seagullcovelodge.com* *5 bungalows* *Breakfast.*

SPORTS AND THE OUTDOORS

SCUBA DIVING AND SNORKELING

Boca Chica is the most convenient base for scuba-diving and snorkeling trips to Parque Nacional Marino Golfo de Chiriquí *(⇨ below)* and to Islas Ladrones and Islas Secas *(⇨ below)*.

SPORTFISHING

The Gulf has superb fishing, especially around the Islas Montuosos and Hannibal Bank. The best fishing is for black marlin and sailfish from January to April. Find huge yellowfin tuna from March to May; dolphin (the fish, not the mammal) abound from November to January. From July to January it's roosterfish and wahoo; catch amberjacks, mackerel, snapper, and grouper year-round.

Gone Fishing. Gone Fishing *(⇨ Where to Stay, above)* offers deep-sea charters or less-expensive inshore fishing that start at $700. *www.gonefishingpanama.com.*

Panama Big Game Fishing Club. Panama Big Game Fishing Club *(⇨ Where to Stay, above)* includes daily fishing trips to the gulf's best spots in their rates. *www.panamabiggamefishingclub.com.*

GOLFO DE CHIRIQUÍ ISLANDS

The vast Gulf of Chiriquí holds dozens of uninhabited islands surrounded by healthy coral formations and excellent conditions for surfing, diving, and fishing. You can base yourself in the Boca Chica/Boca Brava area *(⇨ above)* to explore these islands, but there are also two gulf-island resorts that provide more immediate access. Isla Ensenada, in the gulf's northeast corner, is near five of the country's best and most remote breaks, accessed from the Morro Negrito Surf Camp. The beautiful, remote **Islas Secas** (Dry Islands), a 16-isle archipelago 35 km (21 miles) from the coast, has one luxury eco-lodge but can be visited from Boca Chica or Boca Brava.

GETTING HERE AND AROUND

Transportation to Golfo de Chiriquí lodges is provided by the lodges. The Parque Nacional Marino Golfo de Chiriquí, Islas Secas, and Islas Ladrones can be visited on day trips from Boca Chica and Boca Brava via boat.

Parque Nacional Marino Golfo de Chiriquí (*Chiriquí Marine National Park*). The 36,400 acres of the Parque Nacional Marino Golfo de Chiriquí include more than 20 islands—all but one of which are uninhabited. The islands' beaches are the nicest in Chiriquí Province, with pale sand, clear waters, tropical dry forest, and colorful reef fish just a shell's toss from shore. The loveliest are the palm-lined strands of **Isla Parida** (the largest in the archipelago), **Isla San José, Isla Gamez,** and **Isla Bolaños,** where the sand is snow-white. Various species of sea turtle nest on the islands' beaches, and the water holds hundreds of species including lobsters, moray eels, and schools of parrot fish. You may also see frigate birds, brown pelicans, and green iguanas. Dolphins sometimes cruise the park's waters, and from August to October you may spot humpback whales. There are no lodging facilities; visit on day trips from Boca Chica, 30 to 60 minutes away, depending on the island. ✉ *12 km (7 miles) southwest of Boca Chica* ☎ *507/775–3163 in David* 🎟 *$5* ⏲ *Daily 8–6.*

WHERE TO STAY

For expanded hotel reviews, visit Fodors.com.

★ Fodor's Choice **Islas Secas Resort.** *Resort.* Constant exposure
$$$$ to the bounties of nature, gourmet food, spa services, and other pampering are what you get at this all-inclusive luxury eco-lodge on the Islas Secas. **Pros:** gorgeous, remote loca-

tion; excellent scuba diving; high-end sports equipment; gourmet food. **Cons:** extremely expensive; hard to get to; may be closed during rainy season. *Rooms from: $1350* ✉ *Islas Secas* ☎ *800/377–8877 in U.S.* 🌐 *www.islassecas.com* *7 rooms* *All meals.*

$ **Morro Negrito Surf Camp.** *Hotel.* California surfer Steve Thompson built this basic lodge on a coastal island in the gulf's northeast corner. This simple lodge is near 10 excellent breaks that are usually ridden only by the two-dozen surfers the camp accommodates. **Pros:** great waves with few surfers. **Cons:** basic rooms; shared bathrooms; cold-water showers; bugs can be a problem. *Rooms from: $80* ✉ *Isla Ensenada* ☎ *507/832–2831, 760/632–8014 in U.S.* 🌐 *www.panamasurfcamp.com* *12 rooms, 1 with bath* *All meals.*

SPORTS AND THE OUTDOORS

SCUBA DIVING AND SNORKELING

The Islas Secas and Islas Ladrones are surrounded by more than 50 excellent dive sites, with visibility averaging 70 feet and healthy coral formations surrounded by hundreds of fish species and comparable invertebrate diversity. You might see various species of sea stars and angelfish, elegant Moorish idols, frog fish, and sea turtles.

The **Islas Secas Resort** (⇨ *above*) lies in the middle of the archipelago's coral gardens, and daily scuba dives and snorkeling are included in the rates. Those islands can also be visited on day trips from the Morro Negrito Surf Camp or the Boca Chica/Boca Brava lodges.

SURFING

The Golfo de Chiriquí has some undervisited, remote surf breaks. Surfing is best from June to December when waves consistently break overhead, and faces sometimes reach 20 feet.

Emily. The most convenient wave for guests at the Morro Negrito Surf Camp is Emily, a left that breaks over the reef right in front of the camp. ✉ *Isla Ensenada.*

Nestles. Advanced surfers enjoy the rush of Nestles, a big reef break in front of Isla Silva de Afuera. ✉ *Isla Silva de Afuera.*

P Land. P Land is a year-round left reef break on Isla Silva de Afuera, good for intermediate and advanced surfers. ✉ *Isla Silva de Afuera.*

The Point. The most impressive wave in the gulf is The Point, a tubular reef break that has surfers booking several weeks at the Morro Negrito Surf Camp year after year. ✉ *Isla Ensenada.*

The Sandbar. This long break, which has both lefts and rights, is popular with intermediate surfers and beginners. ✉ *Isla Silva de Afuera.*

PLAYA SANTA CATALINA

190 km (114 miles) east of David, 360 km (223 miles) southwest of Panama City.

★ **Fodor'sChoice** Literally at the end of the road, the tiny fishing village of Santa Catalina sits near some of the best surfing spots in the country and is the closest port to Isla Coiba, Panama's top dive destination. For years, the only people who visited Playa Santa Catalina, technically outside Chiriquí in the province of Veraguas, were adventurous surfers who made the long trip here on rough roads and slept in rustic rooms for the pleasure of riding La Punta, a right point break. The roads and accommodations are better now, and two dive centers have opened. Never fear: This is still a quiet beach town, and you come here to enjoy ocean views through the palm fronds, friendly locals, cheap seafood, and amazing surf and diving.

GETTING HERE AND AROUND

It takes about six hours to drive to Santa Catalina from Panama City, driving west on the Carretera Interamericana to Santiago, and then southwest, via Soná, the 110 km (68 miles) to Playa Santa Catalina.

WHERE TO EAT AND STAY

For expanded hotel reviews, visit Fodors.com.

$ ✕ **Pinguino Cafe.** *Italian.* Smack at the end of the main road to Santa Catalina, this beachside restaurant has a fine selection of seafood and Italian dishes, with recipes for *pollo a la scalopina* and *filete de pescado a la mediterránea* taken straight from the cookbook of the Italian owner's mother. With a great sunset view of the bay at Playa Santa Catalina, finer dining in a more sandals-optional location won't be found. *Average main: $6* ✉ *End of Carretera Nacional, right side facing the beach* ▭ *No credit cards.*

$ **La Buena Vida.** *B&B/Inn.* Charming fauna-themed villas showcase the U.S. owners' attention to detail at this small lodge. **Pros:** central location close to dive shops, beach, and restaurants; great value. **Cons:** often booked full. *Rooms from: $66* ✉ *Carretera Nacional, on left in front of school* ☎ *507/6635–1895* 🌐 *www.labuenavida.biz* *3 rooms* *No credit cards* *No meals.*

$ **Oasis Surf Camp.** *Resort.* This rustic, Italian-owned lodge is right on Playa Santa Catalina, amid the coconut palms and mere steps from the surf. **Pros:** on the beach; laid-back atmosphere; good food. **Cons:** basic rooms; you have to wade through or cross in an adequate vehicle a shallow river to reach property; impossible to find space over Panamanian holidays. *Rooms from: $45* ✉ *Playa Catalina* ☎ *507/6588–7077* 🌐 *www.oasissurfcamp.com* *10 rooms* *No meals.*

SPORTS AND THE OUTDOORS

SCUBA DIVING AND SNORKELING

Playa Santa Catalina is the closest embarkation point to Isla Coiba *(⇨ below)*, which has Panama's best scuba diving, but there are numerous other spots nearby. Visibility and sea conditions can change from one day to the next, but in general the diving is better during the rainy season than during the dry season. Many of the dive spots around Isla Coiba require ocean-diving experience, but some closer to town are appropriate for novices or for snorkeling. Within an hour of Santa Catalina are dive sites such as **Punta Pargo** and **Palo Grande,** where you might see moray eels, parrot fish, various types of puffers, and big schools of jacks, among other things.

Coiba Dive Center. Coiba Dive Center offers the complete slate of PADI courses, as well as multiday diving excursions to Isla Coiba with overnight stays in the National Environment Authority (ANAM) cabins. ✉ *Calle Principal, on right before beach* ☎ *507/6780–1141* 🌐 *www.coibadivecenter.com.*

Scuba Coiba. Santa Catalina's first dive center offers boat dives at dozens of nearby spots and multiday trips to Isla Coiba with overnights in the ANAM cabins there. They also offer PADI certification courses and snorkeling/beach trips to other nearby islands as well. ✉ *Calle Principal, on left before beach* ☎ *507/6980–7122* 🌐 *www.scubacoiba.com.*

SURFING

Isla Cebaco. An excellent alternative to the coastal breaks is Isla Cebaco, a 90-minute boat ride from Santa Catalina, which has both a beach break and point break.

La Punta. Santa Catalina's legendary point break, known simply as La Punta, is one of the country's best. The waves break over a rock platform in front of a point just east of town, forming both lefts and rights, though the rights are more hollow and longer. It is best surfed from mid- to high tide and usually needs a four- to five-foot swell to break. When a good swell rolls in, the faces can get as big as 15 to 20 feet.

Panama Surf Tours. Panama Surf Tours offers five- and eight-day surf packages that include a guide and transportation to and from Playa Santa Catalina. The company also offers lessons and surf tours in other parts of Panama. ☎ *507/6671–7777* 🌐 *www.panamasurftours.com.*

Playa Santa Catalina. An easier alternative to La Punta is the nearby beach break at Playa Santa Catalina, which is usually smaller and less treacherous.

Punta Brava. If La Punta is too small or crowded, a 30-minute hike west of town takes you to Punta Brava, where a fast left tubes over a rocky bottom. The waves here are often bigger than at La Punta, but it can only be surfed from low to mid-tide.

PARQUE NACIONAL COIBA

50 km (31 miles) southwest of Santa Catalina.

GETTING HERE AND AROUND

Most people visit Isla Coiba on fishing, diving, or nature tours offered by the companies listed above. It is possible to organize your own trip, in which case you would hire a boat in Playa Santa Catalina. Most fishermen there charge about $200 for a day trip to Isla Coiba, and more if they must stay overnight on the island.

★ Fodor's Choice **Parque Nacional Coiba.** Remote and wild, Panama's largest island and one of the world's largest marine parks offers the country's best scuba diving, world-class fishing, and palm-lined beaches. About 80% of the island is covered with tropical dry forest, home to an array of wildlife.

Isla Coiba began its human history as a penal colony—it was Panama's version of Devil's Island—where 3,000 convicts toiled on farms carved out of the dry forest, growing food for the country's entire prison system. The Panamanian government declared the island a national park in

1991, but it took more than a decade to relocate the prisoners. Parque Nacional Coiba now protects 667,000 acres of sea and islands, of which Isla Coiba itself constitutes about 120,000 acres.

The marine life of the park is as impressive as that of the Galápagos. The extensive and healthy reefs are home to comical frog fish, sleek rays, and massive groupers. The national park holds more than 4,000 acres of reef, composed of two-dozen different types of coral and 760 fish species. The park's waters are also visited by 22 species of whale and dolphin, including killer whales and humpback whales, fairly common there from July to September.

The wildlife on Coiba doesn't compare to that on the Galápagos, but its forests are home to howler monkeys, agoutis (large rodents), and 150 bird species, including the endemic Coiba spinetail, the rare crested eagle, and the country's biggest population of endangered scarlet macaws. Several trails wind through the island's forests; the **Sendero de los Monos** (Monkey Trail), a short boat trip from the ranger station, is the most popular. Crocodiles inhabit the island's extensive mangrove swamps, and sea turtles nest on some beaches from April to September. The most popular beach in the park is on the tiny **Granito de Oro** (Gold Nugget) island, where lush foliage backs white sand, and good snorkeling lies a short swim away.

Options for visiting Isla Coiba range from a day trip out of Playa Santa Catalina to one-week tours, or small-ship cruises that include on-board lodging. The National Environment Authority (ANAM) offers accommodations ($20 per bed; five beds per building) in air-conditioned cement buildings with communal kitchen—you have to bring your own food—near the ranger station. There is also space for 15 campers ($10 per two-person tent). Reserve at least a month ahead of time during the dry season. ☎ *507/998–4271 in Santiago* 🎫 *$20.*

SPORTS AND THE OUTDOORS

SCUBA DIVING AND SNORKELING

Isla Coiba has Panama's best scuba diving, and some of the best diving in Central America, with vast reefs inhabited by hundreds of species of fish. On any given dive there you may see spotted eagle rays, white-tip reef sharks, sea turtles, giant snapper and grouper, moray eels, stargazers, frog fish, pipefish, angelfish, and Moorish idols. The reefs hold plenty of invertebrates, whereas offshore pinnacles attract big schools of jacks, Pacific spadefish, and other species.

Among the park's best dive spots are **Santa Cruz,** a vast coral garden teeming with reef fish; **Mali Mali,** a submerged rock formation that is a cleaning station for large fish; **La Viuda,** a massive rock between Islas de Coiba and Canales that attracts major schools of fish; and **Frijoles,** submerged rocks where divers often see sharks, large eels, and manta rays. Many of the dive spots around Isla Coiba require a bit of ocean-diving experience, but there are also dive spots that are appropriate for novices and good snorkeling areas.

Eco Circuitos. Eco Circuitos, based in Panama City, has a one-week snorkeling and hiking tour to Isla de Coiba with overnights in the ANAM cabins and in Santa Catalina. ☎ *507/315–1305, 800/830–7142 in U.S.* ⊕ *www.ecocircuitos.com.*

Scuba Coiba. Santa Catalina's Scuba Coiba are the local experts, offering boat dives at dozens of spots in the park on trips with overnights in the ANAM cabins. ✉ *Santa Catalina* ☎ *507/6980–7122* ⊕ *www.scubacoiba.com.*

SPORTFISHING

Catch-and-release fishing is permitted inside Coiba National Park, but the fishing is just as good outside the park. Blue marlin, black marlin, and Pacific sailfish run here in significant numbers from December to April, with January to March being the peak months. The area also holds legions of wahoo, dolphin (mahimahi), and tuna, which often run bigger than 200 pounds. The fishing is less spectacular from April to December, but there are still plenty of roosterfish, mackerel, amberjack, snapper, and grouper. Some of the area's best fishing is around **Isla Montousa** and the **Hannibal Banks,** 65 to 80 km (40 to 50 miles) west of Isla Coiba.

Coiba Adventure Sport Fishing. Captain Tom Yust's Coiba Adventure Sportfishing runs fishing tours around Isla Coiba on a 31-foot Bertram, or a 22-foot Mako, with overnights at the ANAM cabins. ☎ *800/800–0907 in U.S.* ⊕ *www.coibadventure.com.*

Panama Yacht Tours. Panama Yacht Tours, based in Panama City, offers fishing tours to the waters around Isla Coiba with overnighters at the ANAM cabins or land-based stays at more upscale lodges in Santa Catalina. ☎ *507/6614–1114* ⊕ *www.panamayachtours.com.*

Pesca Panama. Pesca Panama offers one-week fishing tours to the waters west of Isla Coiba with overnights on a barge near David. ☎ *800/946–3474* 🌐 *www.pescapanama.com.*

THE MOUNTAINS

Nestled in the Cordillera de Talamanca, which towers along the province's northern edge, are the lush mountain valleys of Boquete, Cerro Punta, and Bambito, each with unique scenery. The mountain range's upper slopes are covered with lush cloud forest, which is kept wet by the mist that the trade winds regularly push over the continental divide. That mist not only keeps the landscape green, it creates the perfect conditions for rainbows, commonly sighted during the afternoon. Mountain streams feed half a dozen rafting rivers up here, and abundant forests are excellent areas for bird-watching, hiking, horseback riding, or canopy tours. The area's captivating beauty and charming restaurants and inns make it a favorite among many visitors to Panama.

BOQUETE

38 km (24 miles) north of David.

This pleasant town sits at 3,878 feet above sea level in the always springlike valley of the Río Caldera. The surrounding mountains are covered with forest and shade coffee farms, where coffee bushes grow amidst tropical trees. It's superb for bird-watching, and the roads and trails can be explored on foot, horseback, mountain bike, or four wheels.

Though the surrounding countryside holds most of Boquete's attractions, the town itself is quite appealing, with tidy wooden houses and prolific flower gardens. Around 30,000 people live here, most of them scattered around the valley. The town center holds a simple *parque central* (central park), officially the Parque de las Madres, surrounded by shops, the town hall, and roads lined with patches of pink impatiens and the pale trumpetlike flowers of the Datura, also known as jimson weed or devil's trumpet. Streams meander through town, and the Río Caldera flows through a wide swath of boulders along its eastern edge.

Make no mistake though: Boquete is booming these days as one of Panama's top real estate destinations. Among the population are now several thousand foreigners who have chosen to make the town their new (or second) home. With a four-lane highway heading out from David and the

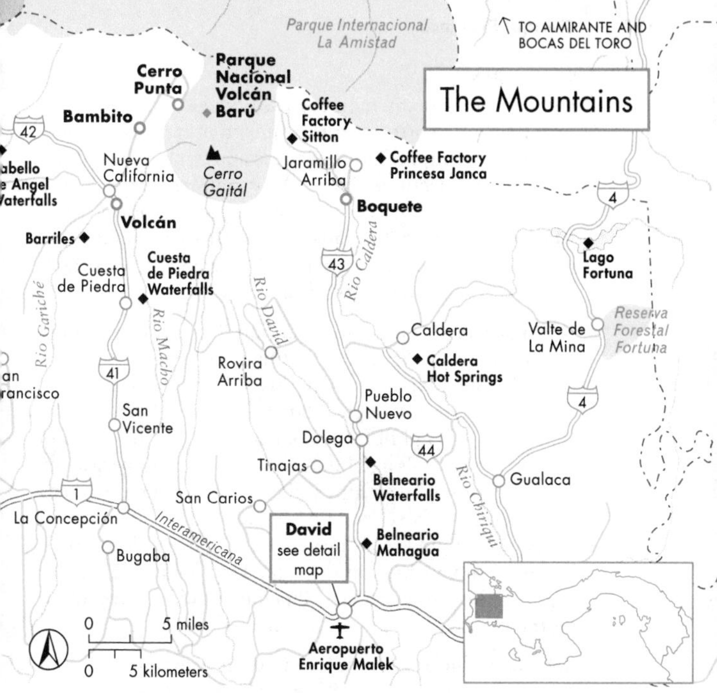

coming expansion of that city's airport, growth is expected to continue, which longtime residents have mixed feelings about.

GETTING HERE AND AROUND

It's an easy 45-minute drive to Boquete from David, where you follow Avenida Obaldía north, which becomes a four-lane highway. Buses depart from David's terminal every 30 minutes and take about 60 minutes to reach Boquete.

Boquete's local transportation is via vans that depart regularly from Avenida Central just north of the parque central for either the Alto Quiel/Bajo Mono loop or the Alto Lino/Palo Alto loop. They pick up and drop off passengers anywhere en route for $1. Taxis wait around the parque central and charge $1–$5 for valley trips.

Contacts **Boquete Shuttle Service.** Boquete Shuttle Service runs direct transfers between hotels in Boquete and David's airport for $10. ☎ *507/720–1635* 🌐 *www.aventurist.com.* **Daniel Higgins.** Daniel Higgins is an English-speaking driver who'll take you to David, Boca Chica, or Cerro Punta. He can also drive you to or from Almirante, the gateway to Bocas del Toro, for $150; it's a beautiful four-hour drive. ☎ *507/6617–0570.*

EXPLORING

Unlike most Panamanian towns, Boquete was settled by European and North American immigrants at the beginning of the 20th century. This lineage is apparent in everything from the architecture to the faces of many residents. Plenty of Ngöbe people migrate to Boquete from the northeast of Chiriquí to work in the orange and coffee harvests. Recently the valley has become popular with foreign retirees, drawn by the climate and beauty of the area.

★ **Bajo Mono Road.** The road, near San Ramón, leads to the trailhead for the **Sendero Los Quetzales** *(⇨ Cerro Punta, below)*, which winds its way through the forest between Cerro Punta and Boquete. Start that hike in Cerro Punta, though; it's all uphill from Boquete. Head to Bajo Mono to look for quetzals and hundreds of other bird species; the best area for bird-watching is the beginning of the Sendero Los Quetzales, above the Alto Chiquero ranger station. Two other good hiking trails head off of the Bajo Mono road: the **Sendero Culebra,** on the right 1½ km (1 mile) up the road to Alto Chiquero, and **Pipeline Road,** a gravel track on the left that leads to a canyon and waterfall.

Café Ruiz. The Ruiz family has been growing coffee in Boquete since the late 1800s, and their coffee-roasting and packaging plant just south of Mi Jardín Es Su Jardín offers a 45-minute tour that includes a taste of the coffee on sale here. A full three-hour tour visits the family farm and processing plant in the mountains above town. Because it has plenty of trees and uses few chemicals, the farm is a good place to see birds. Do the tour in the morning between October and May, during harvest. Reserve a tour by phone or via the Web site. ✉ *Av. Central, ½ km (¼ mile) south of park, on right* ☎ *507/720–1000* 🌐 *www.caferuiz.com* 🎫 *Plant tour $9, coffee-tasting tour $20, full tour $30* ⊙ *Mon.–Sat. 8–12 and 1–4.*

CEFATI Information Center. If you're driving, stop at the town's official visitor center, on the right at the BOQUETE arch at the south entrance to town. The center offers free information on local sights and services, but the main reason to stop is to admire the view of the Boquete Valley. The building also has a small café and gift shop. ⚠ **Beware of any businesses that advertise themselves as a "Tourist Center" or "Visitor Center" near the main park on Avenida Central. Unlike CEFATI, they operate solely on commission and generally steer travelers toward operations for which they can increase**

service rates. Additionally, their information and prices are not always reliable. ✉ *Av. Central, at south entrance to town* ☎ *507/720–4060* ⏲ *Daily 9:30–5:30.*

★ Fodor's Choice **Finca Lérida.** On the eastern slope of Volcán Barú, this coffee farm encompasses nearly 650 acres of bird-filled cloud forest. The farm is recommended in *A Guide to the Birds of Panama* as the place to see quetzals, and that's practically a guarantee between February and June. You may also see silver-throated tanagers, collared trogons, clorophonias, and about 150 other species. The farm's resident guide can take you along its 10 km (6 miles) of hiking trails, one leading to a small waterfall, or you can explore them on your own. The guide is invaluable if you're looking for quetzals. The coffee tour here gives you insight into the harvesting and processing of Boquete's most famous product. The farm has a great view and a moderately priced restaurant ($–$$) serving Panamanian food, homemade desserts, and fresh-roasted coffee. ✉ *7 km (4 miles) northwest of second Y, via Callejón Seco, Alto Quiel* ☎ *507/720–2285* 🌐 *www.fincalerida.com* 🎟 *$10, coffee tour $25, guided hike or bird-watching $65* ⏲ *Daily 7 am–8 pm.*

Kotowa Coffee Tour. In the hills of Palo Alto, this farm produced one of Boquete's best coffees, available at a small chain of coffee shops. The farm still has the original coffee mill from 1920. Today the Kotowa Estate is recognized for its innovation such as burning coffee bean husks for fuel. Tours provide a close look at the cultivation, harvest, and processing of coffee. Go during the October-to-May harvest and reserve your tour a day in advance for free transport from your hotel. ✉ *Palo Alto* ☎ *507/720–3852* 🌐 *www.coffeeadventures.net* 🎟 *Tour $35* ⏲ *Tour Mon.–Sat. at 2 pm by reservation.*

Mi Jardín Es Su Jardín (*My Garden Is Your Garden*). A few blocks north of the parque central, Avenida Central veers left at a "y" in the road. Just past the junction is a garden surrounding an eccentric Panamanian's vacation home. Cement paths wind past vibrant flower beds and bizarre statues of animals and cartoon characters, which make this place a minor monument to kitsch. ✉ *Av. Central ½ km (¼ mile) north of park, on right* 🎟 *Free* ⏲ *Daily 9–5.*

4

CLOSE UP

The Quetzal and the Cloud Forest

Central American cloud forests remain the natural habitat of the resplendent quetzal (Pharomachrus mocinno), one of six quetzal species, and the forests above Boquete are one of the best places in the world to see this elusive creature. The quetzal has been revered since the days of the ancient Maya, who called it the winged serpent. Although the female quetzal is attractive, the male, with its distinctive crimson belly, blue-green back, and long tail, is spectacular. Though a mature bird stands just 14 inches tall (think "robin" for body size), male quetzals have two- to three-foot tail feathers that float behind them and more than double their length. Its unforgettable appearance notwithstanding, the quetzal can be difficult to spot in the lush foliage of the cloud forest. You might want to hire a local birding guide who can take you to spots where they commonly feed, or reproduce during the February to June nesting season. (In the spirit of equality between the sexes, male and female take turns incubating the eggs.) Even if you have little interest in bird-watching, taking a tour to Finca Lérida or one of the other spots above Boquete where quetzals are common, is highly recommended. Though you may not catch a glimpse of the legendary resplendent quetzal, you're bound to see dozens of other spectacular birds, and the quetzal's cloud-forest habitat is a magically beautiful ecosystem. If you do catch a glimpse of this bird-watcher's Holy Grail, consider yourself fortunate.

WHERE TO EAT

$ × **El Oasis.** *International.* Perched on the banks of Caldera River, this pleasant restaurant is Boquete's go-to place for an intimate meal. The smoked trout and pasta with prawns are delicious, but it's the rack of lamb in a mint and rosemary crust that is a local favorite. For a romantic dinner, the fireside gazebo has the best view. A more social setting can be found at the bar, appropriately named "La Roca" (The Rock) for a boulder that washed onto the property during a rainstorm in 1970; the boulder remains. There's often live music, making it a great place to enjoy a glass of wine or the richly decadent triple mousse dessert. Lighter fare of soups, salads, and sandwiches are also on the menu. *Average main: $12* ✉ *From Av. Central, over Caldera River bridge, 50 meters to the right* ☎ *507/720–1586* 🌐 *www.oasisboquete.com.*

$ ✕ **La Casona Mexicana.** *Mexican.* Owned by a local woman who lived in Mexico for many years, this open-air restaurant on the south end of town serves a decent selection of Aztec taste treats. The menu includes Tex-Mex classics such as burritos, soft tacos, fajitas, enchiladas, and *flautas* (deep-fried tacos), as well as more original items such as *pechuga Michoacán* (chicken breast in an orange sauce). The food itself isn't spicy, but hot sauce is offered on the side. The restaurant's stucco walls are painted wild colors and decorated with a few Mexican souvenirs. *Average main: $9* ✉ *Av. Central, 1 block south of Texaco gas station* ☎ *507/720–1274.*

$ ✕ **Machu Picchu.** *Peruvian.* The local branch of Panama City's popular Peruvian restaurant chain serves the same selection of spicy delicacies. The dining room is a bit plain, despite paintings of Peruvian landscapes and colorful woven tablecloths, but you can't go wrong with such classics as ceviche, *ají de gallina* (chicken in a chili cream sauce), *seco de res* (Peruvian stewed beef), and *sudado de mero* (grouper in a spicy soup). Be careful with their *ají* hot sauce; it packs a real punch. *Average main: $10* ✉ *Av. Belisario Porras, behind Banco Nacional* ☎ *507/720–1502.*

★ Fodor's Choice ✕ **Restaurante Panamonte.** *Latin American.* $ Though Boquete's first hotel now faces stiff competition, its charming restaurant remains one of the best in town. Inventive dishes based on traditional Panamanian cuisine include pumpkin soup, shrimp-and-plantain croquettes, mountain trout sautéed with almonds, and grilled beef tenderloin topped with a three-pepper sauce. It's served in a historic European atmosphere that's hardly changed over the past century. Sunday breakfast is popular. *Average main: $12* ✉ *Panamonte Inn & Spa, right at first Y north of town, on left* ☎ *507/720–1324.*

$ ✕ **Ristorante e Pizzería Il Pianista.** *Italian.* There is something ★ European about the stone building that houses this restaurant a short drive northeast of town, which is made complete with authentic Italian cuisine. The small dining room is on the ground floor overlooking a stream surrounded by trees and impatiens; an outdoor patio sits beside a small waterfall. The menu includes fresh pastas such as vegetable lasagna and fettuccine *del Chef* (with prawn-and-mushroom cream sauce) or *napolitano* (with tomato-clam sauce). Other specialties include *trucha al forno* (trout baked with tomatoes and mushrooms) and *calamares rellenos* (squid stuffed with tomatoes, cheese, and pine nuts). You can also build your own pizza or calzone or grab a pizza to go. *Average main: $14* *Right at first Y north of town, left after the bridge, 3½ km (2 miles) north on right, Arco Iris* *507/720–2728* *No credit cards* *Closed Mon. and Oct.*

WHERE TO STAY

For expanded hotel reviews, visit Fodors.com.

Hotels in Boquete don't need air-conditioning. Theft has been a problem at some Boquete hotels, so lock your valuables in a safe if you can.

Boquete Garden Inn. *B&B/Inn.* As the name suggests, this small hotel's grounds hold plenty of flowers, as well as trees, a few boulders, and a nature path. **Pros:** lovely grounds on river; friendly staff; spacious rooms; good value. **Cons:** limited views, no-see-ums can be a problem. *Rooms from: $95* *Right at first Y north of town, 1½ km (1 mile) north of bridge over Río Caldera, Palo Alto* *507/720–2376* *www.boquetegardeninn.com* *10 rooms* *Breakfast.*

$$ **Finca Lérida.** *B&B/Inn.* This working coffee farm on the eastern slope of Volcán Barú above Boquete has almost 650 acres of bird-replete cloud forest, and birders make up the bulk of the clientele here. **Pros:** gorgeous views of the cloud forest; guided bird-watching and coffee tours. **Cons:** eco-lodge lacks greenery nearby; remote. *Rooms from: $150* *7 km (4 miles) northwest of town, turn left at second Y, entrance on left, Callejón Seco, Alto Quiel* *507/720–2285* *www.fincalerida.com* *21 rooms* *Breakfast.*

$ **Hotel Isla Verde.** *B&B/Inn.* Three minutes from the center of town, this garden property has six spacious "roundhouses" and two enchanting suites. **Pros:** creative design; beautiful gardens. **Cons:** minimal parking spaces; inconsistent water temperature in the showers. *Rooms from: $90* *Calle 5, left at Delta Gas, two blocks up the hill on the right* *507/720–2533* *www.islaverdepanama.com* *15 rooms* *No meals.*

$$$ **Los Establos.** *B&B/Inn.* This small, Spanish-style inn with a stirring view of Volcán Barú started out as a horse stable, hence its name, and each room is named after a horse. **Pros:** volcano view from some rooms; nice decor; ample grounds; lovely lounge and porch. **Cons:** most standard rooms lack views; fairly expensive. *Rooms from: $215* *2 km (1 mile) northeast of town, right at first Y north of town, left after bridge, then first right, Jaramillo Arriba* *507/*

720–2685 ☎ 888/481–0656 in U.S. ⊕ www.losestablos.net ⇨ 5 rooms, 2 suites, 4 cottages 🍽 *Breakfast.*

★ Fodor'sChoice **Panamonte Inn & Spa.** *B&B/Inn.* Opened in
$$$ 1914, the Panamonte was long Boquete's only tourist hotel, and these folks still do things right a century later. **Pros:** charming and timeless; nice gardens; great restaurant and bar. **Cons:** some rooms are small, musty, or both; near a busy road. *$ Rooms from: $200 ✉ Right at first Y north of town, on left ☎ 507/720–1324 🖷 507/720–2055 ☎ 800/525–4800 in U.S. ⊕ www.panamonteinnandspa.com ⇨ 18 rooms, 5 suites* 🍽 *No meals.*

$ **The Riverside Inn.** *Hotel.* This large white house with six luxurious suites, cozy lounge, and stone fireplace seems to come right out of New England. **Pros:** luxurious rooms; lovely lounge; good value; nice riverside location; great restaurant. **Cons:** grounds a bit barren. *$ Rooms from: $100 ✉ Right at first Y north of town, left after bridge, then 1½ km (1 mile) on the left, Palo Alto ☎🖷 507/720–1076 ⊕ www.riversideinnboquete.com ⇨ 5 suites, 1 master suite* 🍽 *Breakfast.*

$ **Tinamou Cottage.** *B&B/Inn.* Although it lacks the amenities
★ of a full-service hotel, each cottages is privately situated in a dense forest where monkeys, sloths, and plenty of birds can be found. **Pros:** jungle setting; knowledgeable managers; good beds; organized tours. **Cons:** no restaurant; one-hour walk from town; low water pressure; poor road to the property; no kids under 8. *$ Rooms from: $110 ✉ Near the school, 300 meters up the road on the right, Jaramillo Abajo ☎ 507/720–3852 ⊕ www.coffeeadventures.net ⇨ 1 studio cottage, 2 2-bedroom cottages* 🍽 *Breakfast.*

$ **Valle Del Río.** *Hotel.* This hotel takes pride in reflecting the "great American chain hotels" with comforts like digital TV, Wi-Fi, coffee makers, and minibars in the rooms. **Pros:** great showers; authentic Italian cuisine; on the river. **Cons:** steep parking lot. *$ Rooms from: $115 ✉ Calle Costarica, on the right just before Valle Escondido, Bajo Boquete ☎ 507/720–2525 ⊕ www.valledelrioboquete.com ⇨ 25 rooms, 3 suites* 🍽 *Breakfast.*

$$$ **Valle Escondido.** *Resort.* The main attractions of this lavish resort are its 9-hole golf course and luxury spa. **Pros:** good food; reasonably priced spa treatments; excellent amenities. **Cons:** gaudy decor; gated security entrance sometimes has a long line. *$ Rooms from: $210 ✉ Calle Costarica, just beyond Valle Del Rio Inn, entrance through private gate ☎ 507/720–2454, 866/992–6622 ⊕ www.veresort.com ⇨ 36 rooms, 3 suites* 🍽 *Breakfast.*

4

NIGHTLIFE AND THE ARTS

Panamonte Inn & Spa. A pleasant place for a quiet cocktail is the bar in the Panamonte Inn & Spa, which has a terrace hemmed by gardens, a big fireplace, and lots of couches and cane chairs. ✉ *Right at first Y north of town, on left* ☎ *507/720–1324.*

Zanzibar. The hip crowd hangs at Zanzibar, an attractive lounge with an odd African decor and comfy chairs. ✉ *Av. Central, 2 blocks north of church* ⊙ *Mon.–Sat. 6–11:30 pm.*

SPORTS AND THE OUTDOORS

BIRD-WATCHING

Boquete is a bird-watcher's heaven, and its avian diversity tops 400 species during the dry season. The mountain forests shelter emerald toucanet, collared redstart, sulfur-winged parakeet, a dozen hummingbird species, and the resplendent quetzal. Even the gardens of homes and hotels offer decent birding; they're the best places to see migrant birds wintering in Boquete, from the Tennessee warbler to the Baltimore oriole. The less accessible upper slopes of Volcán Barú are home to rare species like the volcano junco and volcano hummingbird.

One of the best places to see the quetzal and other cloud-forest birds is **Finca Lérida** *(⇨ above)*. Another good place to see quetzal is along the **Bajo Mono Road** just up the road from Finca Lérida. Even experienced birders should hire a local guide, at least for the first day.

Hans and Terry van der Vooren. Terry van der Vooren, who runs coffee tours at the Kotowa Estate, also offers half- to full-day bird-watching and hiking tours ($60–$149). ☎ *507/720–3852.*

Santiago (Chago) Caballero. Boquete's best birding guide is scaling back his excursions a bit these days, but a trip with "Chago," as everyone knows him, is sure to check off new birds on your life list. ☎ *507/6626–2200.*

HIKING

★ Boquete is a great place for hiking, with countless farm roads and footpaths in and around the valley.

Bajo Mono. The Bajo Mono area, near Alto Quiel, has shorter trails into the park that can be explored in a matter of hours. The **Pipeline Road,** a dirt track that heads off the main road to the left, leads into a forested canyon with a waterfall. The **Sendero Culebra** trailhead is on the right from the road to Alto Chiquiero about 1.4 km from the Bajo Mono road.

Sendero Los Quetzales. The most popular area hike is the 9-km (5-mile) Sendero Los Quetzales *(⇨ Cerro Punta, below)*. ✉ *Cerro Punta.*

Volcán Barú. The summit hike to Volcán Barú in Parque Nacional Volcán Barú *(⇨ below)* is a popular area excursion but more demanding than the Sendero Los Quetzales. ⚠ **The weather can change drastically within minutes near the top, where it freezes regularly during the dry season—hypothermia is a real risk if you're caught in a storm.**

HIKING GUIDES AND OUTFITTERS

Aventurist. Aventurist, which owns Boquete Tree Trek, has a four-hour hike ($25) to see waterfalls and wildlife in its private reserve. ✉ *Plaza Los Establos, Av. Central* ☎ *507/720–1635* 🌐 *www.aventurist.com.*

Feliciano González. Feliciano González has been guiding hikers through Boquete's mountains for two decades. In addition to tours of the Sendero Los Quetzales and to Volcán Barú's summit, he leads a six-hour hike through primary forest on the Sendero El Pianista. Tours are $35–$70 per person. ☎ *507/6624–9940.*

HORSEBACK RIDING

Some excellent horseback-riding routes in the mountains around Boquete include panoramic views and exposure to abundant birdlife.

Boquete Tours. Eduardo Cano at Boquete Tours can arrange inexpensive horseback tours, as well as guided hikes down the Sendero Los Quetzales or a Volcán Barú ascent. ☎ *507/720–1750.*

MOUNTAIN BIKING

Aventurist. Aventurist runs a three-hour bike tour ($25), mostly downhill, through the mountains north of Boquete. ✉ *Plaza Los Establos, Av. Central* ☎ *507/720–1635* 🌐 *www.aventurist.com.*

WHITE-WATER RAFTING

Chiriquí has Panama's best white-water rafting, with many rivers to choose from during the rainy season (June–November). ■ TIP→ **Only one river—Río Chiriquí Viejo—is navigable during the December–May dry season.**

The **Río Chiriquí Viejo** is considered Panama's best whitewater river. Of its two rafting routes, the harder is the Class III–IV Palón section, which requires previous experience and can become too dangerous to navigate during the rainiest months. The easier, Class II–III Sabo section is good for beginners. Chiriquí Viejo is a three-hour drive from Boquete each way, which makes for a long day. Unfortunately, it's threatened by government plans to dam it for a hydroelectric project. The **Río Estí** is a Class II–III river fit for beginners that is closer to Boquete and doubles as a good wildlife-watching trip. The **Río Chiriquí** is a fun Class III river with one Class IV rapids; it's a 90-minute drive from Boquete and appropriate for beginners. The **Río Gariche** and **Río Dolega** are Class II–III rivers nearer Boquete and suitable for beginners.

Boquete Outdoor Adventures. Boquete Outdoor Adventures offers multisport trips that combine rafting, kayaking, island tours, hiking, and tree trekking. ✉ *Plaza Los Establos, Av. Central* ☎ *507/720–2284* 🌐 *www.boqueteoutdooradventures.com.*

Chiriquí River Rafting. Chiriquí River Rafting makes safety and eco-friendliness a priority. The company offers trips on all area rivers ($85–$105); the Río Chiriquí Viejo trip is the most expensive. ✉ *Av. Central, across from park* ☎ *507/6879–4382* 🌐 *www.panama-rafting.com.*

Panama Rafters. Panama Rafters is a small, American-owned company that runs easy rafting trips on the Chiriquí and Majagua rivers, and a more expert excursion on the Chiriquí Viejo; trips cost $75–$90, depending on the section and include transportation, lunch, river shoes, and towels. ✉ *Plaza Los Establos, Av. Central* ☎ *507/720–2712* 🌐 *www.panamarafter.com.*

ZIP-LINE TOURS

Boquete Tree Trek. A canopy tour involves gliding along zip-line cables (to which you're attached via a harness), strung between platforms in the high branches of tropical trees. It gives both the sensation of flying through the treetops and a bird's-eye view of the cloud forest. Boquete Tree Trek has trained guides that provide instruction and accompany groups through the tour ($65), which lasts about four hours. Prohibited from the tours are children under six and those weighing more than 250 pounds (men) and 170 pounds (women). ✉ *Office, Plaza Los Establos,*

Av. Central ☎ 507/720–1635 ⊕ www.boquetetreektrek.com ⊙ Tours depart office at 8 am and 1 pm.

SHOPPING

CEFATI. The small shop at CEFATI has a good selection of indigenous handicrafts such as Emberá woven bowls and Ngöbe *chácaras* (colorful woven jute bags). ✉ *Av. Central, at south entrance to town* ☎ *507/720–4060* ⊙ *Daily 9:30–5:30.*

PARQUE NACIONAL VOLCÁN BARÚ

GETTING HERE AND AROUND

You can drive to the park's entrances in a 4WD vehicle or hire a 4WD taxi to drop you off and pick you up.

★ **Parque Nacional Volcán Barú.** Towering 11,450 feet above sea level, Barú Volcano is literally Chiriquí's biggest attraction, and Panama's highest peak. The massive dormant volcano is visible from David and is the predominant landmark in Boquete and Volcán, but Bambito and Cerro Punta are tucked so tightly into its slopes that you can hardly see it from there. The upper slopes, summit, and northern side of the volcano are protected within Barú Volcano National Park, which covers some 35,000 acres and extends northward to connect with the larger Parque Internacional La Amistad, shared by Panama and Costa Rica. The vast expanse of protected wilderness is home to everything from cougars to howler monkeys and more than 250 bird species. You might see white hawks, black guans, violet sabrewings, sulphur-winged parakeets, resplendent quetzals, and rare three-wattled bellbirds in the park's cloud forests. The craggy summit is topped by radio towers and a cement bunker, and unfortunately many of its boulders are covered with graffiti.

The most popular way to take in the park is the **Sendero Los Quetzales**, which has excellent bird-watching and is most easily done starting out in Cerro Punta (⇨ *Cerro Punta, below*). Several other trails penetrate the park's wilderness, including two trails to the summit. The main road to the summit begins in Boquete, across from the church, and is paved for the first 7 km (4 miles), where it passes a series of homes and farms and then becomes increasingly rough and rocky. You pay the park fee at the ANAM ranger station 15 km (9 miles) from town, which takes about 90 minutes to reach in a 4WD vehicle. Park your vehicle at the station, because the road above it can only be ascended in trucks with super-high suspension. From here it's a steep 14-km

(8½-mile) hike to the summit. The other trail to the summit begins 7 km (4 miles) north of Volcán and ascends the volcano's more deforested western slope, a grueling trek only recommended for serious athletes.

For information about hiking in Parque Nacional Volcán Barú, see ⇨Hiking in Boquete, above. ☎507/774–6671 $5 ⏲Daily 8–3.

VOLCÁN

60 km (36 miles) northwest of David, 16 km (10 miles) south of Cerro Punta.

A breezy little town, Volcán has the best view of Volcán Barú, several miles northeast. The town is a dreary succession of restaurants, banks, and other businesses spread along a north–south route.

Bambito and Cerro Punta are more attractive and have the area's best hotels, so there is little reason to stay in Volcán except that it's much warmer than Cerro Punta, which can get cool at night between December and March. It is also a convenient jumping-off point for summiting Barú Volcano via the southern route or bird-watching at Finca Hartmann.

GETTING HERE AND AROUND

Because Volcán's attractions are so spread out, it's best to drive there. From David, head west 22 km (14 miles) on the CA1 to Concepción, where you turn right and drive north 33 km (21 miles) through the mountains to Volcán. Buses depart from David's terminal for Volcán ($2) every 30 minutes during the day.

EXPLORING

Janson Coffee Farm. This large coffee farm near the Lagunas de Volcán gives a tour of the farming and processing of their high-quality beans that ends with a tasting. Do the tour during the October–March harvest. They also offer horseback-riding tours of the farm and nearby lakes. ✉ *Vía Aeropuerto, 2 km (1 mile) south of Volcán ☎507/6867–3884 🌐www.lagunasadventures.com ⏲Mon.–Sat. 8–noon and 1–5; tours by appointment or upon arrival.*

Sitio Barriles. One of Panama's most important archaeological sites and its most visitor-friendly by far, Sitio Barriles is a collection of abandoned digs and pre-Columbian artifacts on a private farm 6 km (3½ miles) south of Volcán. Sitio Barriles was the main town of an agricultural society that farmed the surrounding plains from AD 300 to 600. The farm's current owners manage it under an agreement with the National Culture Institute. Edna Landau, who speaks some English, leads visitors on a 45-minute tour with advance notice. The turnoff for Sitio Barriles is west of the road to Bambito, on the left one block after the road to the airstrip, and is marked Cazán. ✉ *Road to Cazán, 6 km (3½ miles) south of Volcán* ☎ *507/6575–1828* 🎫 *$5* ⏲ *Daily 8–5.*

WHERE TO EAT AND STAY

For expanded hotel reviews, visit Fodors.com.

★ Fodor'sChoice ✕ **Il Forno.** *Italian.* Authentic southern Italian recipes, handed down from generations, are what you'll get here. It might be a challenge, but try not to fill up on the warm baked breads served with roasted garlic and olive oil. On the menu you'll find veal, salmon, chicken, pork, and, of course, brick-oven pizzas. Pastas are all named after women, like "Pasta a la Jessie" served with a bacon and tomato cream sauce. The menu also features lighter options like spinach salad with candied almonds and apples. Adding to the dining experience is the pleasant atmosphere created by wooden tables, a wine room, opera music, and the smell of garlic wafting from the kitchen. 💲 *Average main: $12* ✉ *Left, ¼ mile past the turnoff for Cerro Punta on the road to Volcán* ☎ *507/771–5731* 💳 *No credit cards* ⏲ *Closed Mon.–Tues.*
$

$ 🏨 **Hotel Dos Ríos.** *Hotel.* Volcán's biggest hotel, the Dos Ríos is an original two-story wooden building fronted by a newer cabinlike lobby. **Pros:** best in town; good views; beautiful garden pathways. **Cons:** bar open only in high season; most rooms mediocre. 💲 *Rooms from: $80* ✉ *Road to Río Sereno, 2½ km (1½ miles) north of turnoff for Bambito* ☎ *507/771–5555* 📠 *507/771–5794* 🌐 *www.dosrios.com.pa* 🛏 *17 rooms, 3 bungalows* 🍽 *Breakfast.*

SPORTS AND THE OUTDOORS

HIKING

Volcán Barú. Volcán is a popular departure point for summit hikes of Volcán Barú *(⇨ Parque Nacional Volcán Barú, above).*

BAMBITO

★ *7 km (4 miles) north of Volcán, 8 km (4½ miles) south of Cerro Punta.*

Rather than a town, Bambito is a series of farms and houses scattered along the serpentine Río Chiriquí Viejo valley on the western slope of Volcán Barú, between Volcán and Cerro Punta. Because the people who live in the valley do their shopping in nearby Volcán, it has almost no stores or other businesses—just a few hotels—so it lacks the kinds of architectural eyesores that dominate most Panamanian towns.

The valley's scenery grows more impressive with each hairpin turn. Even if your destination is Cerro Punta, make a few stops to admire the suspension bridges spanning the boulder-strewn river, lush forest clinging to hillsides, wildflowers, and neat wooden farmhouses. Small farms line the road, and several roadside stands sell vegetables, fruit, and preserves—strawberries (fresas) are everybody's favorite here—and fresh fruit *batidos* (smoothies).

GETTING HERE AND AROUND

Turn right at the main intersection in Volcán to reach Bambito. Hotels and restaurants are scattered along the road once it enters the valley. Buses head up and down the valley every 30 minutes and will pick you up and drop you off anywhere.

WHERE TO STAY

For expanded hotel reviews, visit Fodors.com.

$$ ★ **Casa Grande.** *Hotel.* The setting here is idyllic: massive trees shade the wooden buildings and lawns, the Río Chiriquí Viejo is a stone's toss away, and everything is surrounded by dense forest. **Pros:** surrounded by nature; plenty of activities; children's play area. **Cons:** standard rooms are mediocre; potholed, but doable, road last few hundred meters. *Rooms from: $153* ✉ *Road to Cerro Punta, on left after Hotel Bambito* ☎ *507/771–5126, 786/228–8428 in U.S.* 🌐 *www.casagrandebambito.com* *10 rooms, 10 suites.*

$$ **Hotel Bambito.** *Hotel.* This alpine-style resort overlooks sheer rock faces and lush slopes across a wide lawn with fountains. **Pros:** lovely setting; big rooms; covered pool; good restaurant; activities. **Cons:** dated decor. *Rooms from: $152* ✉ *Road to Cerro Punta on right, beginning of valley* ☎ *507/771–4265* 🌐 *www.hotelbambito.com* *37 rooms, 10 suites* *Breakfast.*

CERRO PUNTA

75 km (45 miles) northwest of David, 15 km (9 miles) north of Volcán.

This bowl-shaped highland valley northwest of Volcán Barú offers some splendid bucolic scenery and is bordered by vast expanses of wilderness that invite bird-watchers, hikers, and nature lovers. A patchwork of vegetable farms covers the valley floor and clings to the steep slopes that surround it, and ridges are topped with dark cloud forest and rocky crags. On the eastern side of the valley a steep slope rises up into a wedge of granite for which the area was named—*cerro punta* means "pointed hill." That eastern ridge, part of the country's continental divide, is often enveloped in clouds pushed there by the trade winds. The results are frequent, fleeting rain showers that keep the valley green year-round and produce an inordinate number of rainbows.

Cerro Punta is the highest inhabited area in Panama, nearly 6,000 feet above sea level. It can get chilly when the sun goes down or behind the clouds, though it is usually warm enough for shorts and T-shirts by day. From December to March the temperature sometimes drops down to almost 4°C (40°F) at night, so bring warm clothes and a waterproof jacket, as well as sturdy boots for the slippery mountain trails. The sun is intense, so use sunblock or wear a hat when you aren't in the woods.

GETTING HERE AND AROUND

Reach Cerro Punta by turning right at Volcán's main intersection. Buses come and go every 30 minutes and will let you on and off anywhere.

EXPLORING

★ **Finca Drácula.** Interested in orchids? Finca Drácula holds one of Latin America's largest collections. The farm's name is taken from a local orchid, which has a dark red flower. The main focus here is reproducing orchids for export, but workers also give 40-minute tours, though in limited English and by prior appointment only. The farm has 2,700 orchid species from Panama and around the world, as well as a laboratory where plants are reproduced using micropropagation methods. The best time to visit is between March and May, when flowers are in bloom. If you don't have a 4WD vehicle, walk 20 minutes from Guadalupe to get here. ✉ *Road to Los Quetzales reserve,*

1 km east of Guadalupe ☎ *507/771–2070* 🎫 *$10* ⏲ *Daily 8–11:30 and 1–4.*

★ Fodor'sChoice **Parque Internacional La Amistad** (*PILA*). Parque Internacional La Amistad stretches from the peaks above Cerro Punta down to the remote hills of Bocas del Toro Province, comprising more than 200,000 hectares (more than 500,000 acres) of remote wilderness. It protects a succession of forest types that together hold most of the country's endangered animals, including jaguars and tapirs, and some 400 bird species, from the rare umbrella bird to the harpy eagle. The name *La Amistad*—Spanish for "friendship"—refers to the park's binational (Panama and Costa Rica) status.

Cerro Punta provides the most convenient access to the park entrance and ANAM ranger station at Las Nubes, a 15-minute drive from town up a dirt road, where several trails start. You might see any of more than 150 bird species and mammals such as the coati and olingo. Going with a guide is the easiest way to visit the park. An excellent bird-watching trail is the **Sendero el Retonio,** a 2-km (1-mile) loop over easy terrain that includes cloud forest and a stand of bamboo. If you have a few hours, hike the **Sendero La Cascada,** a 4-km (2-miles) trail to a ridge with views of the valley and a spectacular waterfall. To reach the park, drive around the loop to the intersection near Entre Ríos, on the northern end of the valley, and follow the road all the way to the park, veering left after you drive through the gate. The last stretch is fit for 4WD vehicles only. ✉ *Las Nubes, 5 km (3 miles) north of Cerro Punta* ☎ *507/720–3057 in Boquete* 🎫 *$5* ⏲ *Daily 8–3.*

Los Quetzales Lodge & Spa. Los Quetzales Lodge operates a 1,000-acre private reserve inside Parque Nacional Volcán Barú, a 20-minute drive, or 30-minute hike from the lodge. The reserve has well-maintained trails through the cloud forest, one of which leads to a small waterfall, and all of which pass moss-laden scenery. It is home to more than 100 bird species, including the resplendent quetzal and 12 kinds of hummingbirds. You must be accompanied by one of the reserve's guides. Lodge guests are transported to the reserve every morning for $5. Non-guests pay $20 transport, but it's an easy 30-minute hike. ✉ *3 km (2 miles) east of Guadalupe* ☎ *507/771–2291* 🌐 *www.losquetzales.com* 🎫 *Free for guests, nonguests $5; guide $10 per hour* ⏲ *Daily 6–6.*

★ **Sendero Los Quetzales.** The most popular hike in Cerro Punta is the Sendero Los Quetzales, a footpath through Parque Nacional Volcán Barú that ends in the mountains above Boquete (you can hike it in reverse, but it's entirely uphill). The trail begins at the ANAM station in El Respingo, east of town, where you pay the $5 park admission fee. From there it's a 9-km (5-miles) downhill hike to Alto Chiquero, a short drive from Boquete. The trail winds through the cloud forest and follows the Río Caldera, crossing it several times en route. You might see quetzals, emerald toucanets, collared redstarts, coatis, and other wildlife on the hike, which takes most people three to four hours. ■ TIP→ **Because the trail is not well marked, hire a guide or join an organized tour; the area's bird-watching guides regularly use the trail.** Pack a lunch, lots of water, and rain gear, and wear sturdy waterproof boots. The best option is to have your bags transferred to a Boquete hotel and end there for the night. Hire a taxi in Cerro Punta to drop you off at El Respingo, which should cost $15, and arrange for a Boquete taxi to pick you up in Alto Chiquero. Otherwise, walk 90 minutes from the end of the trail through farmland to Bajo Mono, where you can catch public transportation to Boquete.

4

WHERE TO STAY

For expanded hotel reviews, visit Fodors.com.

★ Fodor'sChoice $ **Cielito Sur.** *B&B/Inn.* The best thing about this B&B is the service provided by its owner. **Pros:** quiet; near nature; great breakfasts; helpful owners; nice rooms. **Cons:** no restaurant; property often booked far in advance; two-night minimum stay Nov.–Apr. *Rooms from: $90* ✉ *4 km (2½ miles) south of Cerro Punta center, Nueva Suiza* ☎ *507/771–2038* *www.cielitosur.com* *5 rooms* *Closed Oct.* *Breakfast.*

$ ★ **Los Quetzales Lodge & Spa.** *B&B/Inn.* You'll find accommodations at this eco-lodge ranging from backpacker dorms to private cabins in the cloud forest. **Pros:** private forest reserve; good restaurant and lounge; lots of activities. **Cons:** remote; need car to stay here. *Rooms from: $85* ✉ *Guadalupe* ☎ *507/771–2291* *www.losquetzales.com* *20 rooms, 9 cabins* *Breakfast.*

SPORTS AND THE OUTDOORS

BIRD-WATCHING

The valley's feathered creatures are most easily spotted around its edges, especially near streams and along the trails that head into the nearby national parks. A good guide can significantly increase the number of species you see.

Ito Santamaría. Guadalupe resident Ito Santamaría is the area's top bird-watching guide and one of the few who speaks English. ☎ *507/6591–1621.*

Los Quetzales Lodge and Spa. The private nature reserve of Los Quetzales Lodge has guides who are good at spotting birds, especially quetzals. ☎ *507/771–2291* 🌐 *www.losquetzales.com.*

HIKING

Between La Amistad and Volcán Barú national parks, there are enough trails around Cerro Punta to keep you hiking for several days. The area's bird-watching guides are familiar with all the local trails and are happy to guide hikers. Wherever you hike, be sure to pack plenty of water, sunscreen, a hat, and warm, waterproof clothing, even if it's sunny, since the temperature can plummet when a storm rolls in.

Bocas del Toro Archipelago

5

WORD OF MOUTH

"Bocas del Toro is my favorite place on Earth. I can't wait to go back there and [I] probably think of it every day. There are great over-the-water hotels and inns to choose from."

—Continental_Drifter

www.fodors.com/forums

Updated by Jeffrey Van Fleet

WITH ITS TURQUOISE WATERS, SUGAR-SAND beaches, and funky island towns, the relatively isolated archipelago of Bocas del Toro has the same attractions as major Caribbean destinations with a fraction of the crowds, development, and price. An astounding variety of flora and fauna cover its six major islands, 52 cays, and 200 islets, with an overlay of a fascinating Afro-Caribbean and indigenous culture.

Bocas del Toro—the term means "mouths of the bull" and no one agrees on the origin of the name—refers to the archipelago itself, its entire province that encompasses northwest Panama, and its provincial capital. (Most visitors use the term in the last sense, but five minutes here, and you'll shorten it to "Bocas" as everyone else does.) The town offers an ample selection of affordable hotels and good restaurants. On any given morning dozens of boats depart from the port, carrying locals and visitors to nearby islands, beaches, reefs, and rain forests, making the town a good base from which to explore.

The only caveat is that the archipelago's rain forests result from copious and frequent downpours, which have dampened more than a few vacations. Heavy showers are often over in a matter of hours, but an entire week of rain isn't out of the question some months of the year. Apart from March, September, and October, avoid booking your entire vacation here, since the likelihood of getting sunny days elsewhere in Panama is greater. But don't let the rain scare you away, because when it's sunny, Bocas del Toro is simply amazing.

ORIENTATION AND PLANNING

GETTING ORIENTED

The Bocas del Toro Archipelago scatters across a shallow lowland gulf. Tourism centers on Bocas del Toro town, which occupies a spit of land on the southern tip of Isla Colón, the westernmost island. Many visitors arrive and depart from the tiny airport here. Water taxis and a ferry ply the waters between the town and the mainland port of Almirante, from which roads lead southeast to Chiriquí and the rest of Panama and west to banana farms and the Costa Rican border. East of Isla Colón lie several other islands with communities and isolated hotels—Islas Carenero and Bastimentos the most popular—and by day, private boats and water taxis travel regularly between the islands.

TOP REASONS TO GO

Idyllic Islands. Jungle-hemmed beaches, coconut palms growing in pale sand, emerald waters . . . the archipelago has the stuff of tropical fantasies.

Funky Bocas Town. The offbeat, colorful town of Bocas offers a mix of historic architecture, mellow locals, good food, nightlife, and abundant views of the surrounding sea and islands.

Neptune's Gardens. The submarine wonders—from the sponge-studded reef beneath Hospital Point to the seemingly endless coral gardens of the Cayos Zapatillas—can keep you diving for days.

The Jungle. Though the sea and sand are the big attractions, the rain forests that cover much of the archipelago are home to hundreds of bird species as well as everything from howler monkeys to tiny poison dart frogs.

Caribbean Cultures. Bocas del Toro's cultural mix of Afro-Caribbean, Panamanian, and indigenous Ngöbe tradition adds layers to the islands' personality.

PLANNING

WHEN TO GO

The big drawback of Bocas del Toro is the rain. Rain sometimes falls for days on end any time of year. Statistically, March is the sunniest month. September and October are the next-driest months, and May and June tend to be nice as well. Waters are calm and ideal for snorkeling and diving from mid-August to October. Since May, June, and (especially) September and October are the rainiest months in the rest of Panama, Bocas del Toro is the place to be at those times. December is the wettest month, and July and August are right behind it, though it tends to be sunny about a third of the time. Despite this, December, July, and August are good months for surfing in the archipelago but the worst months for diving. In January and February the odds of enjoying sunny days are about fifty-fifty. Many of the outlying lodges and some restaurants close during May and June, the lowest of the low season.

GETTING HERE AND AROUND

AIR TRAVEL

The Aeropuerto Internacional Bocas del Toro (BOC), the archipelago's tiny airport, is five blocks from the center of Bocas Town, at the west end of Avenida E. Domestic carrier Air Panama flies twice daily to and from Panama City.

Costa Rican airline Nature Air flies three mornings weekly between Bocas and San José. You'll pay an international departure tax of $15.

Carriers **Air Panama** ☎ *507/316–9000* 🌐 *www.flyairpanama.com.* **Nature Air** ☎ *507/757–9075 in Panama, 800/235–9272 in the U.S.* 🌐 *www.natureair.com.*

BOAT AND FERRY TRAVEL

Boats are the most common means of transportation in Bocas del Toro, and the town of Bocas has several water-taxi companies and dozens of boatmen who provide transportation between Islas Colón, Carenero, and Bastimentos, as well as day tours. The water-taxi companies Bocas Marine Tours, Jam Pan Tours, and Taxi 25 have trips every 30 minutes between Bocas and Almirante ($4), where you can catch a bus to David. It takes 20 minutes to reach Almirante, with departures every half-hour from 6 am to 6:30 pm. Jam Pan also provides transport to the other islands, as do independent boatmen who depart from the dock next to the Farmacia Rosa Blanca, on Calle 3 in Bocas. The fare to Carenero is $1.50, to Old Bank, $2.

If you are heading to Isla Carenero or Bastimentos, it can be less expensive to do as the locals do and travel with boatmen who wait at the dock next to Farmacia Rosa Blanca. Most boat trips cost between $2 and $20, though the farthest lodges can be much more expensive to reach.

TIP→ **A car is of little use here.** No in-town hotel has parking and roads are scarce to nonexistent elsewhere. A car ferry, run by Trasbordadores Marinos, travels between Almirante and Bocas daily except Monday, departing from Almirante at 8 am and Bocas at 4 pm. The trip takes an hour and costs $20–$30, depending on the size of the vehicle.

Contacts **Bocas Marine & Tours** ✉ *Calle 3, at Av. C, Bocas del Toro* ☎ *507/757–9033* 🌐 *www.bocasmarinetours.com.* **Jam Pan Tours** ✉ *Calle 1, at Av. D, Bocas del Toro* ☎ *507/757–9619* 🌐 *www.jampantours.com.* **Taxi 25** ✉ *Calle 1, at Av. Central, Bocas del Toro* ☎ *507/757–9028.* **Trasbordadores Marinos** ✉ *Town port, Almirante* ☎ *507/6490–7193.*

5

BUS AND TAXI TRAVEL

Transporte Boca del Drago has two shuttle vans that travel the length of Isla Colón, from Bocas del Toro to Bocas del Drago, five times daily on weekdays. The cost is $4 per person. Share taxis run up and down Bocas's main streets, charging $1 for most trips in town.

Bocas del Toro can be reached from Panama City by land and water. The direct bus from Panama City to Almirante (and vice versa) takes eight hours but is comfortable and costs $30. If you're in Chiriquí you can bus or taxi from David or Boquete to Almirante (3½ hours), where water taxis depart for Bocas every half-hour.

Boquete-based taxi driver Daniel Higgins provides transportation between Boquete and Almirante for $150. Caribe Shuttle offers daily transportation between the Southern Caribbean coast of Costa Rica (Puerto Viejo/Manzanillo/Cahuita) and Bocas del Toro. The $36 rate includes hotel pickup and the 30-minute boat trip to Isla Colon.

Contacts **Almirante Bus** ☎ *507/774–0585.* **Caribe Shuttle** ☎ *507/6092–8599* 🌐 *www.caribeshuttle.com.* **Daniel Higgins** ☎ *507/6617–0570.*

ABOUT THE RESTAURANTS

The town of Bocas has an ample restaurant selection, with such surprising options as Thai and Indian cuisine to complement the traditional seafood. Dining is casual and the pace is slow, so be patient for your meal. Local specialties include lobster, whole-fried snapper, octopus, and shrimp served with *patacones* (fried plantain slices) or *yuca frita* (fried cassava strips). At restaurants, opt for bottled water over a glass with ice because tap water is usually unsafe to drink. Almost no restaurant here accepts credit cards. Although tipping is not obligatory in Bocas, it is greatly appreciated by the locals.

Prices in the reviews are the average cost of a main course at dinner or, if dinner is not served, at lunch.

ABOUT THE HOTELS

Accommodations here range from traditional wooden buildings in town to rustic but enchanting bungalows nestled in the wilderness of Isla Bastimentos. All of them have private baths, and all but the eco-lodges have air-conditioning and Internet. Although Bocas del Toro town has an array of budget and moderately priced hotels, the out-of-town lodges tend toward the expensive, though hardly luxurious. Other advantages of staying in town are the local color and the selection of restaurants, shops, and nightlife. The downside is noise from neighbors and revelers, which is a problem at some in-town hotels. Lodges outside town provide more natural, tranquil settings.

Prices in the reviews are the lowest cost of a standard double room in high season. For expanded reviews, facilities, and current deals, visit Fodors.com.

ESSENTIALS

EMERGENCIES

Although slated for major improvements in coming years, for now the hospital in Bocas is good only for minor matters. Serious medical problems should be treated in Panama City or David.

Emergency Services **Fire** ☎ *911 in Bocas del Toro.* **Police** ☎ *911 in Bocas del Toro.*

MONEY MATTERS

There are two ATMs at the Banco Nacional de Panama. They give cash withdrawals from Visa and MasterCard and from Cirrus- and Plus-affiliated debit and credit cards.

SAFETY

Bocas is a safe town, but it has acquired a few sidewalk hustlers and drug dealers in recent years, so don't wander its side streets late at night. The main dangers in the archipelago, however, are sunburn and bug bites. Take a hat, sunscreen, and insect repellent. Drowning is also a real danger, and there are no lifeguards. Don't swim at the beaches if the waves are big, unless you are an experienced surfer, and don't let a boatman take you into rough water in a dugout canoe.

THE WESTERN ARCHIPELAGO

The westernmost island in the archipelago, Isla Colón, is also the most developed, with a road running across it and the provincial capital occupying a peninsula on its southern tip. Across a channel from that urbanized headland is the smaller Isla Carenero. Boats regularly travel between the two communities that are home to the bulk of the archipelago's residents and most of its hotels and restaurants. Most travelers stay in Bocas del Toro town and make day trips to the other islands, beaches, and dive spots.

BOCAS DEL TORO

550 km (341 miles) and one hour by air northwest of Panama City, 170 km (105 miles) north of David.

The town of Bocas del Toro, which the locals simply call Bocas, sits on a little headland connected to the island's primary landmass by a narrow isthmus and is a neat grid packed with homes, businesses, and government offices. The town is surrounded by water on three sides, which gives it plenty of ocean views. The nearest beach, on the isthmus that connects it to Isla Colón, is not the island's best. The town itself holds few sights, but is a laid-back town with wide streets, weathered Caribbean architecture, and plentiful greenery. To play in the surf and sand you either have to boat to Isla Bastimentos or take a bike, taxi, bus, or boat to one of the beaches on Isla Colón. An abundance of boatmen, dive shops, and tour operators are eager to show you paradise.

Most of Bocas's restaurants and other businesses are on or near Calle 3, its main drag sometimes called Calle Principal. This wide, north–south track stretches from one end of town to the other (seven blocks) and runs along the sea for

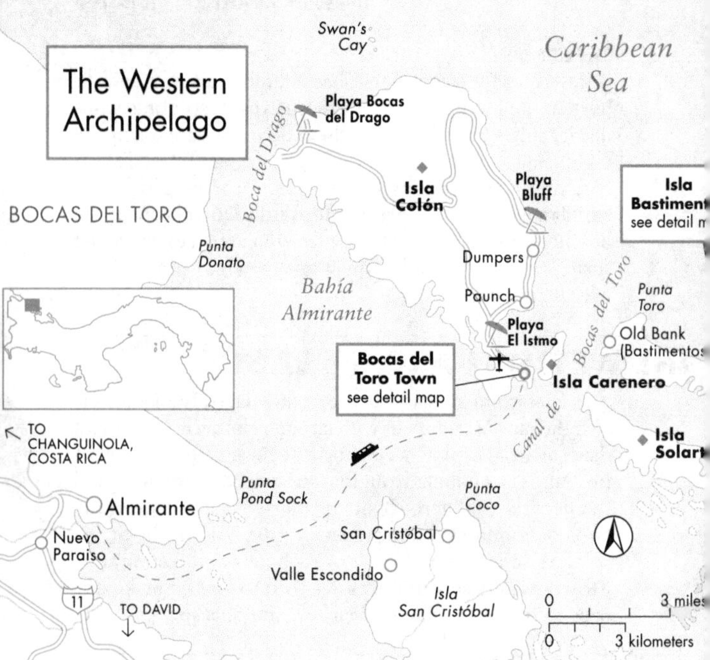

its southern half. Boats to the mainland and other islands depart from docks along that stretch, as do tours bound for fun in the sun, while people from the other islands arrive here to shop and run errands.

BIKING BOCAS: BOCAS BICIS. Bocas del Toro is a perfect town for biking, which is a good way to get to Bluff Beach. Various businesses rent bikes for about $3 an hour or $15 per day. Among them is Bocas Bicis. ✉ ***North end of Calle 3 at Av. F*** ☎ ***507/6446–0787.***

GETTING HERE AND AROUND

All arrivals from elsewhere in Panama and internationally from Costa Rica put you here in Bocas town. (⇨ *See Getting Here and Around above.)*

EXPLORING

ATP (Autoridad de Tourismo Panama). The local office of the Panamanian Tourism Authority, ATP (Autoridad de Tourismo Panama), housed in a large Caribbean-style building on the water, can supply you with all the standard info about Bocas and Panama. A small museum sits on the second floor with information about the area's ecology and history. ✉ *Calle 1, next to Policía Nacional* ☎ *507/757–9035* 🌐 *www.visitpanama.com* ⏲ *Daily 9:30–5:30.*

Bocas Butterfly Garden. A few minutes west of town by boat is the Bocas Butterfly Garden, where a dozen native butterfly species inhabit a screened flyway and a trail leads through a small forest reserve. ✉ *Macca Hill, near Bocas Marina* ☎ *507/757–9008* 🎫 *$5* ⏲ *Mon.–Sat. 9–3, Sun. 9–noon.*

Finca Los Monos Botanical Garden. Finca Los Monos Botanical Garden has a large collection of heliconia, ginger, palm, and fruit trees in a rain-forest setting with plenty of wildlife. In addition to the standard tours offered twice a week, morning bird-watching tours can be arranged with prior reservation. ✉ *Idaan Hill, just past the Smithsonian Institute* ☎ *507/757–9461, 507/6729–9943* 🌐 *www.bocasdeltorobotanicalgarden.com* 🎫 *$10* ⏲ *Tours Mon. at 1 and Fri. at 8:30 or by appointment.*

5

Parque Simón Bolívar. The town's central park site near the north end of Calle 3 and is shaded by mango trees and royal palms. Children play here, and locals chat on its cement benches in the evening. North of the park stands the **Palacio Municipal,** a large cement building that houses various government offices. ✉ *Calle 3, at Av. Central.*

Playa Bocas. Playa Bocas stretches along the narrow isthmus that connects the town to Isla Colón, overlooking tranquil Bahia Chitre (Sand Flea Bay). Its a mediocre beach but will do in a pinch. If you have the time and energy, rent a bike and make the *rough* 40-minute ride out to Bluff Beach (4 km [2½ miles] north of Bocas Town, on Isla Colón), which is gorgeous. ✉ *Av. Norte, 1 km (½ mile) northwest of Calle 3.*

WHERE TO EAT

$ ★ ✕ **Buena Vista Bar and Grill.** *American.* Perched over the water, the back deck of this wooden building is one of the most pleasant places in town to have a meal since it overlooks the sea and nearby Isla Carenero. Boats zip by, and waves wash against the pilings under the floor. The menu ranges from such gringo standards as T-bone steak to the more daring jambalaya, enchiladas, and ginger-orange shrimp. Their selection of salads, burgers, and sandwiches made with imported meats and cheeses makes it a popular lunch spot. Save room for the Bocas Brownie made with organic Cerutti chocolate. $ *Average main: $8* ✉ *Calle 1, at Calle 2* ☎ *507/757–9035* ⏲ *Closed Tues.*

$ ✕ **Gringo's.** *Mexican.* "Dive," . . . "hole in the wall," . . . "joint," . . . Bocas's expat community has various terms of endearment for this Mexican restaurant a block west of the central park. All agree that the fresh Mexican food here is top-notch. The homemade salsas crafted with roasted onion, tomato, and pepper dress up the enchiladas, burritos, and taco salads. Dine inside the small restaurant itself—Mexican music videos are usually playing—or outdoors on the more spacious covered patio. *Average main: $8 ✉ Av. E at Calle 4, Bocas del Toro ☎ 507/6902–4759 No credit cards Closed Sun.*

★ Fodor's Choice ✕ **Guari-Guari.** *Mediterranean.* Wooden tables, $$$ plastic chairs, and a tin roof hardly do justice to the spectacular six-course, prix-fixe dinner served here. A great deal of effort (and love) goes into each dish, prepared by Spanish chef Monica, who abandoned her law profession to be with German engineer "Ossi" (who serves as the restaurant's charming waiter). Together they have managed to break the barriers of Bocas typical fare with a tasting menu that includes tuna carpaccio, spinach salad, and pork tenderloin with roasted potatoes and blue cheese sauce. Adding to the experience is the sound of crashing waves near the open-air restaurant. The menu changes daily, and special vegetarian courses can be provided upon request. Since the restaurant is surrounded by lush vegetation, mosquito coils are lit beside each table to keep the bugs away. *Average main: $20 ✉ 2 km (1 mile) outside Bocas Town, between La Bomba gas station and the Smithsonian ☎ 507/6627–1825 Reservations essential No credit cards Closed Tues.–Wed.*

$$ ✕ **Lemon Grass.** *Asian.* This restaurant's location on the second floor of an old wooden building over the water gives it a great view of the turquoise sea and nearby islands. Tables sit beneath parchment-paper lamps that dangle from a tin roof that roars on rainy days. The sea here provides the perfect ingredients for Asian-fusion recipes that include spicy crab cakes, steak teriyaki, various curries, and fish-and-chips. Scribbled on a chalkboard menu are creative cocktails like "Lemon Grass Lips," a punchy blend of rum, lemon juice, and cranberries. The changing dessert selection could include such decadent inventions as Oreo-Baileys cheesecake and a cappuccino tiramisu sundae. *Average main: $10 ✉ Calle 2, at Avenida D ☎ 507/757–9630 No credit cards Closed Thurs. No lunch.*

$ ✕ **Om Café.** *Indian.* You can get authentic Indian cuisine in Bocas del Toro at this cozy café atop a surf shop. Owner

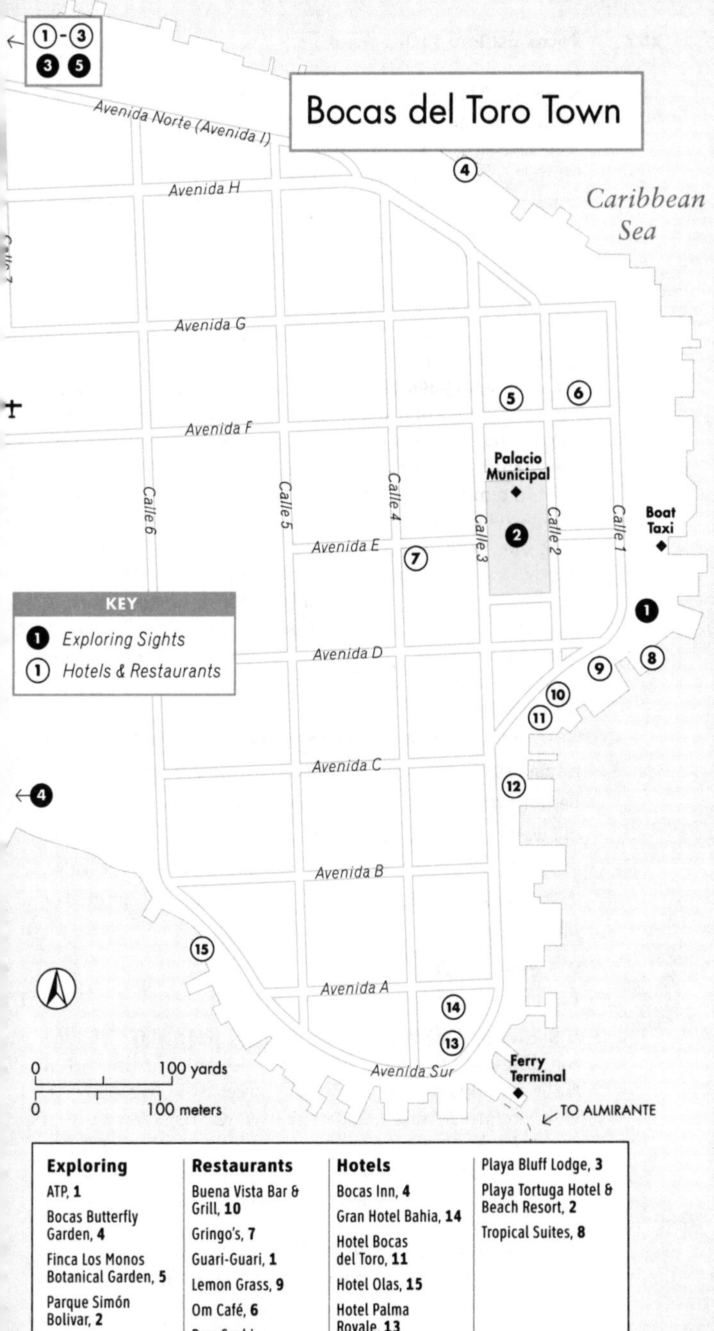
Bocas del Toro Town
Caribbean Sea
Avenida Norte (Avenida I)
Avenida H
Avenida G
Avenida F
Avenida E
Avenida D
Avenida C
Avenida B
Avenida A
Avenida Sur
Calle 6
Calle 5
Calle 4
Calle 3
Calle 2
Calle 1
Palacio Municipal
Boat Taxi
Ferry Terminal
TO ALMIRANTE
KEY
Exploring Sights
Hotels & Restaurants
0 100 yards
0 100 meters
Exploring
ATP, 1
Bocas Butterfly Garden, 4
Finca Los Monos Botanical Garden, 5
Parque Simón Bolivar, 2
Playa Bocas, 3
Restaurants
Buena Vista Bar & Grill, 10
Gringo's, 7
Guari-Guari, 1
Lemon Grass, 9
Om Café, 6
Raw Sushi + Martini Bar, 12
Hotels
Bocas Inn, 4
Gran Hotel Bahia, 14
Hotel Bocas del Toro, 11
Hotel Olas, 15
Hotel Palma Royale, 13
Hotel Swan's Cay, 5
Playa Bluff Lodge, 3
Playa Tortuga Hotel & Beach Resort, 2
Tropical Suites, 8

Sunanda Mehra is a Canadian of Punjabi descent who raided her aunt's cookbook before running off to Panama. You can savor such improbable delicacies as her prawn vindaloo, *palaak paneer* (fresh cheese in a spinach sauce), chicken tandoori, or any of half-dozen vegetable dishes. In the morning, treat yourself to an Indian breakfast, which includes vindaloo eggs in a roti wrap and *chana bhatura* (garbanzo curry with fried bread), accompanied by a refreshing fruit *lassi* (yogurt smoothie). *Average main: $10 Av. F at Calle 2 507/6624–0898 No credit cards Closed Wed. and May–June. No lunch.*

$ **Raw Sushi + Martini Bar.** *Sushi.* Is there any better name than "Raw" for a sushi restaurant? The Canadian owner prefers to refer to her restaurant's cuisine as Japanese fusion, and the menu here expands beyond classic sushi to include shrimp tempura and salad rolls. This newish, lively place has become a favorite among Bocas's large expat community, but all are welcome, resident and visitor alike. Dine inside if your group counts more than two. The tables overlook the water. Smaller tables line a long pier jutting out into the bay. Raw does a brisk business each evening during its 6–7 pm happy hour. *Average main: $10 Calle 3 at Av. C, Bocas del Toro 507/6938–8473 Closed Mon. No lunch.*

CONSERVING WATER. **As unlikely as it may seem in a place where it rains as much as it does in Bocas del Toro, the town suffers periodic water shortages, because it has outgrown its decades-old water system. The best hotels have massive water tanks to ensure they don't run out, but do your part, and conserve water. ⚠ The tap water in Bocas isn't potable, so drink only bottled or filtered water.**

WHERE TO STAY

For expanded hotel reviews, visit Fodors.com.

$ **Bocas Inn.** *B&B/Inn.* This small lodge in an older wooden building over the water has a great location at the end of Calle 3 and is buffered from the street by a large garden, so it's relatively quiet. **Pros:** great views; organized tours; good breakfast. **Cons:** no TV; no Internet. *Rooms from: $99 Av. Norte at Calle 3 507/757–9600 507/269–9415 in Panama City www.anconexpeditions.com 7 rooms Breakfast.*

$ **Gran Hotel Bahia.** *B&B/Inn.* Histoy abounds at the town's quaintest hotel, a two-story wooden building that was the headquarters of the United Fruit Company in the 1930s. **Pros:** good value; comfortable, historic building. **Cons:** off water; small windows. *Rooms from: $80* *Calle 3 and Av. A* *507/757–9626* *www.ghbahia.com* *18 rooms* *Closed June* *Breakfast.*

★ Fodor'sChoice **Hotel Bocas del Toro.** *Hotel.* This attractive
$$ water-front hotel was designed by a boat builder, so it's no coincidence that guest rooms, with their polished hardwoods and nautical decor, look as if they could be on a yacht. **Pros:** on the water; superb staff; very clean rooms. **Cons:** expensive for in-town Bocas, but good value for offerings. *Rooms from: $129* *Calle 2, next to Hotel Limbo* *507/757–9771* *507/757–9018* *www.hotelbocasdeltoro.com* *10 rooms, 1 suite* *Breakfast.*

$ **Hotel Olas.** *Hotel.* Hidden at the south end of town, this
★ large wooden hotel is one of the best deals in Bocas, comparable to more centrally located inns that charge twice as much. **Pros:** inexpensive; on the water; communal computer; quiet. **Cons:** rooms smallish. *Rooms from: $48* *Av. Sur at Calle 6* *507/757–9930* *www.hotelolas.com* *24 rooms* *No credit cards* *Breakfast.*

$ **Hotel Palma Royale.** *Hotel.* At four stories, a veritable skyscraper for Bocas, this newly constructed, ochre, all-suites hotel at the south end of town climbs in number of amenities as you climb the floors. **Pros:** quiet, attentive service; save money by cooking for yourself. **Cons:** a few blocks removed from the center of action. *Rooms from: $95* *Southern end of Calle 3, Bocas del Toro* *507/757–9979* *www.palmaroyale.com* *15 rooms* *Breakfast.*

$ **Hotel Swan's Cay.** *Hotel.* This two-story wooden complex behind the Palacio Municipal fits into Bocas well enough, but inside the lobby it feels like Old Europe. **Pros:** reasonable rates; pool by the sea; restaurant. **Cons:** incongruous decor. *Rooms from: $72* *Calle 3, between Avs. F and G* *507/757–9090* *507/757–9027* *www.swanscayhotel.com* *47 rooms, 2 suites* *No meals.*

$$ **Playa Tortuga Hotel & Beach Resort.** *Resort.* Everything, but everything is here at Bocas's newest, flashiest, resort-iest hotel. **Pros:** myriad activites; ocean views; good value for what is offered. **Cons:** not a good option if you crave solitude; outside of Bocas town. *Rooms from: $125* *2 km (1 mile) north of town on road to Playa Bluff, Bocas del Toro* *507/757–9050* *507/757–9044* *507/300–1893 in Panama City* *www.hotelplayatortuga.com* *74 rooms, 43 suites* *Multiple meal plans.*

5

$$ **Tropical Suites.** *Hotel.* The spacious rooms here evoke fully furnished Florida condos, with their tropical colors, ★ tile floors, ceiling fans, and sliding glass doors that open onto balconies (half have ocean views). **Pros:** decent value for offering; spacious rooms; great ocean views. **Cons:** questionably clean swimmng area. *Rooms from: $139* *South end of Calle 1* *507/757–9081* *507/757–9080* *www.bocastropical.com* *16 suites* *Breakfast.*

NIGHTLIFE AND THE ARTS

Bocas livens up when the sun goes down, because the temperature becomes more conducive to movement. The decks of the town's various waterfront restaurants are pleasant spots to enjoy a quiet drink and conversation.

Barco Hundido. Barco Hundido is a funky, open-air affair with tropical gardens. Wooden platforms stretch over the water, surrounding a small shipwreck that's lit at night so you can watch the fish. It's an obligatory stop if you wish to partake of the rowdier side of Bocas. *Calle 1, at Av. E* *507/6512–9032* *Daily 8 pm–midnight.*

Bocas Bambu Beach. A large, semi-open-air bar and restaurant in the center of town projects reggae music videos on a big screen. You're sure to hear "No Woman, No Cry" and all the standards here. *Calle 3, at Avenida C, Bocas del Toro* *507/757–9227* *Mon.–Sat. 6–11.*

La Iguana. La Iguana, in a wooden building over the water, gets packed with locals on Thursday nights, when ladies drink for free. *Calle 1, at Avenida D* *Mon.–Sat. 7–midnight.*

★ Fodor's Choice **The Wine Bar.** Tucked away on the second floor of a Calle 3 building, this comfortable wine bar is a nice change from the typical Bocas evening revelry. Here, you can actually hear yourself talk. Some nights there's food—a dish or two, light fare, whatever the owner decides to prepare—but you'll always find Bocas's best selection of wine. *Calle 3, at Av. C, Bocas del Toro* *507/6627–5906* *Mon.–Sat. 5–11.*

SPORTS AND THE OUTDOORS

SCUBA DIVING AND SNORKELING

Bocas is primarily a base for exploring the wonders of the surrounding archipelago, the most impressive of which are the acres of colorful coral reefs. More than a dozen dive spots are within five minutes to one hour by boat from the town's several good dive centers. Snorkeling excursions usually cost \$20–\$30, depending on the destination and number of passengers, and depart at 8 or 9 am. You can guarantee a lower rate for everyone if you organize a small group. Two-tank boat dives cost \$75–\$150, depending on distance.

Bocas Water Sports. The town's original dive shop, Bocas still maintains the best reputation. Diving is offered at a dozen sites, and you can take enriched air nitrox and certification courses. The company also offers daily snorkeling tours to the Cayos Zapatillas and other spots. Snorkeling equipment and kayaks can be rented. ✉ *Calle 3, 1 block south of Parque Bolívar* ☎ *507/757–9541* 🌐 *www.bocaswatersports.com.*

Dive Panama. This multilingual Dutch-owned outfitter offers inexpensive boat dives, snorkeling excursions, and PADI certification courses. ✉ *Avenida Norte, betwen Calles 3 and 4, Bocas del Toro* ☎ *507/6567–1812* 🌐 *www.thedutchpirate.com.*

La Buga. La Buga offers diving and snorkeling trips to outer reefs, ship wrecks, and Tiger Rock, as well as the complete slate of PADI courses. ✉ *Calle 3, next to Farmacia Rosa Blanca* ☎ *507/757–9534* 🌐 *www.labugapanama.com.*

Starfleet Scuba. Starfleet Scuba offers various two-tank boat dives and snorkeling excursions, and has open-water certification courses for \$250. ✉ *Calle 1* ☎ *507/757–9630* 🌐 *www.starfleetscuba.com.*

SURFING

Bocas is a short boat ride from the breaks on Islas Colón, Carenero, and Bastimentos, which makes it a great base for surfers.

Azucar Surf. Azucar Surf offers board rentals and surf lessons, as well as boat charters for groups of one to six people to the best spots around the islands. It also runs "girls only" surf packages. ✉ *Av. Norte, at Calle 6* ☎ *507/6491–2595* 🌐 *www.azucarsurf.com.*

Mondo Taitu. Mondo Taitu, a hostel on the north side of town, rents surfboards. ✉ *Av. G, at Calle 5* ☎ *507/757–9425* 🌐 *www.mondotaitu.com.*

5

Tropix. Surf shop Tropix is a good place to get advice, wax, or a board. ✉ *Calle 3, across from Parque Simón Bolívar* ☎ *507/757–9415* 🌐 *tropixsurf.tripod.com.*

SHOPPING

Although souvenir shops are limited in town, several Panamanian vendors sell arts and crafts at the north and south ends of Calle 3.

Artesanías Bri Bri. Artesanías Bri Bri sells hammocks, clothing, and local handicrafts, such as the jute bags made by indigenous Ngöbe people. ✉ *Calle 3, at Av. B* ☎ *507/757–9020* ⏲ *Daily 8–7.*

Super Gourmet. Stop in at this boutique food market for a yummy selection of organic chocolate made on-site. A huge collection of kosher food items is also available. ✉ *Calle 3 at Av. A, Bocas del Toro* ☎ *507/757–9357* 🌐 *www.supergourmetbocas.com* ⏲ *Mon.–Sat. 9–6.*

ISLA COLÓN

2 km (1 mile) north of Bocas Town.

Once you're outside of Bocas town, Isla Colón is a wild and beautiful place, with just two dirt roads, two lovely beaches, and significant swaths of tropical forest.

GETTING HERE AND AROUND

Avenida G leads north from Bocas town over an isthmus to the rest of Isla Colón, where the road soon forks. Veer right for Playa Bluff and the surf breaks of Paunch and Dumpers, which can be reached in about 30 minutes on a very rough road by bicycle, or in an hour on foot. A taxi takes about 40 minutes, and costs $20. A boat to Paunch or Dumpers from Bocas town should cost $10. Bocas del Drago is accessible by boat, taxi, or bus.

EXPLORING

Playa Bluff. The nicest and biggest beach on Isla Colón is Bluff Beach, a 7-km (3½-miles) stretch of golden sand backed by tropical vegetation and washed by aquamarine waters. It's a great place to spend a day, or even an hour, but it has virtually no facilities, so pack water and snacks. When the waves are big, Playa Bluff has a beach break right on shore, but it can also develop rip currents, so swimmers beware. When the sea is calm it's a decent swimming beach—always exercise caution—and the rocky points at either end have decent snorkeling. Leatherback turtles nest here from April to September, when a local group runs night tours to look for them. If you're lucky, you may find baby turtles on the beach between June and December. ✉ *4 km (2½ miles) north of Bocas Town* ✣ *Veer right at the Y heading out of Bocas Town, continue 4 km (2½ miles) north on the coastal road.*

Boca del Drago. Boca del Drago is a tiny fishing community in the northwest corner of the island that overlooks the mainland. The water at the coconut palm–lined beach is *usually* calm, which makes for good swimming and snorkeling. It's a popular destination for boat tours. A small restaurant on the beach serves decent seafood and always has plenty of cold beer. ✉ *14 km (9 miles) northwest of Bocas town.*

Swan's Cay (*Isla de los Pájaros*). Swan's Cay is a rocky islet off the north coast of Isla Colón that is commonly visited on boat tours to Boca del Drago. The swan it was named for is actually the red-billed tropicbird, an elegant white seabird with a long tail and bright-red bill that nests on the island in significant numbers. The rugged island has a narrow, natural arch in the middle of it that boatmen can slip through when the seas are calm. The surrounding ocean is a good scuba-diving area. ✉ *5 km (3 miles) northeast of Boca del Drago.*

5

WHERE TO STAY

For expanded hotel reviews, visit Fodors.com.

$ **Playa Bluff Lodge.** *Hotel.* It's still pretty remote out here in Playa Bluff, but this comfy place is an oasis at the end of a rugged road. **Pros:** friendly, knowledgeable owners; wonderfully secluded; eco-friendly. **Cons:** rough road to get here. *Rooms from: $95* ✉ *Playa Bluff, Isla Colón* ☎ *507/6798–8507* 🌐 *www.playablufflodge.com* *5 rooms* *No credit cards* *Breakfast.*

★ $$$$ Fodor'sChoice **Punta Caracol Acqua-Lodge.** *Resort.* This collection of spacious bungalows above the turquoise shallows off Isla Colón's western coast is both gorgeous and innovative. **Pros:** gorgeous setting; charming rooms; eco-friendly. **Cons:** expensive for Bocas; sometimes buggy, minimum stay is two nights. *Rooms from: $316* ✉ *10 km (6 miles) northwest of Bocas town* ☎ *507/757–9718* 🌐 *www.puntacaracol.com* *9 cabanas* *Some meals.*

SPORTS AND THE OUTDOORS

SCUBA DIVING AND SNORKELING

Isla Colón doesn't have great diving, but it does have good snorkeling, mostly along the west side of the island, which has scattered reefs along the mangrove islets, one of the best of which is in front of the Punta Caracol Acqualodge. Excursions to Boca del Drago and Swan's Cay also include snorkeling.

SURFING

There are three good surf breaks on Isla Colón, all of them 5–7 km (3–4 miles) from Bocas. The best months for surfing are November to March, though there are often good swells in July and August. They all require intermediate or expert skills. September and October tend to be the flattest months. There are waves about half the time the rest of the year.

Paunch is a reef break 5 km (3 miles) north of town, around the bend from the Playa Mango Resort, that you have to walk over a coral platform to reach. The best way to get there from town is by boat. It breaks mostly left, and is for intermediate to expert surfers. **Dumpers** is an excellent left reef break on the point north of Paunch, 7 km (4 miles) north of town. It is a quick, hollow wave that gets dangerous when big. **Playa Bluff** has a powerful beach break close to shore when there's a good swell.

TURTLE WATCHING

Playa Bluff. Playa Bluff is a nesting beach for the rare leatherback turtle from April to September, when night tours are led there by members of the Grupo Ecológico Bluff, a local Ngöbe group. ✉ *Coastal road, 4 km (2½ miles) north of Bocas Town.*

ISLA BASTIMENTOS

Isla Bastimentos covers 20 square miles of varied landscapes, including lush tropical forest, mangrove estuaries, a lake, and several of the archipelago's nicest beaches. It also has several Afro-Caribbean and Ngöbe indigenous communities, and some excellent snorkeling and surfing spots. Old Bank, the archipelago's second-largest town, overlooks a cove on the island's western tip. The northern coast holds four beaches separated by rocky points, the longest of which, Playa Larga, lies within Parque Nacional Marino Isla Bastimentos. This park also protects a swath

of rain forest and the nearby islands of Cayos Zapatillas. Mangrove forests and islets line Bastimentos's southern side. There you can find the indigenous community of Bahia Honda.

The island's long southeast coast is more distant and remote, taking 40 minutes to reach from Bocas by boat. The coast's southern point, Macca Bite, is hemmed by mangroves, perfect for kayak exploration, and is next to the archipelago's most popular snorkeling spot, Crawl Cay. A short boat ride to the east of either point takes you to the bleached sand and vast coral gardens of the paradisiacal Cayos Zapatillas.

OLD BANK (BASTIMENTOS)

4 km (2½ miles) and 10 minutes by boat east of Bocas Town.

Spread along a bay on the island's western tip, between the ocean and forested hills, is a colorful, crowded, poor collection of simple wooden buildings known as Old Bank. It is a predominantly Afro-Caribbean community where

Guari-Guari—a mix of patois English and traces of Spanish—is the lingua franca. Most people live in elevated wooden houses, some awfully rudimentary, that line sidewalks and dirt paths instead of streets. Old Bank doesn't have a proper sewage system, so avoid swimming in the bay, even though the local kids do. Head to one of the nearby beaches instead.

GETTING HERE AND AROUND

Small boats regularly carry people between Bocas and Old Bank during the day. They depart Bocas from the dock next to the Farmacia Rosa Blanca and Bastimentos from the Muelle Municipal (the long dock in the middle of town). The trip takes 10 minutes and costs $2 each way.

WORD OF MOUTH. **"Isla Bastimentos is a beautiful island with great beach and jungle options—also a 15-minute boat ride to Bocas." —mad**

WHERE TO EAT AND STAY

For expanded hotel reviews, visit Fodors.com.

$ ★ ✕ **Roots.** *Caribbean.* Perched over the sea near the center of Old Bank, this rustic, open-air restaurant is known for serving authentic *bocatoreña* food. House specialties include Caribbean chicken (in a mildly spicy sauce), fresh lobster, shrimp, and conch, listed as "snail" on the menu. They are served with a hearty mix of coconut rice, red beans, and a simple cabbage salad. The ambience—a thatch roof with tables and chairs made from tree trunks—is equally authentic. *Average main: $8 On the water east of police post 507/6473–5111 No credit cards Closed Tues.*

★ $$$ Fodor'sChoice **Eclypse de Mar.** *Resort.* Built over the water on stilts, this luxurious eco-lodge is the ultimate Caribbean fantasy. **Pros:** friendly staff; remote location; innovative design. **Cons:** basic breakfast; loud music can sometimes be heard from Old Bank. *Rooms from: $250 Bastimentos Island 507/6430–7576, 507/6627–3000 www.eclypsedemar.com 2 rooms, 6 bungalows Breakfast.*

SURFING

Bastimentos's north coast has half a dozen surf breaks, some of which are hard to reach. **Wizard's Beach** has a fun beach break when the waves are small, but when the swell is big, it requires serious experience. **Silverbacks** is an experts-only reef break in front of the point west of Wizard's Beach that is the only place to surf when a big swell hits.

RED FROG BEACH AND BAHIA HONDA

8 km (5 miles) east of Bocas, 4 km (2½ miles) east of Old Bank.

A couple of miles east of Old Bank, Isla Bastimentos gets narrow—a mere ½ km (¼ mile) wide—and the sea to the south is dotted with mangrove islets. Here you can find a small dock that marks the entrance to a footpath across the island to Red Frog Beach, one of the loveliest spots in the archipelago, with its golden sand shaded by tropical trees, but undergoing major real estate development in 2012. East of the beach, the island becomes wide again, and is largely covered with lush rain forest that is home to everything from mealy parrots to white-faced capuchin monkeys and countless tiny, bright-red poison dart frogs. The scattered homes of local Ngöbe line the bay to the south, known as Bahia Honda, where an indigenous organization has cut a trail through the forest and built a rustic restaurant for tourists. To the east is Parque Nacional Marino Isla Bastimentos and to the south a narrow channel through the mangroves that is the main route to the island's eastern coast and the Cayos Zapatillas.

GETTING HERE AND AROUND

Most day tours to Crawl Cay cost around $25 and include a stop at Dolphin Bay, Hospital Point, and Red Frog Beach before heading back to Bocas. Boat operators will drop you off at Red Frog Beach for $3–$5 from Old Bank and $6–$10 from Bocas, and will pick you up at a specified time.

EXPLORING

Red Frog Beach. Remarkable natural beauty and relative accessibility (a five-minute walk from a dock) combine to make Red Frog Beach one of the most popular spots in Bocas del Toro. The beach is almost a mile long, with golden sand backed by coconut palms, Indian almond trees, and other tropical greenery. It's the perfect spot for lounging on the sand, playing in the sea, and admiring the amazing scenery. Red Frog has, unfortunately, become a victim of its own popularity with a 170-acre condo devlopment and a 150-boat marina under construction. ⚠ **Red Frog is usually a good swimming beach, but when the surf's up, rip currents can make it dangerous, so don't go beyond waist-deep if the waves are big.** ⊠ *4 km (2½ miles) east of Old Bank.*

WHERE TO STAY

For expanded hotel reviews, visit Fodors.com.

★ Fodor'sChoice **La Loma Jungle Lodge.** *Resort.* A boat ride through mangroves and a walk across wooden planks will lead you to the tastefully rustic bungalows at this eco-lodge, part of a 60-acre working cacao farm. **Pros:** in the jungle; friendly; environmentally conscientious; good tours of Bastimentos bat caves. **Cons:** very rustic; steep climb to rooms; paths are extremely dark at night. *Rooms from: $200 Bahía Honda 507/6619–5364 www.thejunglelodge.com 3 bungalows No credit cards All meals.*

SPORTS AND THE OUTDOORS

Bastimentos Sky Canopy Tour. Neighboring Costa Rica gave the world the so-called zip-line canopy tour, and they have sprung up around the world, including here in the Red Frog complex on Isla Bastimentos. The concept: A series of cables, seven in this case with one up to 1,000 feet long and 150 feet above the ground, zip you from tree to tree, courtesy of helmet and very secure harness. This facility also includes a rappel line and a Tarzan swing. Though billed as a way to get close to nature and observe life in the rain-forest canopy—hence the name "canopy tour"—your screams of delight will probably scare away any animal life within a mile. Think of it more like a two-hour amusement-park ride. Reservations are required. *507/757–8021 www.redfrogbeach.com $55; boat transport from Bocas town $4 one-way, $7 round-trip Daily at 10 am, 1, and 3:30 pm.*

MACCA BITE

20 km (12 miles) southeast of Bocas.

Bastimentos's southernmost point has an odd name, and its origin is as mysterious as Bocas del Toro's, though the theory is that wild macaws once lived there (there are now tame ones at the eponymous lodge). That hilly headland hemmed by mangroves and draped with lush rain forest is a mere 30 minutes from Bocas by boat, yet it feels like the end of the world.

Crawl Cay (*Coral Cay*). Just east of Macca Bite is Crawl Cay, a large reef that holds an impressive array of coral heads, colorful sponges, large sea fans, and hundreds of small reef fish. It is an excellent spot for snorkelers, who can simply float over the reef and watch the show. The reef also has enough marine life in and around its innumerable crannies to entertain experienced divers. It is sufficiently sheltered that the water there is usually calm and clear, even when the sea is too rough for diving at Cayos Zapatillas.

GETTING HERE AND AROUND

Tranquilo Bay lodge provides free transportation to and from Bocas on Wednesday and Saturday but charges $100 for the trip on other days. Hotel Macca Bite charges $50 for round-trip transportation. Rates are per trip, not per passenger.

WHERE TO STAY

For expanded hotel reviews, visit Fodors.com.

$$$ **Hotel Macca Bite.** *Resort.* Perched at the edge of the point, between the mangroves and the sea, this comfortable hotel has inspiring views of crystalline waters dotted with coral heads, the ocean horizon, and nearby Isla Popa. **Pros:** on the water; great view; well-equipped rooms; snorkeling; excursions. **Cons:** remote; no transportation at night; occasional no-see-ums. *Rooms from: $200* *Crawl Cay* *507/6673–5155* *www.hotelmaccabite.com* *8 room, 3 suites* *Some meals.*

★ Fodor's Choice **Popa Paradise Beach Resort.** *Resort.* On the
$$ northeastern tip of Isla Popa, this barefoot luxury resort sits on a white-sand beach backed by 25 acres of tropical rain forest. **Pros:** family-friendly; excellent food; courteous staff. **Cons:** remote; paths are dark at night. *Rooms from: $160* *Isla Popa* *507/6550–2505* *www.popaparadisebeachresort.com* *9 cottages, 5 lodge rooms, 2 suites, 1 penthouse* *Breakfast.*

$$$$ **Tranquilo Bay.** *All-Inclusive.* This jungle lodge is geared
★ toward active travelers—you can kayak, snorkel, hike, surf, or fish, or just stroll the beach and lounge in a hammock, all amid amazing scenery. **Pros:** varied activities; wild surroundings; nice rooms; good food. **Cons:** expensive; remote; three-night minimum stay; fixed arrival and departure days. *Rooms from: $743* *Macca Bite* *713/589–6952 in U.S.* *www.tranquilobay.com* *6 bungalows* *Closed June* *All-inclusive.*

SPORTS AND THE OUTDOORS

Macca Bite's lodges lie near some of the archipelago's best dive sites and offer daily snorkeling excursions and kayaking. Tranquilo Bay also offers jungle hiking, sportfishing, and surfing.

5

PARQUE NACIONAL MARINO ISLA BASTIMENTOS

★ **Parque Nacional Marino Isla Bastimentos** (*Bastimentos Island National Marine Park*). About one-third of Isla Bastimentos and the Cayos Zapatillas, to the southeast, lie within Parque Nacional Marino Isla Bastimentos. The park's 32,000 acres comprise an array of ecosystems ranging from sea-grass beds to rain forest and include some spectacular and ecologically important areas. Much of the park is virtually inaccessible, especially the island's forested interior, but you can see most of its flora and fauna in the private reserves of adjacent jungle lodges. That wildlife includes tiny, bright-red poison dart frogs, green iguanas, two-toed sloths, ospreys, parrots, toucans, and collared manakins. The park's coral reefs protect even greater biological diversity, including spiny lobsters, sea stars, barracuda, various snapper species, and countless colorful reef fish.

Most people experience the park's reefs at the postcard-perfect, coconut-palmed **Cayos Zapatillas,** two cays southeast of Bastimentos that are the park's crown jewels. The Cayos' most impressive scenery is actually in the surrounding ocean, which holds 1,200 acres of protected coral reef ranging from a shallow platform around the islands to steep walls pocked with caves. Scuba divers explore the reef's outer expanses, while snorkelers enjoy views of the shallow platform adorned with some impressive coral formations. The park tends to have more fish than Crawl Cay and other unprotected dive spots, and divers can expect to see tiny angelfish, parrot fish, squirrelfish, octopi, eels, stingrays, and countless other marine creatures. When seas are rough (as they often are between December and March), scuba diving is limited to the leeward side of the island, making Crawl Cay a more attractive dive spot at that time. The island has a ranger station and a small nature trail through the forest. Bring sunblock, insect repellent, a hat, a towel, water, and snorkeling gear. ☎ *507/758–6603* 🎫 *$10* ⏲ *Daily 6–6.*

Eastern Panama

WITH GUNA YALA (SAN BLAS ISLANDS) AND THE DARIÉN

6

WORD OF MOUTH

"My best memories of our trip to Panama are the two nights we spent in the San Blas Islands. Sort of a hassle to get to, but, a memorable experience."

—JeanH

www.fodors.com/forums

By David Dudenhoefer

THE EASTERN PROVINCES OF GUNA Yala and the Darién are Panama at its most pristine, with spectacular scenery, wildlife, and indigenous cultures that have barely changed since the first Spanish explorers arrived here more than five centuries ago.

The region's riveting tropical nature ranges from the colorful diversity of Caribbean coral reefs to amazing birdlife of the rain forest. The traditional Guna (formerly Kuna), Emberá, and Wounaan communities that live here offer a fascinating alternative to the modern world. The combination of nature and culture provides the ingredients for unforgettable journeys, on which you might imagine you've traveled back in time or perhaps to the very ends of the Earth. Yet most of the region's lodges lie within a 60-minute flight from Panama City, which is often followed by a dugout canoe trip over aquamarine waters or up a jungle-shaded river. And the flights themselves take you over vast expanses of pure jungle. When it comes to Guna Yala and the Darién, more than in any other part of Panama, the adventure begins with the trip here.

Nevertheless, true adventure has its price, and it's not for everyone. This region's remarkable but remote attractions lie far from the nearest paved road, convenience store, or ATM, and may require that you put up with conditions you wouldn't stand for at home. Tours and accommodations can be expensive; for the cost of a suite in Panama City you may have to settle for a thatched hut. You may also have to deal with insects or less-than-fantastic food, but the prize is exposure to splendid scenery, and unique indigenous cultures. Your adventure may include boat trips to breathtaking islands, jungle hikes, snorkeling over coral reefs, or witnessing ancient rituals. And at night you'll hear only the calls of jungle critters, or the slosh of waves against coral.

ORIENTATION AND PLANNING

GETTING ORIENTED

Guna Yala (aka Kuna Yala) stretches along Panama's northeast coast from the Central Caribbean eastward to the border with Colombia, comprising forested mountains, coastal lowlands, the 365 San Blas Islands, and the surrounding sea. The entire province was once called San Blas, but it is known now by its indigenous name, Guna Yala,

TOP REASONS TO GO

Indigenous Cultures. Eastern Panama's indigenous Guna, Emberá, and Wounaan villages are amazingly traditional, colorful places that provide visitors with unforgettable cross-cultural experiences.

San Blas Islands. The islands of Guna Yala have ivory beaches shaded by coconut palms and washed by turquoise waters—scenery fit for the covers of travel magazines or the daydreams of snowbound accountants.

Ocean Treasures. Guna Yala's crystalline sea holds countless coral reefs awash with living rainbows of fish and invertebrates, whereas the white-sand shallows of its islands are idyllic spots for a tranquil swim.

Spectacular Wildlife. The eastern provinces' lush rain forests, mangrove estuaries, and cloud forests together hold more than about 500 bird species, and everything from crocodiles to capuchin monkeys.

Fabulous Fishing. More than 250 sport-fishing records have been set in the sea south of the Darién, which is accessible from one of the world's best fishing lodges.

which translates as "Land of the Guna." Only one road penetrates the otherwise isolated province, a dirt track called the Camino Llano-Cartí that traverses its western end. The eastern half of the narrow indigenous territory borders the vast Darién province, the southern half of which holds Parque Nacional Darién, various smaller reserves, and two *comarcas* (indigenous territories). The Carretera Interamericana (Inter-American Highway) dead-ends in the Darién at a frontier town called Yaviza, beyond which there are virtually no roads. Most travelers consequently fly in and out of both regions. There are daily flights to Guna Yala and twice-weekly flights to the Darién.

PLANNING

WHEN TO GO

It rains almost every afternoon from May to December in the Darién, though the rain lets up a bit in July and August. Most people consequently visit the region from January to May. Guna Yala has similar seasons, though it gets less rain in September and October, and more in December and January. The sea tends to be rough here from January to

April. The best diving months are August to November, when the seas tend to be calm and visibility is better.

GETTING HERE AND AROUND

AIR TRAVEL

The easiest way to get to Guna Yala or the Darién is to fly. The domestic airline Air Panama offers daily flights to several airstrips in Guna Yala (Achutupo, El Porvenir, and Playón Chico) and two flights per week to the Darién (Bahía Piñas). ⚠ **Flights often land at several airstrips, so make sure you get off at the correct one!** There are neither airline offices nor airports in this region, only simple airstrips.

BOAT TRAVEL

Motorized dugouts are the most common form of transportation in Guna Yala and the Darién, where most people travel via jungle rivers. Some of the better lodges in Guna Yala transport guests in small fiberglass boats, whereas the Tropic Star fishing lodge, in southwest Darién, uses more seaworthy vessels. Most visitors to this region go to either the Darién or Guna Yala, since direct travel between the two provinces is time consuming.

Boat transportation is included in the rates of all Guna Yala hotels. The company San Blas Sailing runs sailboat cruises to Guna Yala that combines visits to Guna villages with time on pristine outer islands, such as the Cayos Holandeses.

Several cruise lines, including CruiseWest, Holland America, Princess, Seabourn, Silversea, and Windstar make port calls in the San Blas Islands on select Panama Canal and western Caribbean itineraries; CruiseWest also sails to an Emberá village in the Darién. You'll be tendered ashore. The Guna levy a $5 tax on cruise visitors. It may or may not be included in the price of your shore excursion. The total absence of restaurants means that cruise visits are kept short—usually just under a half-day—with time to be back on ship for the next meal.

CAR TRAVEL

Several people provide transportation between Panama City and Cartí, in Guna Yala, in four-wheel-drive vehicles; you will be picked up at your hotel. It's possible to drive to Cartí in a four-wheel-drive vehicle and leave it there while you visit nearby islands. Ancon Expeditions transports guests to and from its lodge on Punta Patiño with a combination of driving and a boat.

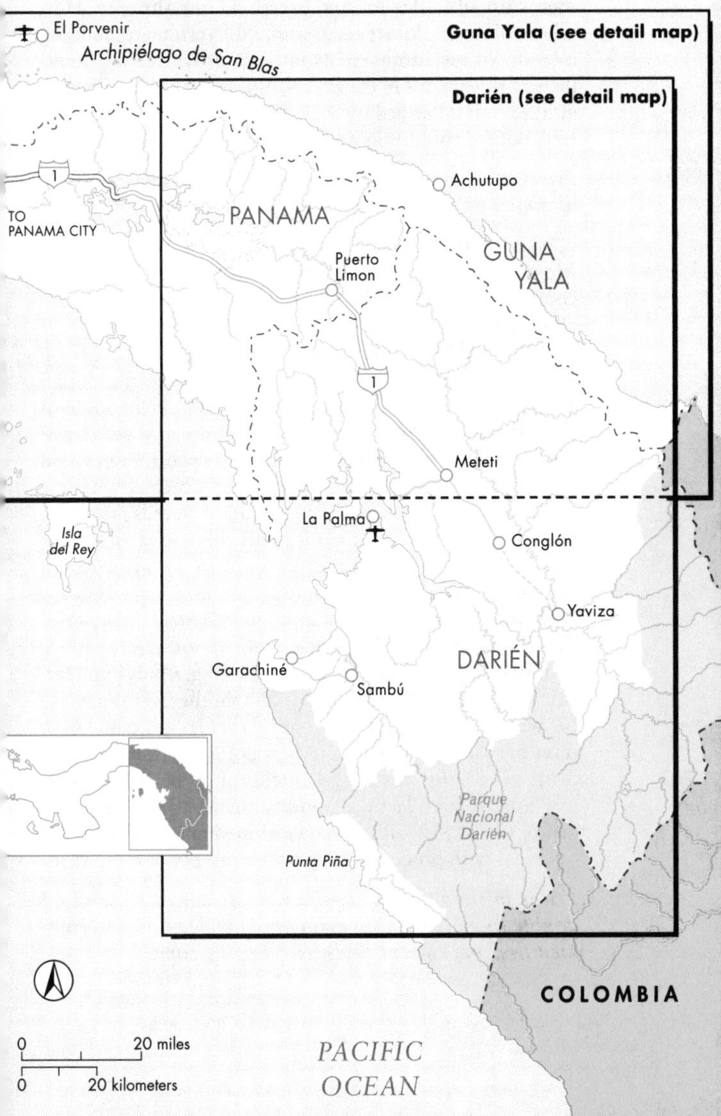
Eastern Panama
Caribbean Sea
El Porvenir
Archipiélago de San Blas
Guna Yala (see detail map)
Darién (see detail map)
1
TO PANAMA CITY
PANAMA
Achutupo
GUNA YALA
Puerto Limon
1
Meteti
La Palma
Conglón
Isla del Rey
Yaviza
Garachiné
Sambú
DARIÉN
Parque Nacional Darién
Punta Piña
COLOMBIA
0
20 miles
0
20 kilometers
PACIFIC OCEAN

ABOUT THE RESTAURANTS

This isn't the part of Panama you head to for epicurean delights. You can count on fresh seafood in Guna Yala—and little else. If you don't eat seafood, you should mention it when you reserve and again when you arrive. Establishments usually offer lobster, except March through May, when fishing for lobster is prohibited. Nothing resembling a sit-down restaurant exists in these provinces, so hotels include three meals in their rates, usually served family-style at fixed times. Purified water, coffee, tea, and fruit juices are free; bottled soft drinks and alcoholic beverages cost extra.

Prices in the reviews are the average cost of a main course at dinner or, if dinner is not served, at lunch.

ABOUT THE HOTELS

Most accommodations in this part of Panama range from comfortably rustic to downright primitive. Only Guna are allowed to own businesses in Guna Yala; a waga (foreigner) is prohibited from holding property here. Lodges are basic as a result—most have no hot water, no air-conditioning, and only a few hours of electricity at night—but some of those thatched bungalows have priceless ocean views. There are a few nice Guna lodges, but the less expensive ones tend to be dirty and serve lamentable food, which is why few are listed in this book. Since most Guna lodges lack offices, only three accept credit cards. The alternative is to visit Guna Yala on a day trip and sleep at Coral Lodge, 26 km (16 miles) away, which has most of the comforts of home (⇨ *Santa Isabela in "The Canal and Central Panama")*. The Darién currently has few lodging options, but they are comfortable, and include air-conditioning. One characteristic all lodges in this region share is that they are expensive for what you get, but keep in mind that rooms come with three meals, guided tours, and transportation. Rates usually drop by 10% for stays of two nights or more. All lodgings in Guna Yala collect a mandatory per-person, per-night visitor tax of $10—it's usually included in the price you're quoted—with proceeds going to community development.

Prices in the reviews are the lowest cost of a standard double room in high season. For expanded hotel reviews, facilities, and current deals, visit Fodors.com.

A BIT OF PANAMA HISTORY

In 1510 conquistador Vasco Nuñez de Balboa founded the first Spanish town in Central America, Santa María la Antigua del Darién, in a bay on the eastern end of what is now Guna Yala. Three years later, Balboa departed from Santa María with a group of men to look for a sea that local people had told him lay to the south. After hiking through the Darién jungle, Balboa reached the Gulf of San Miguel, where he became the first European to lay eyes on an ocean he dubbed "Pacífico," referring to the gulf's calm waters. Shortly thereafter the Spaniards discovered gold in the mountains of the Darién; mines here became so productive that Spain brought in African slaves, as the region's indigenous population succumbed to old-world diseases and inhumane working conditions. Meanwhile, a late 17th-century attempt by Scotland to colonize the Darién failed miserably. Some historians credit the so-called Darién Scheme with so weakening Scotland economically that it had no choice but to agree to a 1707 union with England.

When the conquistadors first arrived in Panama, the Guna lived in the jungles of northern Colombia, but in the 16th century they began moving up the coast into present-day Panama, where they eventually established their villages in the San Blas Islands. During the 17th and 18th centuries the Guna allied themselves with French and English pirates, providing them safe harbor and food in exchange for protection from Spain. Guna warriors often joined the pirates on raids of Spanish gold mines and ports. The Spaniards never subjugated the Guna, who lived independently until the early 20th century, when the new Republic of Panama government tried to establish a military presence in the San Blas Islands.

In 1925 the Guna rebelled against the Panamanians, killing or capturing all government officials in their territory in what the Guna call the Revolución de Tule. Subsequent negotiations led to the creation of the Comarca Guna Yala, an independent territory governed by the Congreso General Guna, a democratic congress of Guna chiefs. Decades later the Guna model was copied by the Emberá and Wounaan, who now share two *comarcas* in the eastern and western lowlands of the Darién, though they gained their autonomy through political pressure rather than revolution.

ESSENTIALS

Guna Yala and the Darién may have pristine nature and traditional cultures, but both provinces lack ATMs and pharmacies, and they have only rudimentary clinics, simple stores, and few phones. Although the Darién lodges have bilingual guides, few Guna lodges have English speakers, though you can hire a guide in Panama City to accompany you. Flights to Guna Yala depart at 6 am, and ground transportation often leaves at 5 am—at least the lodges serve you breakfast when you arrive. Bring plenty of sunblock, a hat, insect repellent, a water bottle, and cash.

⚠ **If you have serious health problems in either Guna Yala or the Darién, get on the next flight to Panama City.**

EMERGENCIES

The larger islands have police stations with radios to call Panama City for help in an emergency and tiny *centros de salud* (health centers) that can provide first aid. Lodges in Punta Patiño and Bahía Piñas have satellite phones to call Panama City for an air ambulance in case of emergencies.

MONEY MATTERS

There are no ATMs in this part of Panama, so bring all the money you'll need during your trip. Stock up on small bills in Panama City, since the indigenous vendors, and even some hotels, are usually short on change.

SAFETY

The main dangers in Guna Yala are the sun and sea creatures such as Portuguese man o' war, which are rare. Visiting Parque Nacional Darién and the area around it is currently not advisable because armed Colombian guerrilla groups have been known to slip into Panamanian territory; some hikers were kidnapped there years ago. When hiking through the rain forest anywhere in Panama, be careful where you put your hands and feet because there are plenty of palms with spiny trunks, some stinging insects, and the occasional poisonous snake.

TELEPHONES

Telephone access is spotty in this region. Hotels near El Porvenir have cell-phone reception, but most areas of Guna Yala have only pay phones—usually one or two per island.

Tour Companies **San Blas Sailing** ☎ *507/314-1288, 507/314-1800* 🌐 *sanblassailing.com.*

GUNA YALA (SAN BLAS)

The San Blas Archipelago and surrounding sea are the main attractions in Guna Yala—an indigenous *comarca* (autonomous territory) stretching more than 200 km (120 miles) along Panama's northeast coast—but the traditional culture of the Guna is a close second. The comarca is composed of a thin strip of land dominated by a mountain range called the Serranía de San Blas and the 365 San Blas Islands that dot the coastal waters. Although much of the world still refers to this region by its former name, San Blas, you'll endear yourself to residents by using the name they give to their home, Guna Yala. ■TIP→ **Note that you may also see it spelled Kuna Yala, but Guna leaders voted to change the spelling from Kuna to Guna in 2010.**

This is a lush and stunning region of forest-cloaked mountains, white-sand beaches, vibrant coral reefs, and timeless villages. Your trip here can consequently combine time on heavenly islands, jungle hiking, handicraft shopping, and exposure to a proud and beautiful indigenous people. Since coral reefs surround nearly every island, snorkeling is practically obligatory in the archipelago. Most lodges include the use of snorkeling equipment in their rates, and all of them provide daily trips to beaches with reefs nearby. You don't need to swim to appreciate the area's beauty, though, because the scenery topside is just as impressive; coconut groves shade ivory sand, dugout canoes with lateen sails ply turquoise waters, and cane huts with thatch roofs make up island villages.

Guna Yala's greatest beauty, however, may be in the traditional dress of its women, whose striking clothing includes hand-stitched *molas* (appliqué fabric pictures), colorful skirts and scarves, and intricate beadwork on their calves and forearms. ■TIP→ **Note that women and children commonly expect a payment of $1 if you photograph them.** Men, however, have gradually abandoned traditional clothing in favor of jeans, polo or tropical cabana shirts, and derby hats (for older men) or baseball caps (for younger men). Times are changing, even in Guna Yala.

THE GUNA FLAG. As befits a self-governing region, the flag of Guna Yala flies proudly here, with Panama's blue-white-red national flag little in evidence. Don't be alarmed at what you see: the local flag contains a black reverse *swastika* on a field of yellow, an ancient Guna symbol representing an octopus. Like the

Sanskrit swastika you'll see almost everywhere in India, it has nothing to do with Nazi Germany.

EL PORVENIR, CARTÍ, AND RÍO SIDRA

95 km (60 miles) northeast of Panama City.

The most accessible and popular part of Guna Yala is the cluster of islands on its western end, the most prominent of which are the provincial capital of El Porvenir, and Cartí Suitupo and Rio Sidra, which are the area's largest communities. This area holds the same kinds of timeless indigenous villages and paradisiacal islands as the rest of Guna Yala, the differences being that it receives more visitors, especially during the New Year, Carnaval, and Easter holidays and its hotels are geared toward backpackers, whereas lodges to the east provide a higher level of comfort and service.

GETTING HERE AND AROUND

Western Guna Yala can be reached by flying Air Panama to El Porvenir (PVE). Flights depart at 6 am, and are met by guides from the area's lodges.

Cartí is the only part of Guna Yala that can be reached by land, via the Llano-Cartí road, which runs between the village of El Llano, on the Interamerican Highway, north to the rudimentary port of Cartí. Lam Tours offers daily service between Panama City and Cartí in a four-wheel-drive vehicle.

Río Sidra is accessible by land, via the Llano-Cartí road, or by air, via El Porvenir. Lam Tours offers a daily taxi service between Panama City and Cartí, Air Panama has daily flights to El Porvenir (PVE). Río Sidra lodges can pick you up at either Cartí or El Porvenir.

Air Panama ☎ *507/316–9000* 🌐 *www.flyairpanama.com.*

Lam Tours. The only part of Guna Yala that can be reached by road is the western El Porvenir area, via the Llano–Cartí road, which crosses the lushly forested Serranía de San Blas. Lam Tours runs a bus/taxi service from Panama City to Cartí, where boats from lodges near El Porvenir and Río Sidra pick up guests. Lam Tours will pick you up at your hotel at 5:30 am, reaching Cartí around 9:30 am, and returns to Panama City shortly thereafter. ☎ *507/6676–6384, 507/6706–2810.*

Guna Yala

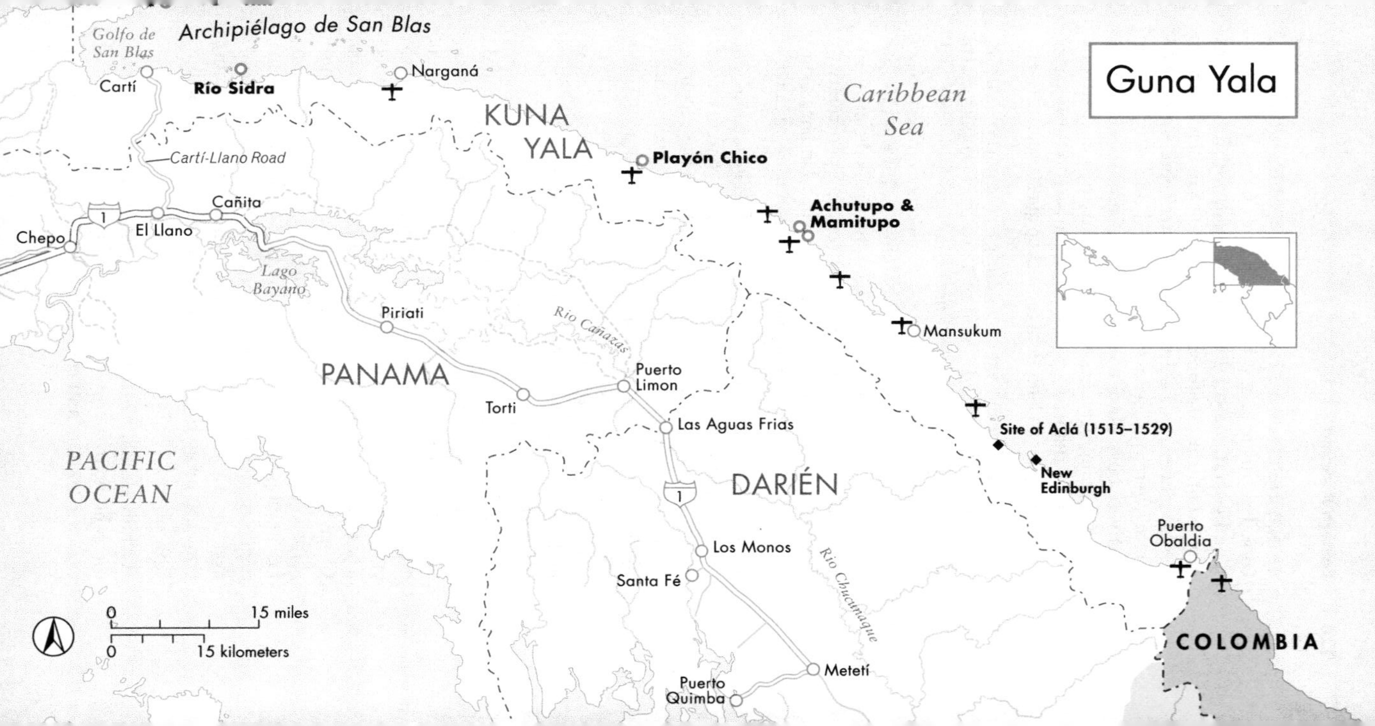

Guna Yala
Archipiélago de San Blas
Golfo de San Blas
Cartí
Río Sidra
Narganá
Caribbean Sea
KUNA YALA
Playón Chico
Achutupo & Mamitupo
Mansukum
Site of Aclá (1515–1529)
New Edinburgh
Puerto Obaldia
COLOMBIA
Cartí-Llano Road
Cañita
El Llano
Chepo
1
Lago Bayano
Piriati
Río Cañazas
PANAMA
Torti
Puerto Limon
Las Aguas Frias
DARIÉN
1
Los Monos
Santa Fé
Río Chucunaque
Metetí
Puerto Quimba
PACIFIC OCEAN
0
15 miles
0
15 kilometers

EXPLORING

Cartí. This rustic port is the only part of Guna Yala accessible by land, via the Llano-Cartí road, which winds its way over the lushly forested Serranía de San Blas between the Interamerican Highway and Carti. There is no community here, just a few buildings and docks, but it is a relatively busy place most mornings, because people and goods moving between more than a dozen Guna communities and Panama City pass through here. ■ TIP→ **Lodges near El Porvenir and Río Sidra can pick up guests here.** ✉ *Cartí.*

Cartí Suitupo. The closest community to the port of Cartí is the densely populated island of Cartí Suitupo (aka Cartí Sugdub). Here visitors will find a collection of thatched huts, cement stores, and plenty of handicraft hawkers. Near the school is a large thatched building called the Casa de la Cultura, where sahilas (chiefs) from across the province gather once or twice a year. Aside from an opportunity to experience life in a Guna community, the island has a tiny museum dedicated to traditional Guna culture. ✉ *Cartí.*

Museo de la Cultura Guna. This small, family-run museum is housed in a typical Guna home, with a thatched roof, cane walls, and sand floor. It's packed with the accoutrements of traditional Guna life, such sleeping hammocks, woven baskets and fans, ceremonial wooden staffs and statues, and traps and gear for hunting and fishing. There is also a display of skulls of the animals they hunt for meat in the nearby rain forest. ✉ *Cartí Suitupo, Cartí* ☎ *507/299–9074* 🎫 *$3* ⏲ *Daily 8–4.*

El Porvenir. Though it is technically the provincial capital, this island is practically uninhabited. It has a police station, an office of the Guna congress, a rustic hotel, and an airstrip, which makes it the arrival point for many travelers. Guides from lodges on nearby islands meet the flights. There are two small islands nearby that hold traditional Guna villages and rustic lodges, and are visited by cruise ships: Wichub Huala and Nalunega. These islands are fascinating to explore, but their lack of sewage systems means the sea around them is unsafe for swimming. However, there are several uninhabited, white-sand cays a short boat trip away that are idyllic swimming and snorkeling spots. ✉ *El Porvenir.*

Wichub Huala. This tiny island, just south of El Porvenir, is home to a crowded Guna village with a mixture of thatch-roof huts and cement buildings that are separated by narrow sand paths. Papaya and breadfruit trees grow in back patios, dugout canoes crowd the shore, and children play in the sandy streets. Expect to encounter a number of women trying to sell you molas and other handicrafts as you explore, because this is one of the village's main sources of income. ✉ *Wichub Huala, El Porvenir.*

Nalunega. The slightly larger island of Nalunega lies just to the south of Wichub Huala. Like Wichub Huala, it has a collection of huts and cement structures, including the archipelago's original lodge, the rundown Hotel San Blas, founded in 1972. This a good place to see how the Guna live, and where you can purchase handicrafts. ✉ *Nalunega, El Porvenir.*

Río Sidra. To the east of Cartí Suitupo is the island community of Río Sidra, which is a good place to visit if you want to experience how the Guna live. Several sparsely populated islands, which are farther out, have lodges on them. To get here, lodges pick up guests in Cartí and El Porvenir. ✉ *Río Sidra.*

Río Masargandi. The Río Masargandi, a small river that flows out of the mountains near Río Sidra, provides access to the rain forest and a 30-foot waterfall. Local lodges offer half-day trips to the mainland for an additional charge. ⚠ **Excursions to see wildlife are best done early in the morning, but slather yourself with insect repellent.** ✉ *Río Sidra.*

WHERE TO STAY

For expanded hotel reviews, visit Fodors.com.

Accommodations in this part of Guna Yala are very rustic. Most bungalows have sand floors, cane walls, thatch roofs, and shared bathrooms. Those who can do without comforts, however, are rewarded with phenomenal island scenery and great snorkeling.

Most accommodations on or near El Porvenir are geared toward backpackers, the best option in the area is Cabañas Coco Blanco.

$$$ **Cabañas Coco Blanco.** *B&B/Inn.* Occupying half of the small island of Ogobsibudup, Coco Blanco has the nicest accommodations in western Guna Yala: rustic bungalows with private bathrooms steps away from a white-sand beach. **Pros:** nice beach; private bathrooms; near various uninhabited islands. **Cons:** rustic; no English spoken. $ *Rooms from: $190* ✉ *Ogobsibudup, El Porvenir*

☎ *507/275–2853, 507/6123–5457 Roberto, 507/6967–4849 Ligia* ⇒ *8* ▭ *No credit cards* 🍽 *All meals.*

$$ **Cabañas Narasgandup.** *B&B/Inn.* Though quite rustic, this lodge has a great setting on a sparsely inhabited island shaded by coconut palms with a lovely beach. **Pros:** great beach; friendly service; day trips. **Cons:** very rustic; no English spoken. *Rooms from: $180* ✉ *Ogobsibudup, Río Sidra* ☎ *507/256–6239, 507/6501–6033* ⊕ *www.sanblaskunayala.com* ⇒ *6 bungalows, 2 with bath* ▭ *No credit cards* 🍽 *All meals.*

$$ **Kuanidup.** *B&B/Inn.* With a small beach and hammocks strung between palm trees, this remote island is an idyllic spot. **Pros:** gorgeous island; great snorkeling. **Cons:** tiny, rustic rooms; shared bathrooms can get crowded; no English spoken. *Rooms from: $150* ✉ *Kuanidup Island, near Río Sidra, Río Sidra* ☎ *507/6635–6737, 507/6656–4673* ✉ *kuani9@hotmail.com* ⊕ *kuanidup.8k.com* ⇒ *12 huts* ▭ *No credit cards* 🍽 *All meals.*

SPORTS AND THE OUTDOORS

The lodges in this area have good snorkeling nearby and there are several uninhabited islands that can be visited on excursions, the most popular of which is Achutupu (aka Isla Perro),which has a small shipwreck offshore. (⇨ *See Achutupu, below.*)

SHOPPING

It would be a shame to visit Guna Yala and not buy a mola. Women usually set up shop outside their homes. Bring plenty of small bills, and try to buy from various vendors to benefit as many families as possible.

PLAYÓN CHICO

150 km (93 miles) northeast of Panama City.

This community of about 3,000 people lies just offshore, with a wooden footbridge connecting it to the mainland, where the town's school and landing strip are located. Most homes in Playón Chico are traditional thatched buildings, with small gardens shaded by breadfruit, mango, or citrus trees. It was an important place in the 1925 revolution that led to Guna autonomy, because it held one of the Panama military outposts that were captured by Guna warriors.

The lowlands around the landing strip hold farms, but a nearby hill is topped with the burial ground that resembles a small village. The Guna bury family members together under thatched shelters complete with the tools and utensils that their spirits require to survive. Forested mountains stand beyond the farmland where a trail leads to a waterfall. Insect repellent is essential on the mainland due to sand fleas. There are several uninhabited islands in the area with pale beaches and coral reefs offshore that local lodges take guests to for snorkeling and beach time.

GETTING HERE AND AROUND

Air Panama flies to Playón Chico airstrip (PYC) most days, departing from Panama City's Albrook Airport at 6 am and returning at 7 am. A guide from your lodge will meet you at the airstrip.

WHERE TO STAY

For expanded hotel reviews, visit Fodors.com.

$$$$ **Sapibenega.** *B&B/Inn.* With spacious rooms and an attractive restaurant perched over the sea, this is one of the better lodges in Guna Yala, but it is also the most expensive. **Pros:** big rooms; good food; friendly staff. **Cons:** rooms lack privacy; no beach on island; little English spoken; overpriced. *Rooms from: $340 ✉ Playón Chico ☎ 507/215–1406 ⊕ www.sapibenega.com ⇨ 6 rooms 🍽 All meals.*

★ Fodor's Choice **$$$** **Yandup Island Lodge.** *B&B/Inn.* Not only does Yandup offer the nicest accommodations in Guna Yala, it is also the best deal in the province. **Pros:** lovely bungalows and island; friendly staff; good food. **Cons:** sand fleas can be a problem at night. *Rooms from: $230 ✉ Yandup Island ☎ 507/202–0854 ☎ 507/6579–2911 ⊕ www.yandupisland.com ⇨ 10 bungalows 🍽 All meals.*

ACHUTUPO

190 km (118 miles) northeast of Panama City.

Achutupo, or Isla Perro in Spanish, is a medium-size community on an island near the mainland in the eastern half of Guna Yala. Because this is the most distant area that you can visit in Guna Yala, it's a good destination if you're especially interested in Guna culture. The people on Achutupo and nearby Aligandi see few tourists, and offer handicrafts of a higher quality than you'll find on the province's western end. There are several uninhabited islands and plenty of coral near Achutupo, which means it's also a good area for beaches and snorkeling. It's also possible to hike into the rain forest to a waterfall on the mainland (bring insect repellent). A tour to the local burial ground is another

MOLAS 101

The Guna are famous for their *molas:* fabric pictures made using a reverse appliqué technique, and Panama's most famous souvenir. Guna women wear these designs on their blouses, but they are also used to decorate everything from purses to pillows to hot pads to wall hangings. The original molas echoed the geometric designs employed by the Guna as body paint—Christian missionaries' influence in the 19th century brought modest body covering to the region for the first time, and the word *mola* means "clothing" in Dulegaya, the Guna language. Over the decades, designs have taken on abstract nature scenes, and, today, even a few TV and cartoon characters show up in the artwork. Regarding the traditional geometric designs, look closely before you buy: some molas feature a reverse swastika, an ancient Guna symbol. You may not want one of those. Mola production is a major source of income in Guna Yala, and you'll often see women sewing them as they chat with neighbors. Expect to pay $20 or more for a well-made mola. Number of layers used increases the price; two is most common, but the premium works incorporate several more layers. Fineness of stitching, up to the point of being nearly invisible, also means a finer mola. Embroidery frequently enhances a mola's design, but a top-notch product creates its design strictly through reverse appliqué technique. Oddly, a bit of wear or fading is not considered to be a flaw. Perhaps a panel had a previous life as a piece of someone's blouse and is now being used in another work. Such a "blemish" adds to the mola's authenticity and means that it wasn't created strictly for tourists.

Bargaining is expected, but don't haggle too hard. Molas are usually already reasonably priced when you consider the labor that went into their production, and those few extra dollars will mean much more to the vendor than to you. If you plan on buying multiple molas, try to buy from a variety of women. You'll benefit more families that way.

interesting option, especially early in the morning, when you may see Guna women leaving gifts of food for their ancestors.

GETTING HERE AND AROUND

Air Panama flies from Panama City's Albrook Airport to the airstrip at Achutupo (ACU) departing from Albrook at 6 am and returning at 7 am. A guide from your lodge will meet you at the airstrip.

EXPLORING

Aligandi. A short trip to the west of Achutupo is the island community of Aligandi, which played an important role in the Guna revolt of 1925. You'll see the orange-and-yellow Guna flag displayed here, as well as a statue of the local revolutionary Simral Colman, one of the architects of the autonomous Guna state.

WHERE TO STAY

For expanded hotel reviews, visit Fodors.com.

$$$$ **Akwadup Lodge.** *B&B/Inn.* This lodge's wooden bungalows are perched over the sea and just a short walk from a small beach. **Pros:** comfortable bungalows; decent snorkeling and swimming. **Cons:** island has trash on it; no-see-ums can be a problem. *Rooms from: $320* *Akwadup Island, Achutupo* *507/396–4805 in Panama City, 213/533–2211 in USA* *www.akwaduplodge.com* *7 bungalows* *All meals.*

$$$ ★ **Dad Ibe Lodge.** *B&B/Inn.* This hotel occupies a tiny island that's hardly bigger than a basketball court: it must have looked like something from a comic book before locals undertook the construction of five thatched bungalows and an open-air restaurant on either end of it. **Pros:** great beach; good guide. **Cons:** bungalows quite rustic. *Rooms from: $240* *Isla Dad Ibe* *507/293–8795, 507/6112–5448* *www.dadibelodge.net* *5 bungalows* *No credit cards* *All meals.*

$$$ **Dolphin Island Lodge.** *B&B/Inn.* (*Uaguinega*). **Pros:** spacious bungalows; friendly staff; Internet access. **Cons:** no beach on island. *Rooms from: $250* *Uaguinega Island* *213/533–2211 in USA, 507/396–4805 in Panama City* *www.uaguinega.com* *10 bungalows* *All meals.*

SHOPPING

Shopping is inevitable here, because the streets of Achutupo and Aligandi fill with mola hawkers whenever tourists arrive. In addition to molas, you can often purchase beadwork, wood carvings, or shells.

6

THE DARIÉN

The easternmost province of the Darién is Panama's wildest, least accessible region; home to extraordinary flora, fauna, and indigenous communities. Its remote eastern and southern extremes are dominated by mountain ranges cloaked with dense jungle, whereas its lowlands are drained by serpentine rivers that flow into the Pacific Ocean at the Golfo de San Miguel. Much of its wilderness is sequestered within Parque Nacional Darién and several nearby protected areas. Those preserves hold imposing, primeval forests dominated by massive tropical trees such as mahogany, strangler fig, and barrel-trunked *cuipos*. They are home to an array of wildlife that includes more than 450 bird species and everything from boa constrictors to strange and wonderful butterflies. Although most of that wilderness is inaccessible, or unsafe to visit, there are a few spots that provide access to the region's wonders, the most comfortable of which is the field station in the Reserva Natural Punta Patiño.

The Darién is a lush and rainy region with muddy rivers lined with the tangled roots of mangroves and thick swaths of elephant grass, where the most popular form of transportation is the dugout canoe. The province's rivers are dotted with dozens of indigenous Emberá and Wounaan villages that probably look much as the region's towns did when Balboa hiked across the isthmus five centuries ago. Villages such as Mogue and La Marea are set up to receive visitors: a day or two spent in these communities can be an unforgettable experience. The Darién has Panama's best bird-watching and sport fishing, but it is also a good destination for anyone interested in tropical nature and traditional cultures or travelers who simply want to stray from the beaten path.

LA PALMA

176 km (109 miles) southeast of Panama City.

La Palma, the capital of the Darién, is a perfect illustration of just how undeveloped this province is. At the end of a peninsula where the Tuira River flows into the Golfo de San Miguel, La Palma has just one commercial street with a handful of government offices, basic restaurants, and rustic hotels. It has one of the Darién's few airstrips, but commercial flights were suspended in 2012, so the nearby Reserva Natural Punta Patiño and Emberá villages of La

Darién
Naraganá
GUNA YALA
Ailigandí
TO
PANAMA CITY
Ustupu
Caribbean
Sea
Interamericana
Puerto
Limon
Mulatupu
PANAMA
Río Sabanas
Puerto
Obaldia
Los Monos
Río Chucunaque
1
Meteti
COMARCA
EMBERÁ
WOUNAAN
ÁREA #1
Puerto
Quimba
La Palma
Conglón
Reserva
Forestal
Changlón
Mogue
Golfo de
San Miguel
Punta
Patiño
Yaviza
Ensenada de
Garachiné
Taimatí
El Real de
Santa María
Garachiné
Sambú
DARIÉN
Río Sambú
CIFIC
CEAN
Serranía de Pirre
COMARCA
EMBERÁ
WOUNAAN
ÁREA #2
Santa Cruz
de Cana
Parque
Nacional
Darién
Puerto
Piña
Punta Piña
Tropic Star Lodge
Bahía Piñas
Jaqué
0
15 miles
0
15 kilometers
COLOMBIA

THE DARIÉN GAP

The impenetrable jungle that covers the eastern and southern Darién occupies the only interruption in the Pan-American Highway, which would otherwise run continuously from Alaska to southern Chile. The United States began promoting and underwriting that regional road system in the 1940s, but they asked Panama to leave a so-called "Darién Gap" intact to help prevent foot-and-mouth disease from spreading north from South America. An outbreak of the disease did occur in Colombia in 2009, but there's a more compelling reason to maintain the gap today. Panama is likely in no hurry to complete a road into a neighboring country with numerous armed groups and drug traffickers. This is good news for conservationists, who lament that the highway is flanked by deforested landscapes in the rest of the country. The highway, which is called the *Carretera Interamericana* (Inter-American Highway) in Panama, becomes a muddy track in the Darién, dead-ending about 50 km (31 miles) short of the Colombian border, at the town of Yaviza. To the east and south of that frontier town are dozens of indigenous villages and the biggest remaining expanse of tropical wilderness in Central America, which will hopefully remain intact for generations to come.

Marea and Mogue can only be reached by a combination of road and boat from Panama City, or from a cruise ship.

GETTING HERE AND AROUND

As of 2012, there were no commercial flights to La Palma (PLP), so the only way to visit this area is on a cruise, or with a Panama City tour company, which transport guests to their lodges by a combination of road and river.

EXPLORING

★ **La Marea.** A fascinating option for adventurous travelers is to spend three nights in the Emberá village of La Marea, a 48-km (30-mile) boat ride southeast of La Palma. Advantage Tours Panama *(⇨ Chapter 8, Outdoor and Learning Vacations)* offers four-day tours to La Marea that include nights in rustic accommodations and hiking tours into the nearby rain forest to look for wildlife such as spider monkeys, blue-and-gold macaws and harpy eagles. ⊠ *La Marea.*

Mogue. You can experience Emberá life up close in the village of Mogue (pronounced MOE-gay) on a bank of a river of the same name, about 30 km (19 miles) southwest of La Palma. That trip there takes you up a winding river through a thick forest to a traditional Emberá community, where people live in thatched huts perched above the ground on wooden posts. From there, you can hike to the nearby rain forest, which has plenty of wildlife. Some cruise ships visit as a day trip. The tour company Eco Circuitos (⇨ *Chapter 8, Outdoor and Learning Vacations)* has a four-day tour to Mogue with overnights in traditional Emberá dwellings, but it needs to be reserved six months ahead of time.

Reserva Natural Punta Patiño. The most comfortable accommodations near La Palma are in the Reserva Natural Punta Patiño, a private nature reserve 32 km (20 miles) southwest of town managed by ANCON, the country's biggest conservation group. A former ranch in the midst of ecological restoration, the reserve consists of 26,000 hectares (65,000 acres) of mature forest and former pastureland. It is home to crab-eating raccoons, crocodiles, capybaras (the world's largest rodent), and hundreds of bird species, ranging from the delicate mangrove swallow to the mighty harpy eagle. Ancon Expeditions (⇨ *Chapter 8, Outdoor and Learning Vacations)* offers four-day tours to the Punta Patiño Lodge, on the north end of the reserve.

6

WHERE TO STAY

For expanded hotel reviews, visit Fodors.com.

$$$$ ★ **Punta Patiño Lodge.** *B&B/Inn.* This eco-lodge inside the Reserva Natural Punta Patiño sits on a hill with views of secondary forest and the sea. **Pros:** nice rooms; air conditioning; expert guides. **Cons:** remote location; takes seven hours to get here. *Rooms from: $500* ✉ *Punta Patiño* ☎ *507/269–9415 in Panama City* 🌐 *www.anconexpeditions.com* *10 bungalows* *Closed Oct. and Nov.* *All meals.*

BAHÍA PIÑAS

230 km (143 miles) southeast of Panama City.

Nestled in the southwest corner of the Darién, just north of the Jaque River, lies remote and beautiful Bahía Piñas, a deep bay with a rocky coastline, where mountains are covered with virgin rain forest and the aquamarine sea teems with an array of marine life. In fact, it's the marine life that draws most people to Piñas Bay, since the quality of its fishing is legendary, with more than 250 world fishing records set in the surrounding waters. Zane Grey fished in the area in the 1950s, and John Wayne and Lee Marvin hooked plenty of billfish here in the '60s. Since then, thousands of anglers have followed in their wake, heading out to Zane Grey Reef in search of sailfish and blue, black, and striped marlin. The Tropic Star Lodge, in Bahía Piñas, provides convenient access to some of the best sport fishing in the world.

GETTING HERE AND AROUND

Charter flights are included in the Tropic Star Lodge packages, as is transportation in Panama City.

WHERE TO STAY

For expanded hotel reviews, visit Fodors.com.

$$$$ ★ **Tropic Star Lodge.** *Hotel.* The Tropic Star Lodge offers access to world-class sport fishing in a comfortable, friendly atmosphere. **Pros:** great fishing; good food. **Cons:** expensive if you're not fishing. *Rooms from: $649* *Piñas Bay* *507/232–0143 in Panama City, 800/682–3424 in the U.S.* *www.tropicstar.com* *18 rooms, 1 suite* *Closed Oct. and Nov.* *All meals.*

SPORTS AND THE OUTDOORS

The ocean around Piñas Bay has Panama's best fishing, with sailfish and blue and black marlin biting most of the year. December through February are the best months for black marlin—many people book their weeks at the Tropic Star Lodge years in advance. The marlin fishing drops off in March, improving again from May to September. Sailfish are common in the area from April to September. Fishing at Tropic Star is catch-and-release for billfish, whereas fish for eating, such as tuna and dolphin, are served for dinner. There are plenty of big tuna and dolphin in the area, and smaller fighters such as roosterfish, wahoo, and mackerel inshore, where you can also troll deep for snapper and grouper.

Outdoor and Learning Vacations

7

WORD OF MOUTH

"Traveling [on a private tour] with Ancon [Expeditions] (or another travel company) means no driving and no buses (definitely would not ride the wild and crazy independent buses). A great way to go with limited time."

—eyemom84

www.fodors.com/forums

PLANNING YOUR ADVENTURE

CHOOSING A TRIP

Adventure Tours. Adrenaline-pumping sports and thrills for the active traveler.

Beaches and Relaxation. Find a place to hang your hammock after a volcanic mud bath.

Cultural Tourism. Live and learn with local culture.

Diving Trips. Panama's Caribbean coastline is one of the world's major diving destinations.

Ecotourism. Spot a resplendent quetzal while staying at a thatched jungle lodge in pristine cloud forests.

Language Schools. Learn Spanish while staying with a local family.

How strenuous do you want your trip to be? Adventure vacations are commonly split into "soft" and "hard." Hard adventures, such as strenuous treks or Class IV rafting, generally require excellent physical conditioning and previous experience. Most hiking, biking, canoeing/kayaking, and similar soft adventures can be enjoyed by persons of all ages who are in good health and are accustomed to a reasonable amount of exercise. Recognize your own level of physical fitness and discuss it with the tour operator before signing on.

How far off the beaten path do you want to go? Depending on your tour operator and itinerary, you'll often have a choice between relatively easy travel with comfortable accommodations or more strenuous activities with overnights spent in basic lodgings or at campsites. Ask yourself if it's the *reality* or the *image* of roughing it that appeals to you. Go with a company that provides what you're looking for.

Is sensitivity to the environment important to you? If so, determine whether the environment is equally important to your operator. Does the company protect the fragile environments you'll be visiting? Does the company designate any profits for conservation efforts? Are they put back into the communities visited? Does it encourage indigenous people to dress up (or dress down) so that your group can get great photos, or does it respect their cultures? Many of the operators listed here are actively involved in environmental conservation and projects with indigenous communities.

Their business's future depends on keeping this fragile ecological and cultural mix alive.

What sort of group is best for you? Do you enjoy mixing with people from similar backgrounds, or do you prefer travel with people of different ages and backgrounds? Inquire about group size. Many companies have a maximum of 10 to 16 members, but groups of 30 or more are not unknown. The larger the group, the more time will be spent (or wasted) at rest stops, meals, and hotel arrivals and departures.

Do you want a custom trip? If groups aren't your thing, most companies will customize a trip for you. Your itinerary can be as flexible or as rigid as you choose. Such travel offers the conveniences of a package tour, but the "group" is composed only of those you've chosen as your travel companions. Many operators also offer family trips, with itineraries carefully crafted to appeal to both children and adults.

How much preparatory help do you want? Gorgeous photos and well-written tour descriptions go a long way toward selling a company's trips. Once you've chosen your trip, though, there's a lot of room for your operator to either help you out or leave you out in the cold. For example, does the operator provide useful information about health, such as suggested or required immunizations? Will you get a list of frequently asked questions and its answers? What about recommended readings? Does the company provide equipment needed for sports trips? Can the company provide a list of client referrals? All of these things can make or break a trip, and you should know before you choose an operator whether you want help getting answers to all these questions.

Are there hidden costs? Make sure you know what is and what is not included in basic trip costs when comparing tour companies. International airfare is almost always extra. Domestic flights in-country are usually add-ons, but some companies do provide charter air service as a part of their basic trip cost. Is trip insurance required, and if so, is it included? Are airport transfers included? Departure taxes? Gratuities? Although some travelers prefer the option of an excursion or free time, many (especially those visiting a destination for the first time) want to see as much as possible. Paying extra for a number of excursions can significantly increase the total cost of the trip. Don't assume that roughing it will save you money, as prices rise with limited access.

MONEY MATTERS

Tours in Panama come at all prices, but local operators can usually offer the best deal and also give the greatest monetary benefit to the local economy. These types of tours are not always listed in guidebooks or on the Internet; often they have to be found in-person or by word of mouth. Safety and date specificity can fluctuate. Guides might not speak English and are not always certified. Amenities such as lodging and transportation may be very basic in this category. Some agencies pay attention to the environment while others do not. You really have to do your research on every operator to be sure you are getting exactly what you need. The payoff in terms of price and quality of experience can be considerable if you find the right match for your needs.

On the other end of the spectrum, large tour agencies such as Abercrombie & Kent, G Adventures, International Expeditions, Panama Trails, and others may be expensive, but they provide the greatest range of itinerary choices and highest quality of services. These companies often use the best transportation, such as private planes, buses, and boats, which rarely break down. First-rate, safe equipment and reliable English-speaking guides are the norm. Dates and times are set in stone, so you can plan your trip down to the time you step in and out of the airport. Food and lodging are generally of high quality. If you like to travel in comfort, look for operators at this end of the spectrum.

LODGING

Lodging costs vary greatly within Panama. Independent travelers tend to favor budget hotels and hostels costing little more than a few dollars a night. Conversely, luxurious five-star hotels geared to package tourists are becoming as common as howler monkeys. Your preference will help determine what type of tour operator is best for you. Most multiday tours include lodging, often at a discounted rate, and they generally offer options for a variety of budgets. Many hotels have their own tour agencies or sell tours at a discounted rate to particular agencies. You can book either way depending on the specific tours and hotels that interest you. In many instances you don't necessarily have to book accommodation through your tour agency, although you can often save money if you are combining services such as transportation, food, tours, and guides. If you are interested in specific hotels, beach resorts or eco-lodges, your best tour options will be directly through those establishments.

EQUIPMENT

Good gear is essential: Bring sturdy shoes, a small flashlight, rain gear, sunscreen, mosquito protection, and basic medications with you no matter what kind of tour you're taking. For more technical sports, tour operators can generally provide equipment, but quality may vary. If you're using provided equipment, ask your operator for a written statement concerning the gear to be used. When you arrive, check that your expectations have been met, and complain if they haven't. Many companies do use top-of-the-line equipment; however, the occasional company will cut corners. Prices on equipment purchased in Panama tend to be significantly more expensive (roughly 20% higher) than in North America. If you prefer or require a specific brand of equipment, bringing your own is a good idea. Airlines accommodate most types of equipment and will likely have packing suggestions if you call ahead. For instance, most bicycle shops can take apart and box up your bike for plane transport. Bringing your own surfboard, however, will cost you $175 each way on most airlines, and the boards are seldom handled with care. Airlines charge additional fees for surpassing size and weight limits. Shipping equipment to Panama gets expensive.

ADVENTURE AND LEARNING VACATIONS

ADVENTURE TOURS

MULTISPORT TOURS

Season: Year-round

Locations: Central Panama, Chiriquí, Bocas del Toro, Guna Yala, Chagres National Park

Cost: From $1,245 for eight days from Panama City for package tours; from $180 to $700 for daily tours.

Tour Operators: BikeHike Adventures, Boquete Outdoor Adventures, Classic Journeys (⇨ *International Tour Companies)*, Coral Lodge (⇨ *Lodges and Resorts)*, Extreme Panama, Islas Secas (⇨ *Lodges and Resorts)*, Mountain Travel Sobek, Seakunga, Tranquilo Bay (⇨ *Lodges and Resorts)*

Hordes of adventure companies have opened up a new frontier of touring here. Boquete Outdoor Adventures offers a nine-day trip combining rafting, sea kayaking, island tours, hiking, and tree trekking. Mountain Travel Sobek has nine-day kayaking trips led by Guna guides that take you camping in Guna Yala for a total of 60 to 80 miles of paddling. Seakunga Adventures' eight-day kayaking trip centers on Guna Yala, but adds rafting and hiking in Chagres National Park.

The high-end Classic Journeys' well-balanced presentation of all Panama has to offer mixes hiking, bird-watching, and rafting, with coffee tasting and visits to the canal and fortifications at Portobelo. BikeHike Adventures and Extreme Panama run one- to two-week tours that combine biking, hiking, rafting, snorkeling, kayaking, and other sports. Comfortable eco-lodges Coral Lodge, Islas Secas, and Tranquilo Bay offer packages that include skin diving, fishing, and other activities in pristine areas.

HORSEBACK RIDING

Season: Year-round

Locations: Central Panama, Chiriquí, Bocas del Toro

Cost: $45 per day

Tour Operators: Boquete Outdoor Adventures *(⇨ Adventure Tours)*, Los Quetzales Lodge *(⇨ Lodges and Resorts)*, Margo Tours

For a country with such a long ranching tradition, horseback tours are in short supply. Boquete Outdoor Adventures has half-day trips to Caldera's hot springs. Margo Tours offers a half-day trail ride in the hills outside Panama City, but the best equestrian options are available through hotels in El Valle de Antón, Boquete, and Cerro Punta.

KAYAKING

Season: Year-round

Locations: Central Panama, Chiriquí, Bocas del Toro, Guna Yala

Cost: $80 to $190 per day

Tour Operators: Boquete Outdoor Adventures *(⇨ Adventure Tours)*, Expediciones Tropicales

Many coastal hotels have sit-on-top kayaks available for their guests, but serious kayakers should consider outfitter Expediciones Tropicales, which offers a sunset paddle on the canal, day trips down the lower Chagres River, and multiday sea-kayak tours of Guna Yala. Boquete Outdoor Adventures has programs that combine sea kayaking with other outdoor activities.

CLOSE UP

Tour Operators

ADVENTURE TOUR OUTFITTERS

BikeHike Adventures ☎ *888/805–0061 in the U.S.* 🌐 *www.bikehike.com.*

Boquete Outdoor Adventures ✉ *Boquete* ☎ *507/720–2284 in Panama* 🌐 *www.boqueteoutdooradventures.com.*

Extreme Panama ✉ *Panama City* ☎ *507/360–2030* 🌐 *www.extremepanama.com.*

G Adventures ☎ *800/800–4100* 🌐 *www.gadventures.com.*

Mountain Travel Sobek ☎ *888/831–7526* 🌐 *www.mtsobek.com.*

Seakunga Adventures ☎ *800/781–2269* 🌐 *www.seakunga.com.*

BEACHES

Adventure Life ☎ *800/344–6118* 🌐 *www.adventure-life.com.*

Wildland Adventures ☎ *800/345–4453* 🌐 *www.wildland.com.*

BIRD-WATCHING

Canopy Tower Family ✉ *Panama City* ☎ *800/930–3397* 🌐 *www.canopytower.com.*

Exotic Birding ☎ *877/247–3371 in U.S.* 🌐 *www.exoticbirding.com.*

Field Guides ☎ *800/728–4953 in U.S.* 🌐 *www.fieldguides.com.*

Nattur Panama ✉ *Colón* ☎ *507/442–1340* 🌐 *www.natturpanama.com.*

Panama Audubon Society ✉ *Panama City* ☎ *507/232–5977 in Panama* 🌐 *iap.audubon.org.*

Victor Emanuel Nature Tours *(VENT).* ☎ *800/328–8368 in U.S.* 🌐 *www.ventbird.com.*

DIVING

Bocas Water Sports ✉ *Bocas del Toro* ☎ *507/757–9541 in Panama* 🌐 *www.bocaswatersports.com.*

Coral Dreams ✉ *Contadora* ☎ *507/6536–1776 in Panama* 🌐 *www.coral-dreams.com.*

La Buga ✉ *Bocas del Toro* ☎ *507/757–9534 in Panama* 🌐 *www.labugapanama.com.*

Panama Divers ✉ *Portobelo* ☎ *507/314–0817 in Panama* 🌐 *www.panamadivers.com.*

Scuba Coiba ✉ *Santa Catalina* ☎ *507/6980–7122* 🌐 *www.scubacoiba.com.*

Scuba Panama ✉ *Panama City* ☎ *507/261–3841 in Panama* 🌐 *www.scubapanama.com.*

Starfleet Scuba ✉ *Bocas del Toro* ☎ *507/757–9630* 🌐 *www.starfleetscuba.com.*

FISHING

Coiba Adventure Sport Fishing ✉ *David* ☎ *800/800–0907 in U.S.* 🌐 *www.coibadventure.com.*

Panama Canal Fishing ✉ *Panama City* ☎ *507/315–1905 in Panama* 🌐 *www.panamacanalfishing.com.*

Panama Fishing & Catching ✉ *Panama City* ☎ *507/6622–0212 in Panama* 🌐 *www.panamafishingandcatching.com.*

Pesca Panama ☎ *800/946–3474 in U.S.* 🌐 *www.pescapanama.com.*

CLOSE UP

Tour Operators (continued)

HIKING AND WALKING

Advantage Tours ✉ *Panama City* ☎ *507/223–9283 in Panama* 🌐 *www.advantagepanama.com.*

Ancon Expeditions ✉ *Panama City* ☎ *507/269–9415 in Panama, 888/760–3426 in U.S.* 🌐 *www.anconexpeditions.com.*

Coffee Adventures ✉ *Boquete* ☎ *507/720–3852 in Panama* 🌐 *www.coffeeadventures.net.*

Eco Circuitos Panama ✉ *Panama City* ☎ *507/314–0068 in Panama* 🌐 *www.ecocircuitos.com.*

International Expeditions ☎ *800/234–9620* 🌐 *www.ietravel.com.*

Panoramic Panama ✉ *Panama City* ☎ *507/314–1581 in Panama* 🌐 *www.panoramicpanama.com.*

Pesantez Tours ✉ *Panama City* ☎ *507/366–9100* 🌐 *www.pesantez-tours.com.*

Sendero Panama ✉ *Panama City* ☎ *507/390–5526* 🌐 *www.senderopanama.com.*

HORSEBACK RIDING

Margo Tours ✉ *Panama City* ☎ *507/264–8888* 🌐 *www.margotours.com.*

INTERNATIONAL TOUR COMPANIES

Abercrombie & Kent ☎ *800/554–7016* 🌐 *www.abercrombiekent.com.*

Classic Journeys ☎ *800/200–3887 in U.S.* 🌐 *www.classicjourneys.com.*

Collette Vacations ☎ *888/941–8687 in. U.S.* 🌐 *www.collettevacations.com.*

Panama Trails ✉ *Panama City* ☎ *507/393–8334 in Panama, 877/290–2454 in U.S.* 🌐 *www.panamatrails.com.*

Road Scholar ☎ *800/454–5768 in U.S.* 🌐 *www.roadscholar.org.*

KAYAKING

Expediciones Tropicales ✉ *Panama City* ☎ *507/317–1279* 🌐 *www.xtrop.com.*

LANGUAGE SCHOOLS

AmeriSpan Study Abroad ☎ *800/879–6640* 🌐 *www.amerispan.com.*

Habla Ya ✉ *Boquete* ☎ *315/254–2231 in U.S., 507/720–1294 in Boquete, 507/757–7354 in Bocas del Toro* 🌐 *www.hablayapanama.com.*

Spanish at Locations ✉ *Boquete* ☎ *507/720–3456 in Boquete, 507/757–9518 in Bocas del Toro* 🌐 *www.spanishatlocations.com.*

Spanish Panama ✉ *Panama City* ☎ *507/213–3121 in Panama* 🌐 *www.spanishpanama.com.*

SURFING

Panama Surf Tours ✉ *Panama City* ☎ *507/6671–7777 in Panama* 🌐 *www.panamasurftours.com.*

WHITE-WATER RAFTING

Adventures Panama ✉ *Panama City* ☎ *800/614–7214 in U.S.* 🌐 *www.aventuraspanama.com.*

Chiriquí River Rafting ✉ *Boquete* ☎ *507/720–1505 in Panama* 🌐 *www.panama-rafting.com.*

Panama Rafters ✉ *Boquete* ☎ *507/720–2712* 🌐 *www.panamarafter.com.*

CLOSE UP

Tour Operators (continued)

LODGES AND RESORTS

Burbayar Panamá ✉ *Alto Bayano* ☎ *507/236-6061* 🌐 *www.burbayar.com.*

Coral Lodge ✉ *Santa Isabela* ☎ *888/499-2497 in U.S.* 🌐 *www.corallodge.com.*

Finca Lérida ✉ *Boquete* ☎ *507/720-1111 in Panama* 🌐 *www.fincalerida.com.*

Gone Fishing Panama ✉ *Boca Chica* ☎ *786/393-5882 in U.S.* 🌐 *www.gonefishingpanama.com.*

Hacienda del Mar ☎ *866/433-5627 in U.S.* 🌐 *www.haciendadelmar.net.*

Islas Secas ✉ *Islas Secas* ☎ *800/377-8877 in U.S.* 🌐 *www.islassecas.com.*

Los Quetzales Ecolodge and Spa ✉ *Cerro Punta* ☎ *507/771-2291 in Panama* 🌐 *www.losquetzales.com.*

Morro Negrito Surf Camp ✉ *Isla Ensenada* ☎ *760/632-8014 in U.S.* 🌐 *www.panamasurfcamp.com.*

Tranquilo Bay ✉ *Bocas del Toro* ☎ *713/589-6952 in U.S.* 🌐 *www.tranquilobay.com.*

Tropic Star Lodge ✉ *Piñas Bay* ☎ *800/682-3424 in U.S.* 🌐 *www.tropicstar.com.*

WHITE-WATER RAFTING

Season: July–March

Locations: Central Panama, Chiriquí

Cost: \$90–\$175

Tour Operators: Adventures Panama, Chiriquí River Rafting, Panama Rafters

Panama has spectacular white-water rafting, with warm-water rivers that flow through stretches of rain forest. Most of the country's rivers are high enough for rafting only between July and December, but the two best, the relatively easy Río Chagres (Class II/III), near Panama City, and the wilder Río Chiriquí Viejo (Class III/IV), can usually be navigated through March. Adventures Panama runs one- and two-day Chagres trips. Panama Rafters and Chiriquí River Rafting run trips on the Chiriquí Viejo.

BEACHES AND OCEAN SPORTS

BEACHES

Season: Year-round

Locations: Bocas del Toro, Guna Yala

Cost: from $1,250 for seven days from Panama City

Tour Operators: Adventure Life, G Adventures *(⇨ Adventure Tours)*, Seakunga Adventures *(⇨ Adventure Tours)*, Wildland Adventures

Escape the crowds on Panama's Caribbean coast where many spots are reachable only by boat or charter jet. The San Blas Islands are some of the cleanest and most serene islands in the world and are home to the indigenous Guna. There are just a few small guesthouses here, but the waters are crystal clear and the marine life is abundant. Every tour operator in the country will be able to arrange kayaking or sailing trips.

DIVING

Season: Year-round (conditions vary by region)

Locations: Central Caribbean, Gulf of Panama, Isla Coiba, Gulf of Chiriquí, Bocas del Toro, Guna Yala

Cost: From $50 for two-tank boat dive to $450 per day for Isla Coiba dive cruise

Tour Operators: Bocas Water Sports, Coral Dreams, Coral Lodge *(⇨ Lodges and Resorts)*, Islas Secas *(⇨ Lodges and Resorts)*, La Buga, Panama Divers, San Blas Cruises *(⇨ Cruising)*, Scuba Coiba, Scuba Panama, Starfleet Scuba

Panama has some of the best diving in the Caribbean and eastern Pacific and is the only country in the world where you can dive both the Pacific and the Atlantic on the same day. The country's most impressive dive destination is remote Isla Coiba, part of a national park protecting thousands of acres of reef and more than 700 fish species. Scuba Coiba and Panama Divers offer trips that include nights in rustic rooms on the island. Diving around Golfo de Chiriquí is available at the Islas Secas. More accessible sites in the Golfo de Panama can be explored from Isla Contadora with Coral Dreams, or out of Panama City with Scuba Panama, which also offers diving in the Panama Canal and a two-oceans-in-one-day dive trip.

Whereas Panama's Pacific dives offer encounters with schools of big fish, the Caribbean has more coral and sponge diversity and warmer water. Caribbean attractions include vast coral and sponge gardens populated by colorful damselfish, sea stars, and countless other creatures. The most accessible Caribbean diving areas are Portobelo and Isla Grande, about two hours from Panama City, where

Panama Divers and Scuba Panama provide access to miles of barrier reef, sunken ships, and a plane wreck. The most pristine reefs are found in the Escribano Bank, which you can dive out of Coral Lodge, in Santa Isabela. East of there lie Guna Yala's San Blas Islands, where scuba diving is prohibited. Indigenous lodges include snorkeling trips in their rates, but skin divers can visit more pristine reefs and islands on cruises with San Blas Sailing. The other important Caribbean region is Bocas del Toro, with dozens of dive spots and an array of accommodations. Bocas Watersports, La Buga, and Starfleet Scuba offer dives at the impressive Cayos Zapatillas and Tiger Rock.

The Caribbean experiences its best diving conditions from September to November and from April to June. Pacific diving tends to be good everywhere from November to January, when seas are calm. The Gulf of Chiriquí has its best diving conditions between December and July, after which large swells can make dive spots inaccessible and decrease visibility.

FISHING

Season: Year-round (best from January to March)

Locations: Darién, Gulf of Panama, Chiriquí, Gatún Lake

Cost: From $300 per day for Gatún Lake to $1,600 per day for fishing cruises or lodge packages

Tour Operators: Coiba Adventure Sportfishing, Gone Fishing Panama (⇨ *Lodges and Resorts*), Hacienda del Mar (⇨ *Lodges and Resorts*), Islas Secas (⇨ *Lodges and Resorts*), Panama Big Game Fishing Club, Panama Canal Fishing, Panama Fishing & Catching, Pesca Panama, Tropic Star Lodge (⇨ *Lodges and Resorts*)

What can you expect from a country whose name means "abundance of fish"? Though Caribbean fishing is average, Panama's Pacific waters have some of the best fishing in the Western Hemisphere, with massive blue and black marlin, Pacific sailfish, tuna, wahoo, dolphin, roosterfish, mackerel, and other fighters in good supply. The country's top fishing spot is the Darién's remote Bahia Piñas, whose Tropic Star Lodge provides comfortable access to phenomenal fishing. More than 250 world fishing records have been set there, and black marlin average 300 to 600 pounds, and tuna between 100 and 200 pounds are regularly hooked. The Golfo de Chiriquí, to the west, is a close second, with lots of marlin, sailfish, and other big fighters near the Hannibal

Banks, Isla Montuosa, and Isla de Coiba, where catch-and-release fishing is permitted. Those waters can be fished out of lodges with Gone Fishing Panama, Panama Big Game Fishing Club, Pesca Panama, and Coiba Adventure Fishing. Between those two regions lie the Pearl Islands, where good angling is accessible from Hacienda del Mar, on Isla San José. Panama Fishing & Catching has charters in the Gulf of Panama and Pacific estuaries out of Panama City. A less expensive alternative to deep-sea fishing is light-tackle angling on Gatún Lake, in the Panama Canal, which has lots of feisty peacock bass, snook, and tarpon. Panama Canal Fishing has family packages and can guarantee you'll catch plenty of fish year-round.

SURFING

Season: Year-round

Locations: Central Pacific, Chiriquí, Bocas del Toro

Cost: $75–$150 per day

Tour Operators: Morro Negrito Surf Camp *(⇨ Lodges and Resorts)*, Panama Surf Tours

Panama has world-class surf. Most of Panama's surf spots are reef breaks, making them better destinations for experienced surfers than for novices, but surf companies here offer lessons at beaches and less treacherous breaks. Though there are a few breaks in Central Panama, (most notably at Isla Grande and Playa El Palmar), the country's best surf is at Santa Catalina, on the Azuero Peninsula. The best Pacific surfing is from June to December, when the waves regularly break overhead, whereas the Caribbean tends to get its best surf from November to March and July and August.

Surf tours are an excellent option because most of Panama's breaks are quite remote and are often accessible only by boat. Panama Surf Tours has a rustic lodge in Santa Catalina and offers guided trips to the country's best spots. The Morro Negrito Surf Camp, on an island in the Golfo de Chiriquí, provides access to five isolated breaks that are seldom surfed. Bocas del Toro has a few breaks, some of which are a mere 10-minute boat ride from town.

ECOTOURISM

HIKING AND WALKING

Season: Year-round

Locations: Central Panama, Chiriquí, Darién

CRUISING IN PANAMA

Cruise ships regularly transit the Panama Canal, but few actually call at Panamanian ports themselves. Exceptions to this rule are companies that offer cruises on smaller ships that include stops at uninhabited islands and indigenous villages. Alternatively, you can take advantage of less expensive cruising options in Panama, such as weekly partial transits of the canal, or monthly full transits, for a fraction of what a day on a cruise ship costs. Cruises run year-round, with more frequent options from December through May.

Canal & Bay Tours. *Canal & Bay Tours offers partial canal transits every Saturday year-round, with full transits once a month.* ✉ *Panama City* ☎ *507/209–2002* 🌐 *www.canalandbaytours.com.*

Lindblad Expeditions. *Lindblad Expeditions runs cruises that transit the canal and stop at nature-themed sites such as Isla Coiba and Lago Gatún, as well as parks in Costa Rica.* ☎ *800/397–3348 in U.S.* 🌐 *www.expeditions.com.*

Panama Marine Adventures. *Panama Marine Adventures offers partial canal cruises most Fridays and Saturdays year-round and Thursdays December through March. Full transits take place once a month.* ☎ *507/226–8917* 🌐 *www.pmatours.net.*

San Blas Sailing. *San Blas Sailing offers 3- to 14-day sailing cruises to Guna Yala and/or the Pearl Islands.* ✉ *Panama City* ☎ *507/314–1800* 🌐 *sanblassailing.com.*

Tauck. *Tauck combines a Panama Canal transit with visits to Guna Yala, Isla Coiba, and the Darién.* ☎ *800/788–7885 in U.S.* 🌐 *www.tauck.com.*

Windstar Cruises. *Windstar's seven-day sailings take in Guna Yala, Isla Coiba, and a canal transit, along with a few smaller ports of call in Costa Rica.* ☎ *800/240–3707 in U.S.* 🌐 *www.windstarcruises.com.*

Cost: $30 to $175 per day for expeditions

Tour Operators: Advantage Tours, Ancon Expeditions, Burbayar Panamá *(⇨ Lodges and Resorts)*, Canopy Tower Family *(⇨ Bird-Watching)*, Coffee Adventures, Eco Circuitos Panama, Extreme Panama *(⇨ Adventure Tour Outfitters)*, Finca Lérida *(⇨ Fishing)*, International Expeditions, Los Quetzales Lodge and Spa *(⇨ Lodges and Resorts)*, Panoramic Panama, Pesantez Tours, Sendero Panama.

Hiking and walking are a big part of exploring Panama's forests, and options for getting into the country's woods range from an early-morning hike through Panama City's Parque Natural Metropolitano to a two-week trek through the Darién's jungles. All the country's nature-tour operators offer guided hikes and bird-watching trips in parks near Panama City, but only Ancon Expeditions and Eco Circuitos Panama offer multiday trips that include camping in indigenous communities and the rain forest. Ancon Expeditions' Darién Explorer and Camino Real treks are challenging and adventurous, but plenty of shorter hikes take you through pristine forest. For forest hikes intermixed with bird-watching, a canal transit and an introduction to the Emberá people, try International Expeditions. Local operator Sendero Panama offers a variety of nature-theme tours from 7 to 14 days. Choose from hiking, birding, or wildlife viewing. Various lodges with private reserves and trail systems serve as excellent bases for day hikes, such as Burbayar Panamá, Finca Lérida, Los Quetzales Lodge, and lodges run by Ancón Expeditions and Canopy Tower Family. The mountains hold some of the most popular trails, namely El Valle de Antón and Chiriquí's Volcán Barú and La Amistad national parks, near Boquete and Cerro Punta.

BIRD-WATCHING

Season: Year-round (more species October–March)

Locations: Central Panama, Chiriquí, Darién

Cost: From $80 for a day tour to $400 per day for package tour

Tour Operators: Advantage Tours (⇨ *Hiking and Walking*), Ancon Expeditions (⇨ *Hiking and Walking*), Canopy Tower Family, Coffee Adventures (⇨ *Hiking and Walking*), Eco Circuitos Panama (⇨ *Hiking and Walking*), Exotic Birding, Field Guides, Nattur Panama, Panama Audubon Society, Panoramic Panama (⇨ *Hiking and Walking*), Pesantez Tours (⇨ *Hiking and Walking*), Victor Emanuel Nature Tours

With more than 960 bird species in an area smaller than South Carolina, Panama is a bird-watchers Valhalla. It is not only home to such rare and spectacular species as the blue-and-gold macaw, resplendent quetzal, and harpy eagle, it is a place to witness natural phenomena, such as hawk and vulture migrations or island rookeries where tens of thousands of seabirds gather. Several world-class birding lodges complement the avian diversity. The best months for birding are October to April, when Northern migrants boost the local population, so you might spot an emerald toucanet and a Baltimore oriole in the same tree.

You can find birds everywhere in Panama, but the best regions are Central Panama, the mountains of western Chiriquí Province, and the jungles of the Darién. The most popular central areas are Parque Nacional Soberanía, where the Panama Audubon Society has held many world-record Christmas bird counts, and Parque Nacional San Lorenzo, a good place to see the hawk and vulture migrations in October and March. Central Panama has excellent lodges in the middle of the wilderness, such as the Canopy Tower and Canopy Lodge, and Burbayar Panamá. The mountain valleys of Chiriquí's Boquete and Cerro Punta host birds you won't find in other parts of the country, including the resplendent quetzal. Terry van der Vooren of Coffee Adventures is considered Boquete's most knowledgeable bird guide and brings over a decade of experience to the area. The Darién has Panama's most impressive bird diversity, including four macaw species, half a dozen parrot species, and harpy eagles, but it is a most expensive area to visit.

Ancon Expeditions have excellent guides and a comprehensive, affordable "Highlights of Avian Panama" tour. Advantage Tours, Eco Circuitos, and Nattur Panama offer comparable trips. Canopy Tower Family has terrific birding lodges and good guides. Panoramic Panama and Pesantez Tours specialize in shorter trips. Field Guides and Exotic Birding sell Ancon Expeditions' tours but send an expert guide along, whereas Victor Emanuel Nature Tours does the same thing using Canopy Tower Family's lodges. The Panama Audubon Society offers inexpensive weekend excursions that are open to foreigners. In addition, there are a few good, independent birding guides in El Valle de Antón, Boquete, and Cerro Punta.

CULTURAL TOURISM

CULTURAL IMMERSION

Season: Year-round

Locations: Central Panama, Guna Yala

Cost: From $490 for three days from Panama City

Tour Operator: Ancon Expeditions *(⇨ Hiking and Walking)*, Collette Vacations *(⇨ International Tour Companies)*

Ancon Expeditions offers three-day trips to Guna Yala, where you'll flit between islands in traditional dugout canoes and stay in thatched huts belonging to the indigenous Guna. Collette Vacations has eight-day family-oriented trips that combine a bit of everything: indigenous encounters, folklore, nature excursions, and a canal transit.

HISTORY

Season: Year-round

Locations: Central Panama

Cost: From $1,590 for six days from Panama City

Tour Operator: Road Scholar *(⇨International Tour Companies)*

Road Scholar anticipates the Panama Canal's centennial with a canal-themed excursion taking in a full transit, cross-isthmus train ride, and several lectures on the history of the Canal.

LANGUAGE SCHOOLS

Season: Year-round

Locations: Panama City, Boquete, Bocas del Toro

Cost: From $1,600 for four weeks from Panama City

Tour Operators: AmeriSpan Study Abroad, Habla Ya, Spanish at Locations, Spanish Panama

AmeriSpan in Panama City provides 20 hours of classes per week and a private room with a host family in a wealthy suburb. Habla Ya offers group and individual classes in Boquete and Bocas del Toro, as well as discount lodging for visiting students. Spanish at Locations offers 20 to 30 hours of classes per week in Bocas del Toro and Boquete. Spanish Panama, in the capital, offers inexpensive group classes and one-on-one instruction at your hotel, restaurants, while sightseeing, or at their center.

Travel Smart Panama

WORD OF MOUTH

"Panama uses the US dollar as its currency. Don't be confused by its official name, the Balboa—bills are exactly the same. Panamanian coins are of the same value and size as US coins, which are also accepted."

—Isledon

www.fodors.com/forums

GETTING HERE AND AROUND

Panama is the southernmost part of an isthmus that stretches between Colombia and Mexico. Although relatively narrow, the country still has hundreds of miles of Pacific and Caribbean coastline. It is bisected by the Panama Canal, which runs north–south across the center of the country. To the east, the Carretera Panamericana (Pan-american Highway) heads toward the Darién, home to a vast, near-impenetrable jungle, which creates the only break in the whole highway between North and South America. The road starts again on the other side of the Colombian border and continues to Patagonia. A coral atoll known as the San Blas Islands lies off this coast and is accessible only by light airplane or boat. The Carretera Panamericana runs west from Panama City to Costa Rica, passing through David. Two provinces border Costa Rica: Chiriquí, to the south, and Bocas del Toro, to the north. You can reach Bocas by land and boat from Chiriquí.

AIR TRAVEL

From New York or Chicago flying time to Panama City is 5½ hours; from Atlanta 4 hours; from Miami 3 hours; from L.A. 6½ hours; and from Houston 4¼ hours.

Airlines and Airports **Airline and Airport Links.com.** Airline and Airport Links.com has links to many of the world's airlines and airports. 🌐 *www.airlineandairportlinks.com.*

Airline-Security Issues **Transportation Security Administration.** Transportation Security Administration has answers for almost every question that might come up. 🌐 *www.tsa.gov.*

AIRPORTS

Panama's main air hub is Aeropuerto Internacional de Tocumen (PTY), about 17 km (11 miles) northeast of Panama City. All scheduled international flights land here. The airport underwent a $600 million expansion and remodel in 2012 that transformed the space into a beautiful glass-walled construction. Tocumen has two tourist-information booths, shops, a few eating places, ATMs, 24-hour luggage storage, car-rental agencies, and a telephone and Internet center. Arrival and departure formalities are usually efficient. Minimum check-in time is two hours prior to departure; your airline may recommend longer.

Domestic flights operate out of Aeropuerto Marcos A. Gelabert (PAC), more commonly known as Albrook Airport, after the U.S. military base that once stood here. Albrook has a tourist-information stand, an ATM, a small food court, and some car-rental offices.

Airport Information **Aeropuerto Internacional de Tocumen** ✉ *Vía Tocumen, Tocumen, Panama*

City ☎ *507/238–2761* 🌐 *www.tocumenpanama.aero.* **Aeropuerto Marcos A. Gelabert (Albrook Airport)** ✉ *Av. Gaillard, Panama City* ☎ *501–9000.*

GROUND TRANSPORTATION

Taxis are the quickest way into Panama City from Tocumen Airport. The fare is as much as $40, an expensive ride for Panama, so it's worth finding out if your hotel has a shuttle service. Only licensed operators are allowed to offer services as you leave the airport doors. The trip can take between 30 and 60 minutes, depending on traffic, and whether the driver takes the Corredor Sur toll road. Note that taxis are often scarce late at night.

The 15-minute taxi ride from Albrook Airport to the city center costs $3 to $5.

Public buses stop far from Tocumen's terminal and take well over an hour to get into the city. We recommend splurging for a taxi or taking a shuttle if your hotel offers one.

TRANSFERS BETWEEN AIRPORTS

A taxi ride between Tocumen and Albrook airports can top $40, though if you're catching the cab at Albrook you might be able to negotiate a cheaper price. The trip takes about 30 minutes. Alternatively, buses to both airports start and finish at Plaza Cinco de Mayo, but the trip could end up taking a couple of hours.

FLIGHTS

Copa, a United partner, is Panama's flagship carrier. It operates flights from Chicago, Las Vegas, Los Angeles, Miami, New York–JFK, Orlando, Toronto, and Washington Dulles. Copa also flies to many Central and South American cities. You can fly to Panama from Houston and Newark on United, from Atlanta on Delta, from Miami Dallas, New York, and Newark on American, and from Fort Lauderdale on Spirit.

Air Panama is Panama's domestic carrier and serves destinations all over the country, including Guna Yala, Bocas del Toro, David, and the Darién. Domestic flights usually cost $100 to $200 round-trip; you can buy tickets directly from the airline or through a travel agent. Air Panama offers charter flights as well, although these tend to be quite pricey.

Airline Contacts **American Airlines** ☎ *800/433–7300 in North America, 507/269–6022 in Panama* 🌐 *www.aa.com.* **Copa** ☎ *800/359–2672 in North America, 507/217–2672 in Panama* 🌐 *www.copaair.com.* **Delta Airlines** ☎ *800/241–4141 in North America, 507/214–8118 in Panama* 🌐 *www.delta.com.* **Spirit Airlines** ☎ *800/772–7117 in North America, 507/264–2330 in Panama* 🌐 *www.spirit.com.* **United Airlines** ☎ *800/864–8331 in North America, 507/265–0040 in Panama* 🌐 *www.united.com.*

Domestic Airlines **Air Panama** ☎ *507/316–9000 in Panama* 🌐 *www.flyairpanama.com.*

BOAT AND FERRY TRAVEL

For information about Panama Canal boat trips, see The Canal and Central Panama Essentials in Chapter 3. Pan American Seaways' Nissos Rodos operates scheduled ferry service between Colón and Cartagena, Colombia. The ship departs the Colón2000 port Monday, Thursday, and Saturday, and Cartagena each Sunday, Tuesday, and Friday. All departure times are 6 pm and the trip takes 12 hours. The ship carries up to 1,500 passengers and 500 motor vehicles. One-way tickets are $99 for seats, $209 for dorm-style sleepers, and $429 for private cabins.

Pan American Seaways
☎ 507/209–2000 ⊕ www.panaferry.com.

Within Panama, boats are the only way to get between points in the islands of Guna Yala and Bocas del Toro and much of the Darién. There are regular, inexpensive water-taxi services connecting the city of Almirante with Bocas del Toro. In the Darién, water taxis run between Puerto Quimba and La Palma.

Contacts **Mamallena** *☎ 507/6676–6163 ⊕ www.mamallena.com.* **Zuly's Backpackers** *☎ 507/269–2665 ⊕ www.zulysbackpackers.com.*

BUS TRAVEL

DOMESTIC BUS SERVICES

Getting around Panama by bus is comfortable, cheap, and straightforward. Panama City is the main transport hub. Services to towns all over the country (and to the rest of Central America) leave from a huge terminal/mall in Albrook with shops, ATMs, Internet access, and restaurants. To get to smaller cities and beaches, you need to catch minibuses out of regional transit hubs.

THE MATTER OF METERS

In directions and addresses in Panama, "100 meters" means one block, regardless of actual measurements. Likewise, 200 meters is two blocks and 50 meters is half a block.

Long-distance buses are usually clean and punctual. Routes are operated by many different bus companies, and there's no centralized timetable service. Call the bus company or go to the terminal to get departure times. Rates are not set in stone, but estimate $1 to $2 per hour of travel.

For bus company and terminal information, see the Essentials section in each destination chapter.

INTERNATIONAL BUS SERVICES

You can reach Panama by bus only from Costa Rica. Services cross the border at Paso Canoas. The Darién jungle causes a gap in the Panamerican Highway, meaning bus travel to Colombia is impossible.

Ticabus is an international bus company connecting all of Central America. Air-conditioned coaches leave Panama City daily at 11 am and 11 pm and takes 16 hours to get to San José, Costa Rica. One-way tickets cost $55 for the more comfortable "executive service" daytime departure and $40 for the nighttime departure. Ticabus continues to Nicaragua, El Salvador, Honduras, Guatemala, and Mexico.

Panamanian company Expreso Panamá operates air-conditioned coach service from Panama City nightly at 11 pm arriving at San Jose, Costa Rica 16 hours later. The one-way fare is $40.

International Bus Companies

Expreso Panamá ☎ *507/314-6837* 🌐 *www.expresopanama.com*. **Ticabus** ☎ *507/314-6385* 🌐 *www.ticabus.com*.

CAR TRAVEL

Driving is a great way to see Panama. The Panamerican Highway takes you to or near most towns in the country, and with a car you can also visit small villages and explore remote areas more easily. Most secondary roads are well signposted and in reasonable condition.

Panamanian drivers can be a little aggressive, but they're not much worse than New Yorkers or Angelinos. We recommend saving the car for outside Panama City: traffic jams, a dearth of road signs beyond major avenues, and lack of safe parking can make downtown driving stressful.

GASOLINE

Gas stations are plentiful in and near towns in Panama, and along the Panamerican Highway. Some are open 24 hours. On long trips fill your tank whenever you can, as the next station could be a long way away. An attendant always pumps the gas and doesn't expect a tip, though a small one is always appreciated. Both cash and credit cards are usually accepted.

Most rental cars run on premium unleaded gas, which is generally a bit more expensive than in the United States. Gas is sold by the liter.

PARKING

On-street parking generally isn't a good idea in Panama City, as car theft is common. Instead, park in a guarded parking lot—many hotels have them. Many rental agencies insist you follow this rule. Restaurants often have free parking.

RENTAL CARS

Compact cars like a Kia Pinto, Ford Fiesta, VW Fox, or Toyota Yaris start at around $35 a day; for $40–$50 you can rent a Mitsubishi Lancer, a VW Golf, or a Polo. Four-wheel-drive pickups start at $70 a day. International agencies sometimes have cheaper per-day rates, but locals undercut them on longer rentals. Stick shift is the norm in Panama, so check with the rental agency if you only drive an automatic.

Rental-car companies routinely accept driver's licenses from the United States, Canada, and most European countries. Most agencies require a major credit card for a deposit, and most require that you be over 25. Panamanian rental vehicles may not leave the country.

A 4WD (*doble tracción* or *cuatro por cuatro*) is only necessary for exploring the Darién, or for other off-road adventures. Many rental agencies prefer—or even stipulate—that you park your car in guarded lots or hotels with private parking, not on the street.

Contacts **Avis** ☎ *800/230–2898 in North America, 507/278–9444 in Panama* 🌐 *www.avis.com.pa.* **Budget** ☎ *800/472–3325 in North America, 507/263–8777 in Panama* 🌐 *www.budgetpanama.com.* **Dollar** ☎ *866/700–9904 in North America, 507/270–0355 in Panama* 🌐 *www.dollarpanama.com.* **Hertz** ☎ *800/654–3001 in North America, 507/260–2111 in Panama* 🌐 *www.hertzpanama.com.pa.* **National** ☎ *800/222–9058 in North America, 507/265–2222 in Panama* 🌐 *www.nationalpanama.com.* **Thrifty** ☎ *800/847–4389 in North America, 507/238–4955 in Panama* 🌐 *www.thrifty.com.*

RENTAL CAR INSURANCE

If you own a car, your personal auto insurance may cover a rental to some degree, though not all policies protect you abroad; always read your policy's fine print. If you don't have auto insurance, then seriously consider buying the collision- or loss-damage waiver (CDW or LDW) from the car-rental company, which eliminates your liability for damage to the car. Some credit cards offer CDW coverage, but it's usually supplemental to your own insurance and rarely covers SUVs, minivans, luxury models, and the like. If your coverage is secondary, you may still be liable for loss-of-use costs from the car-rental company. But no credit-card insurance is valid unless you use that card for *all* transactions, from reserving to paying the final bill. All companies exclude car rental in some countries, so be sure to find out about the destination to which you are traveling. It's sometimes cheaper to buy insurance as part of your general travel insurance policy.

Car rental agencies in Panama require basic third-party liability insurance, and the fee is included in their cheapest quoted rental price. Optional insurance to cover occupants and the deductible if you are in an accident deemed your fault is about $20 extra per day for a compact car.

ROADSIDE EMERGENCIES

Panama has no private roadside assistance clubs—ask rental agencies carefully about what you should do if you break down. If you have an accident, you are legally obliged to stay by your vehicle until the police arrive, which could take a long time. You can also call the transport police or, if you're near Panama City, the tourist police.

Emergency Services **National police** ☎ *911 for emergencies.* **Tourist police** ☎ *507/511–9262 for information, 911 for emergencies.* **Transport police** ☎ *911 for emergencies.*

ROAD CONDITIONS

The Panamerican Highway is paved along its entire length in Panama, and most secondary roads are paved, too. However, maintenance isn't always a regular process, so worn, pockmarked—or even potholed—surfaces are commonplace. Turnoffs are often sharp, and mountain roads can have terrifying hairpin bends.

In and around Panama City traffic is heavy. An efficient toll highway ($5 one way) connects the capital and the Caribbean port of Colón in under an hour.

Turnoffs and distances are usually clearly signposted. Be especially watchful at traffic lights, as crossing on yellow (or even red) lights is common practice.

FROM PANAMA CITY	TO
Colón	89 km (55 miles)
David	486 km (302 miles)
Boquete	515 km (320 miles)
Costa Rican Border	592 km (368 miles)

RULES OF THE ROAD

You cannot turn right on a red light. Seat belts are required. Cell phone use and texting while driving is prohibited. As you approach small towns, watch out for *topes*, the local name for speed bumps.

TAXI TRAVEL

Panamanian taxis range from sleek air-conditioned sedans to stuffy, banged-up rust buckets that seem to run off the sheer will of the driver. Hailing cabs on the street is widely considered safe during the day and is your cheapest option for private transportation around the city. Short hops are as little as $1; fares within town shouldn't top $3; a trip to an outlying area should run about $5. Airport taxis and hotel taxis are nicer but considerably more expensive, so check to see if your hotel has shuttle service. Don't feel obliged to tip, but city cab drivers who strictly adhere to low city fares are genuinely appreciative (and sometimes surprised by) the extra quarter or two. You may want to ask how much the fare is before getting aboard to avoid a tourist premium.

TRAVEL TIMES FROM PANAMA CITY		
To	By Air	By Bus
Bocas del Toro	1 hour	12 hours (to Almirante)
Colón	N/A	½ hour
David	1 hour	6 hours
Guna Yala	½ hour	N/A
La Palma (Darién)	1½ hours	N/A

TRAIN TRAVEL

Panama's only train service is the Panama Canal Railway, which operates between Panama City and Colón on weekdays. Tracks run alongside the canal itself and over causeways in Gatún Lake. The hour-long trip costs $25 each way; trains leave Panama City at 7:15 am and Colón at 5:15 pm. You can buy tickets at the station before you leave.

Information **Panama Canal Railway** ☎ *507/317–6070* 🌐 *www.panarail.com.*

ESSENTIALS

ACCOMMODATIONS

Panama has plenty of lodging options. "Hotel" isn't the only tag you'll find on accommodation: *hospedaje, pensión, casa de huespedes,* and *posada* also denote somewhere to stay. There are no hard-and-fast rules as to what each name means, though hotels and *posadas* tend to be higher-end places, whereas *hospedajes, pensiones,* and *casas de huespedes* are sometimes smaller and family run. A *residencial* might be a by-the-hour sort of place. Breakfast isn't always included in the room price.

The usual big international chain hotels have rooms and facilities equal to those at home, but usually lack a sense of place. If five-star luxury isn't your top priority, the best deals are undoubtedly with mid-range local hotels. Granted, there's no gym or conference center, but comfortable rooms with private bathrooms, hot water, and much more local character often come at a fraction of the cost of a big chain.

Lodges—both eco- and not-quite-so—are the thing in Guna Yala and Darién. A few are luxurious, most are back-to-nature; all are way off the beaten path, so plan on staying a few nights to offset travel time.

TIP→ **Assume that hotels offer no meals unless we specify that they serve breakfast, some meals, all meals, or are all-inclusive with all meals and most activities).**

FODORS.COM CONNECTION

Before your trip, be sure to check out what other travelers are saying in our Forums on www.fodors.com.

APARTMENT AND HOUSE RENTALS

Short-term furnished rentals aren't common in Panama. Villas International offers several premium villa and apartment rentals. Sublet.com and VRBO deal mostly with modest apartments, often as cheap as $700 a week.

Contacts **Sublet.com** *www.sublet.com.* **Villas International** *800/221–2260 in U.S. www.villasintl.com.* **VRBO** *www.vrbo.com.*

BED-AND-BREAKFASTS

The Panamanian definition of B&B might not coincide with yours: the term is frequently extended to luxury hotels that happen to include breakfast in their price. Indeed, these make up most of the pickings at Bed & Breakfast.com and BnB Finder. Ah! Panamá includes a few homier mid-range establishments. For cheap, family-run places, try Travellerspoint.

Reservation Services **Ah! Panamá** *www.ahpanama.com/travel_and_tourism/bed_and_breakfast.* **Bed & Breakfast.com.** Bed & Breakfast.com also sends out an online newsletter. *512/322–2710, 800/462–2632 www.bedandbreakfast.com.*

BnB Finder.com ☎ *888/469-6663* 🌐 *www.bnbfinder.com.* **Travellers' Point** 🌐 *www.travellerspoint.com.*

ECO-LODGES

In addition to hotels and hostels, Panama does a brisk trade in so-called eco-lodges, most of which are in the Darién and Guna Yala. If you are seriously interested in sustainable accommodation, it pays to do your research. The term *eco-lodge* is used freely, sometimes simply to describe a property in a rural or jungle location rather than somewhere that is truly sustainable. The International Ecotourism Society has online resources to help you pick somewhere truly green.

Information **International Ecotourism Society** 🌐 *www.ecotourism.org.*

COMMUNICATIONS

INTERNET

Contacts **Cybercafés.** Cybercafés lists over 4,000 Internet cafés worldwide. 🌐 *www.cybercafes.com.*

PHONES

The country code for Panama is 507. To call Panama from the United States, dial the international access code (011), followed by the country code (507), and the 7-digit phone number, in that order. Note that cell phones have eight digits. Panama does not use area codes. To make collect or calling-card calls, dial 106 from any phone in Panama and an English-speaking operator will connect you.

CALLING WITHIN PANAMA

Panama's telephone system, operated by Cable & Wireless, is cheap and highly efficient. You can make local and long-distance calls from your hotel—usually with a surcharge—and from any public phone box.

The bright blue public phone boxes all take phone cards and some also accept coins; you insert coins or your card first, and then dial. You can also use prepaid calling cards from them free of charge. Standard local calls cost 10¢ a minute, less with a prepaid calling card (⇨ *Calling Cards, below)* such as ClaroCOM. For **local directory assistance** (in Spanish), dial 102.

CALLING OUTSIDE PANAMA

To make international calls from Panama, dial 00, then the country code, area code and number. The country code for the United States is 1.

Many cybercafés have Internet phone services: rates are often cheap (they're usually posted outside the shop), but communication quality can vary. You can also make international calls from pay phones using a prepaid card such as ClaroCOM. Dialing the international operator lets you make collect international calls. It's possible to use AT&T, Sprint, and MCI services from Panama, but using a prepaid card is cheaper.

CALLING CARDS

ClaroCOM are by far the best prepaid calling cards, and can be used to make local and international calls from any telephone in Panama. Calls both within Panama and to the United States cost as little as 5¢ a minute; cards come in denominations of $3, $5, $10, and $20. To use them, you dial a free local access number, then enter your PIN number and the number you want to call. You can buy cards from ClaroCOM's Web site, or from supermarkets, drugstores, and pharmacies all over the country. Ask for *una tarjeta telefónica de prepago.*

Calling Card Information **ClaroCOM** ☎ *171 in Panama* 🌐 *www.clarocom.com.*

MOBILE PHONES

Mobile phones are immensely popular in Panama. If you have an unlocked tri-band phone and intend to call local numbers, it makes sense to buy a prepaid Panamanian SIM card on arrival—rates will be much better than using your U.S. network. Alternatively, you can buy a cheap handset in Panama for $10–$20.

There are four main mobile-phone companies in Panama: +Móvil (owned by Cable & Wireless), Claro, Movistar, and Digicel. Their prices are similar, but +Móvil has better coverage in farther-flung areas of the country. You pay only for outgoing calls, which cost between 5¢ and 50¢ a minute. You can buy a SIM card (*tarjeta SIM*) from any outlet of either company; pay-as-you-go cards (*tarjeta de prepago para celular*) to charge your account are available from supermarkets, drugstores, gas stations, and kiosks.

You can also rent from companies like CellRent or from top-end hotels. A basic phone costs $5 a day, but you have to pay for incoming and outgoing calls, and for theft insurance, so buying a phone might be cheaper.

CELL PHONE TIPS

You can purchase a cheap cell phone at numerous outlets and simply "top-up" (pay as you go). Incoming calls are free, and with the cheap cell, you'll have service even in many remote places. Have your family call you to save on roaming charges. Check with your cell-phone provider to see if you have international roaming on your phone.

TIP→ **If you travel internationally frequently, save one of your old mobile phones or buy a cheap one on the Internet; ask your cell phone company to unlock it for you, and take it with you as a travel phone, buying a new SIM card with pay-as-you-go service in each destination.**

Contacts **Cellular Abroad.** Cellular Abroad rents and sells GMS phones and sells SIM cards that work in many countries. ☎ *800/287–5072* 🌐 *www.cellularabroad.com.* **Mobal International Cell Phones.** Mobal rents mobiles and sells GSM phones (starting at $49) that operate in 140 countries. Per-call rates vary. ☎ *888/888–9162* 🌐 *www.mobalrental.com.* **Planet Fone.** Planet Fone rents cell phones, but the per-minute rates are expensive. ☎ *888/988–4777* 🌐 *www.planetfone.com.*

CUSTOMS AND DUTIES

You may import 500 cigarettes (or 500 grams of tobacco or 50 cigars) and three bottles of alcohol duty-free. You can import duty-free up to $2,000 of various goods; customs is not overly strict on applying duty to items that are obviously yours for personal use. Prescription drugs should always be accompanied by a doctor's prescription.

U.S. Information **U.S. Customs and Border Protection** *www.cbp.gov.*

EATING OUT

Panama's cosmopolitan history is reflected in its food. Panama City has a great range of restaurants serving both local and international fare. Among the latter, Greek, Chinese, Italian, and American eateries are the most common. Fast-food outlets abound—some are names you'll recognize, others are local chains.

Eateries offering traditional Panamanian fare for locals are cheap—you can get a full plate of beans or lentils and rice and fried chicken for as little as $3. Most restaurants, however, charge U.S.-level prices for meals.

MEALS AND MEALTIMES

A typical Panamanian breakfast (*desayuno*) consists of fried tortillas or hojaldras, washed down with coffee. Most hotels catering to foreigners also offer fruit, toast, and cereal, and you can expect breakfast buffets at five-star hotels.

Lunch (*comida* or *almuerzo*) is the main meal and is generally served around midday. Many restaurants do set-price meals of two or three courses at lunch. In Panamanian homes dinner is often merely a light snack eaten around 9 pm. If you're eating out, dinner is just as big a deal as in the United States, but is usually served until 10:30 pm.

Unless otherwise noted, the restaurants listed in this guide are open daily for lunch and dinner.

PAYING

In restaurants with waiter service you pay the check (*la cuenta*) at the end of the meal. You'll usually have to ask for the check; sometimes more than once. In fast-food restaurants and at food stands, you generally pay up-front. Credit cards are accepted in more expensive restaurants, but it's always a good idea to check before you order, especially as some establishments only accept one kind of credit card.

RESERVATIONS AND DRESS

We only mention reservations when they are essential (there's no other way you'll ever get a table) or when they are not accepted. We mention dress only when men are required to wear a jacket or a jacket and tie.

WINES, BEER, AND SPIRITS

Alcohol is available in just about every restaurant in Panama, though cheaper places have limited selections.

For meals and light drinking, beer—usually lager—is the local favorite. Good brands made in Panama include Balboa, Atlas, Panamá, and Soberana, but North American and European brands are also widely available. For more serious drinking, Panamanians reach for a bottle of *seco,* a fierce white rum that gets you under the table in no time. Seco is often mixed with cranberry juice.

Wine still isn't a big thing in Panama, but most decent restaurants have imported bottles from the United States or Chile and Argentina. Imported liquor is also easy to find in supermarkets.

ELECTRICITY

Electrical current in Panama is 110 volts, the same as in the United States. Outlets take either plugs with two flat prongs or two flat prongs with a circular grounded prong. No converters or adapters are needed.

EMERGENCIES

Dial 911 nationwide for **police, fire**, and ambulance. In a medical or dental emergency, ask your hotel staff for information on and directions to the nearest private hospital or clinic. Taxi drivers should also know how to find one, and taking a taxi is often quicker than an ambulance. Many private medical insurers provide online lists of hospitals and clinics in different towns. It's a good idea to print out a copy of these before you travel.

For theft, wallet loss, small road accidents, and minor emergencies, contact the nearest police station. Expect all dealings with the police to be a bureaucratic business—it's probably only worth bothering if you need the report for insurance claims.

Most embassies in the capital open at 8:30 and close by noon.

The Hospital Nacional is an excellent private hospital with English-speaking doctors, a 24-hour emergency room, and specialists in many areas. The Centro Médico Paitilla is the country's best, and most expensive, hospital. The Clínica Bella Vista is a private clinic with English-speaking doctors. To take advantage of Panama's state-run health care, head to the public Hospital Santo Tomás.

TIP→ **Medical staff at Panamanian public hospitals are well-trained and professional. However, hospitals are underfunded and often lack supplies: as a rule, you're best going to a private clinic, which means medical insurance is a must.**

Pack a basic first-aid kit, especially if you're venturing into more remote areas. If you'll be carrying any medication, bring your doctor's contact information and prescription authorizations. Getting your prescription filled in Panama might be problematic, so bring enough medication for your entire trip.

Foreign Embassies **U.S. Embassy** ✉ *Avenida Demetrio Basilio Lakas no. 783, Clayton* ☎ *507/317–7000* 🌐 *panama.usembassy.gov.*

HEALTH

It's safe to drink tap water and have ice in your drinks in urban areas, but stick to bottled water everywhere else.

Two mosquito-borne diseases are prevalent in Panama: dengue fever (especially in Bocas del Toro) and malaria (in the Darién, Guna Yala, and parts of Chiriquí). Prevention is better than a cure: cover up your arms and legs and use a strong insect repellent containing a high concentration of DEET. Don't hang around outside at sunset, and sleep under a mosquito net in jungle areas.

Sunburn and sunstroke are potential health hazards when visiting Panama. Stay out of the sun at midday and use plenty of high-SPF-factor sunscreen when on the beach or hiking. You can buy well-known brands in most Panamanian pharmacies. Protect your eyes with good-quality sunglasses, and bear in mind that you'll burn more easily at higher altitudes and in the water.

OVER-THE-COUNTER REMEDIES

In Panama *farmacias* (drugstores) sell a wide range of medications over the counter, including some, but not all, drugs that would require a prescription in the United States. Familiar brands are easy to find, otherwise ask for what you want with the generic name. Note that acetaminophen—or Tylenol—is called *paracetamol* in Panama (just as in the U.K.). Farmacias Rey and Farmacias Arrocha are two local drugstore chains with branches all over the country, many of which are open 24 hours.

Information **Farmacias Arrocha** *www.arrocha.com.* **Farmacias Rey** *www.smrey.com.*

SHOTS AND MEDICATIONS

If you're traveling anywhere east of Panama City and the former Canal Zone, a yellow fever vaccination is recommended. Remember to keep the certificate and carry it with you, as you may be asked to show it when entering another country after leaving Panama.

The CDC recommends mefloquine, proguanil, or doxycycline as preventive antimalarials for adults and infants in Panama if entering a malaria zone east of the Panama Canal. Chloroquine is sufficient for western Panama malarial regions. To be effective, the weekly doses must start a week before you travel and continue four weeks after your return. There is no preventive medication for dengue.

Health Warnings **Centers for Disease Control & Prevention** (*CDC*). *877/394–8747 international travelers' health line* *www.cdc.gov/travel.*

MAIL

SHIPPING PACKAGES

Sending packages home through COTEL isn't always reliable, so it's worth paying the extra for certified delivery (*correo certificado*). Most packages take anywhere from a week to a month to arrive in the United States. Many stores—particularly upmarket ones—can ship your purchases for you, for a price. Valuable items are best sent with private express services. International couriers operating in Panama include DHL and FedEx—overnight delivery for a 1-kg (2.2-pound) package starts at about $100. Sending a 1-kg package to the United States with Airbox Express costs $10.50 and takes two to three days.

Contacts **Airbox Express** *507/269–9774* *www.airbox.com.pa.* **DHL Worldwide Express**

☎ 507/271–3451 🌐 www.dhl.com. **FedEx** ☎ 507/271–3838 🌐 www.fedex.com.

MONEY

Although Panama is Central America's most expensive destination, prices compare favorably to those back home. Mid-range hotels and restaurants where locals eat are excellent value. Rooms at first-class hotels and meals at the best restaurants, however, approach those in the United States. Trips into remote parts of the country and adventure travel are also relatively inexpensive.

You can plan your trip around ATMs—cash is king for day-to-day dealings—and credit cards (for bigger spending). U.S. dollars are the local currency; changing any other currency can be problematic. Traveler's checks are useful only as a reserve.

Using large bills is often a problem in Panama, even in big shops or expensive restaurants. Have plenty of ones and fives at hand. Counterfeiting is a problem with $50 or $100 bills. Many businesses won't accept anything larger than $20.

Prices are given for adults. Substantially reduced fees are almost always available for children, students, and senior citizens.

ATMS AND BANKS

ATMs—known locally as *cajeros automáticos*—are extremely common in Panama. In big cities even supermarkets and department stores usually have their own ATM. On-screen instructions appear in English; you are usually prompted to select your language. Make withdrawals from ATMs in daylight rather than at night.

The main ATM network, which accepts cards with both Cirrus and Plus symbols, is called Sistema Clave. Its website lists ATM locations all over the country. Major banks in Panama include Banistmo and Banco General. Many international banks also have branches in Panama City.

Information **Sistema Clave** 🌐 *www.sclave.com.*

CREDIT CARDS

Inform your credit-card company before you travel, especially if you're going abroad and don't travel internationally very often. Otherwise, the credit-card company might put a hold on your card owing to unusual activity—not a good thing halfway through your trip. Record all your credit-card numbers—as well as the phone numbers to call if your cards are lost or stolen—in a safe place, so you're prepared should something go wrong. Both MasterCard and Visa have general numbers you can call (collect if you're abroad) if your card is lost, but you're better off calling the number of your issuing bank, since MasterCard and Visa usually just transfer you to your bank; your bank's number is usually printed on your card.

Credit cards are widely accepted in Panama's urban areas. Visa is the most popular, followed by MasterCard and American Express. Discover is gaining ground. Diners Club is rarely accepted. If possible, bring more than one credit card, as smaller establishments sometimes accept only one type. In small towns only top-end hotels and restaurants take plastic.

Reporting Lost Cards **American Express** ☎ *800/327–1267 in U.S., 001800/545–1171 from Panama* 🌐 *www.americanexpress.com.* **MasterCard** ☎ *800/627–8372 in U.S., 636/722–7111 collect from abroad* 🌐 *www.mastercard.com.* **Visa** ☎ *800/847–2911 in U.S., 410/581–9994 collect from abroad* 🌐 *www.visa.com.*

CURRENCY AND EXCHANGE

Panama's national currency is the U.S. dollar. Don't get confused if you see prices expressed in *balboas*: it's just the local name for the dollar. All bills come in standard U.S. denominations, although Panama also issues its own version of pennies, nickels, dimes, quarters, and 50-cent pieces. New as of 2012 are one-balboa coins, still newfangled enough that much of the population is suspicious of them, with plans for a two-balboa coin on the way. Try to avoid coming to Panama with other currencies, as the exchange rates are generally unfavorable.

PACKING

Think capri pants, skirts, or khakis for urban sightseeing, with something a little dressier for eating out at night. Shorts, T-shirts, tank tops, and bikinis are all acceptable at the beach or farther afield. Leave flashy jewelry behind—it only makes you a target.

"Insect repellent, sunscreen, sunglasses" is your packing mantra; long-sleeve shirts and long pants also help protect your skin from the relentless sun and ferocious mosquitoes. Panama's rainy season lasts from mid-April to December, and rain is common at other times, too, so a foldable umbrella or waterproof jacket is a must. So are sturdy walking boots if you're planning any serious hiking, otherwise sneakers or flats are fine. A handbag-size flashlight is also very useful: blackouts are more common than at home.

In the Darién, a camping mosquito net is invaluable when staying at places with no screens in the windows (or no windows at all). A water purifier and lots of plastic bags are also helpful in the jungle.

Tissues and antibacterial hand wipes make trips to public toilets more pleasant. Finding your preferred brands of condoms and tampons in Panama can be hit and miss, so bring necessary supplies of both. Familiar toiletry brands are widely available.

PASSPORTS AND VISAS

Most travelers from Western countries can visit Panama for up to 90 days with the purchase (on arrival) of a $5 tourist visa; you can buy this upon arrival or at the check-in desk of some airlines. Your passport must be valid for at least six months. The visa may actually say it is valid for only 30 days so ask the usually friendly officer to write "*90 días*" by the stamp on the visa.

Arriving tourists are technically required to show proof that their travels continue beyond Panama. A return ticket will suffice. Airlines are often more demanding than immigration officials on this particular issue: If you don't have a return ticket they might not let you board the plane.

It is nearly impossible to extend your stay in Panama unless you are a retiree investing in property or sponsored by an employer. If you need to stay longer, grab a cheap round-trip flight to Colombia or Costa Rica (or take the bus to Costa Rica) to qualify for a new entry visa.

Information **Consulate of Panama in Washington, D.C.** ☎ *202/483-1407* 🌐 *www.embassyofpanama.org.* **Oficina de Migración** ✉ *Av. Cuba and Calle 28, Panama City* ☎ *507-1800* 🌐 *www.migracion.gob.pa.*

RESTROOMS

Restrooms in Panama use Western-style toilets. Cleanliness standards vary widely, especially in public facilities such as bus and gas stations. Toilet paper isn't guaranteed, so carry tissues in your day pack. Antibacterial hand wipes—for sanitizing you or the facilities—are also useful.

SAFETY

As Latin American countries go, Panama is relatively safe. In most of the country crime against tourists is usually limited to pickpocketing and bag snatching. Taking a few simple precautions is usually enough to keep you from being a target.

In urban areas, strive to look aware and purposeful at all times. Look at maps before you go outside, not on a street corner; and keep a firm hold on your purse. At night exercise the same kind of caution you would in any big American city and stay in well-lit areas with plenty of people around. Ask hotel or restaurant staff to call you a taxi at night, rather than flagging one down. If you're driving, park in guarded lots, never on the street; and remove the front of the stereo if possible.

In Panama City, the Casco Viejo has a sketchy reputation after dark. It's also best to steer clear of the neighborhoods of El Chorrillo, parts of Calidonia away from the parallel thoroughfares of Peru and Cuba avenues, and El Marañón, where muggings are commonplace. (We shade dangerous neighborhoods on our Panama City maps.) Finally, local drivers are a danger to pedestrians in all the city's neighborhoods, so look twice (or thrice) before crossing the street.

Two places in the country are blots on Panama's safety reputation. The city of Colón is a hot spot for violent crime, and locals warn against wandering its streets alone. Bordering Colombia, the Darién Province is a largely impenetrable jungle far from the reach of the law, and thus a hotspot for paramilitary activity and drug smuggling. An organized tour should be your only choice for visiting the Darién.

In the unlikely event of being mugged or robbed, do not put up a struggle. Nearly all physical attacks on tourists are the direct result of their resisting would-be pickpockets or muggers. Comply with demands, hand over your stuff, and try to get the situation over with as quickly as possible—then let your travel insurance take care of it.

Report any crimes to the nearest police station. In Panama City you can also ask English-speaking tourist police (identifiable by a white armband) for help. Panamanian police are usually helpful when dealing with foreigners. However, their resources are limited: they'll happily provide you with reports for insurance claims, but tracking down your stolen goods is pretty unlikely.

In Panama you're legally obliged to carry ID—preferably your passport—with you at all times. If you prefer to keep your passport safe, laminate a color copy of the photo page and carry that, together with your driver's license or other photo ID. You may be asked for proof of your identity when dealing with the police, and you can be fined $10 or hauled away if you don't have ID.

TIP→ **Distribute your cash, credit cards, IDs, and other valuables between a deep front pocket, an inside jacket or vest pocket, and a hidden money pouch. Don't reach for the money pouch once you're in public.**

Contact **Transportation Security Administration** (*TSA*). ⊕ *www.tsa.gov.*

GOVERNMENT ADVISORIES

U.S. State Department travel advisories are known for being very cautious. A perusal of the corresponding sites for other English-speaking countries (Australia, Canada, and the United Kingdom) gives you a larger sampling. All warn against independent travel to the Darién region and recommend avoiding rougher neighborhoods of Panama City and most of Colón.

General Information and Warnings **Australian Department of Foreign Affairs and Trade** ⊕ *www.smartraveller.gov.au.* **Foreign Affairs and International Trade Canada** ⊕ *www.voyage.gc.ca.* **U.K. Foreign & Commonwealth Office** ⊕ *www.fco.gov.uk/travel.* **U.S. Department of State** ⊕ *www.travel.state.gov.*

TAXES

Panama has a value-added sales tax (IVA) of 7%, which is usually included in the displayed price. No tax-refund scheme exists for visitors. Hotels also have a 10% tax. Visitors departing by air are charged an exit tax of $40, though this is usually included in your ticket.

TIME

Panama is five hours behind GMT, the same as U.S. Eastern Standard Time (GMT-5). Panama does not observe Daylight Saving Time.

Time Zones **Timeanddate.com** ⊕ *www.timeanddate.com/worldclock.*

TIPPING

In Panama tipping is a question of rewarding good service rather than an obligation. Restaurant bills don't include gratuities; adding 10% is customary. Bellhops and maids expect tips only in more expensive hotels, and $1–$2 per bag is the norm. You should also give a tip of up to $10 per day to tour guides. Rounding up taxi fares is a way of showing your appreciation to the driver, but it's not expected.

VISITOR INFORMATION

The Autoridad de Turismo Panamá (Panamanian Tourism Authority, ATP) is Panama's official tourism organization. Its bilingual website is an excellent pretrip planning resource with overviews of Panama's regions and links to tour operators and hotels.

ATP has 17 offices around Panama, open weekdays 8–3:30. The English-speaking staff at ATP offices are friendly and helpful. Their resources—mostly brochures—tend to plug local tour companies rather than aid independent touring.

Other resources include *The Visitor,* a small, free paper that can be found at most hotels and travel agencies, and *Panama Planner* an excellent tourism magazine, available at large hotels.

Contacts **Autoridad de Turismo Panamá** (*ATP*). *507/526–7000 in Panama* *www.visitpanama.com.*

ONLINE TRAVEL TOOLS

All About Panama **Explore Panama.** Explore Panama is one-stop shopping for Panama Tourism 101. *www.explorepanama.com.* **Extreme Panama.** Extreme Panama is a good resource for outdoors and adventure travel in Panama. *www.extremepanama.com.* **Hasta Tarde.** Nightlife features heavily in this collection of Spanish-language listings of Panama's cultural goings-on. *www.hastatarde.com.* **Panama Audubon Society.** Audubon is the firt name in bird-watching and bird protection worldwide, and in Panama. *www.panamaaudubon.org.* **Panama Guide.** Part online newspaper, part travel guide, Panama Guide has lots of up-to-date information about what's going on in Panama. *www.panama-guide.com.* **Panama Info.** Packed with maps, listings, and advice, Panama Info is an excellent resource if you're traveling—or moving—to Panama. *www.panamainfo.com.* **The Panama Report.** The Panama Report is full of amusing and helpful articles about travel and life in Panama, as well as lots of investment sales pitches. *www.thepanamareport.com.*

INDEX

PHOTO CREDITS

1, Alex Bramwell / age fotostock. 2, (c) Lmseco | Dreamstime.com. 3 (top), Thompson Paul / age fotostock. 3 (bottom), Piumatti Sergio / age fotostock. 4 (top), Sergio Pitamitz / age fotostock. 4 (bottom), Alfredo Maiquez / age fotostock. 5, (c) Vilainecrevette | Dreamstime.com. 6, Philippe Michel / age fotostock. 7 (top left), Carver Mostardi / Alamy. 7 (top right), Melba / age fotostock. 7 (bottom), Scott B. Rosen / Alamy. 8 (top), (c) Oliviermeerson | Dreamstime.com. 8 (bottom), Alvaro Leiva / age fotostock.

FODOR'S IN FOCUS PANAMA

Writers: David Dudenhoefer, Jeffrey Van Fleet
Series Editor: Douglas Stallings
Editors: Eric Wechter, Alexis Kelly
Editorial Production: Carolyn Roth
Maps & Illustrations: Mark Stroud, David Lindroth, and Ed Jacobus, *cartographers*; Rebecca Baer, *map editor*; William Wu, *information graphics*
Design: Fabrizio La Rocca, *creative director*; Tina Malaney, Chie Ushio, Jessica Ramirez, *designers*; Melanie Marin, *associate director of photography*; Jennifer Romains, *photo research*
Cover Photo: (Lobster restaurant at Coral Cay, Bastimentos Nacional Marine Park) Alfredo Maiquez/age fotostock
Production/Manufacturing: Angela L. McLean

COPYRIGHT

1st Edition

ISBN 978-0-89141-931-0

ISSN 2324–9609

SPECIAL SALES

This book is available for special discounts for bulk purchases for sales promotions or premiums. Special editions, including personalized covers, excerpts of existing books, and corporate imprints, can be created in large quantities for special needs. For more information, write to Special Markets/Premium Sales, 1745 Broadway, MD 3-1, New York, NY 10019, or e-mail specialmarkets@randomhouse.com.

AN IMPORTANT TIP & AN INVITATION

Although all prices, opening times, and other details in this book are based on information supplied to us at press time, changes occur all the time in the travel world, and Fodor's cannot accept responsibility for facts that become outdated or for inadvertent errors or omissions. **So always confirm information when it matters,** especially if you're making a detour to visit a specific place. Your experiences—positive and negative—matter to us. If we have missed or misstated something, **please write to us.** Share your opinion instantly through our online feedback center at fodors.com/contact-us.

PRINTED IN THE UNITED STATES OF AMERICA

10 9 8 7 6 5 4 3 2 1

ABOUT OUR WRITERS

San José, Costa Rica–based freelance writer Jeffrey Van Fleet never passes up the chance to travel to Panama and experience its vibrant, cosmopolitan diversity. He can frequently be seen at the Miraflores Locks admiring the engineering marvel that is the Panama Canal. Jeff updated the Experience Panama, Chiriquí Province, Bocas Del Toro, and Adventure Vacations chapters for this edition. He has also contributed to Fodor's guides to Costa Rica, Guatemala, Los Cabos and Baja California, Peru, Chile, Argentina, and Central and South America.

Freelance journalist David Dudenhoefer began visiting Panama in the early 1990s, when he lived in neighboring Costa Rica. He has returned dozens of times since then to write about everything from the country's politicians to its indigenous peoples. David now lives in Lima, Peru, from where he covers much of South America, but he tries to get back to Panama at least once a year. He updated the Panama City, The Canal and Central Panama, and Eastern Panama chapters.